Liberty & Prosperity:

How the Saxons Created the Modern World

John L. Hancock

LIFE WITHOUT LIBERTY IS A CURSE
www.LibertyLaneMedia.com

ISBN: 0991251229
ISBN-13: 978-0-9912512-2-3
Cover Designed by
Catherine M.C. Martinez-Perez
Author Photo by
Olaiz-Parrish Design

This book is dedicated to my son John and daughter Alejandra. It is their generation that will suffer the consequences of our actions.

Table of Contents

Chapter 1

Introduction

Although he was used to the humid summers of Virginia, the young man could barely tolerate the stifling conditions inside the hall. Not only was it one of the hottest summers Philadelphia has had in recent memory, but the heat from nearly sixty tightly packed men made staying in the room unbearable. But stay they must, for they were making history. The heaviness of the debate -- whether the colonies should declare independence from Britain -- mixed with stifling heat meant that tempers were just as hot as the room itself. Distinguished men, known for their even temperedness, would find themselves losing their composure as they casted barbs and thinly disguised insults at each other.

In exasperation the gentleman from Virginia slowly rose to address the assembly. A stilled hush came over the hall as Thomas

Jefferson, the architect of the Declaration of Independence, cleared his dry throat. He recognized friend and foe among the faces that stared expectantly back at him. He was hot, he was frustrated, and he was tired of the argument that had been raging a few seconds ago. With every bit of his being he knew that independence was the only right course of action. And he knew the of the one form of government that had a history of bringing freedom and prosperity to every nation wise enough to embrace it. It made the United Dutch Republics the freest and most prosperous in Europe, made the English the rulers of the world, and would do the same for the new nation they were creating.

He looked down at his papers, gathering his thoughts as he did so. Clearing his parched throat once more, he looked at the assembled men and asked,

Has not every restitution of the ancient Saxon laws had happy effects? Is it not better now that we return at once into that happy system of our ancestors, the wisest and most perfect ever yet devised by the wit of man...?

Over the last century and half man has witnessed an eruption in the number and variations of political systems or philosophies upon which governments can be established. Just in the 20th century alone, we have seen several variations based on the teachings of Karl Marx. These variations include (but are not limited to) communism, socialism, fascism, Maoism, Stalinism, Nazi-ism, and modern liberalism (a.k.a. Progressivism).

Each one of these variations promises to do or to fix what the other variations do not. Each one claims to be the panacea of all the ills that plague a given society. Yet, for all their claims none of them have been able to fulfill the promises so easily made by their proponents. In fact, history shows us that the outcome is more likely to be the opposite. The eventually prove themselves unsustainable. Any prosperity that a society had prior to adopting these political systems or philosophies is usually depleted within 70 years, often resulting in the loss of liberty.

These political systems are known to most of us but I am certain that you probably have never heard of the Saxon system of government that Jefferson was so in awe of. That is because it is no longer being taught to Americans or even to the British. It has slowly and deliberately been erased from our collective memories. Yet, in 1776, Jefferson did not have to explain what he meant. Every person in that room knew the history. They understood exactly what the young Virginian was referring to. And, for the next 100 years, generations of Americans would also learn this history. As John Motley, who was considered one of the greatest historians of European history of his time, wrote in 1854,

Every schoolchild knows that the so-called revolutions of Holland, England, and America are all links in one chain.

Once, every schoolchild did know this history but today most people have no knowledge of it. The objective of this book to correct this omission in our education and to reconnect us with what had become known as the Saxon model. I will use the story of those three nations -- Holland, England, and America -- as case studies to explain what the Saxon model is and how it has proven itself to be the best form of governance man has ever created. That it is the only system that has a 500 year history of bringing real prosperity and true freedom to the common man. It created the Dutch "Golden Age" of the 1500s, allowed the British to establish the most powerful empire in history, and made the United States of America the most freest and prosperous nation mankind has ever created. In fact, it is no exaggeration to say that the Saxon model not only ended the dark ages, but also created the modern world as we know it.

This is also a fact that modern-day academics have trouble dismissing. John Merriman, Professor of History at Yale University, acknowledges the connection between the Dutch and the English in his course on European Civilization (1648-1945). In the third class of the course he lectures exclusively on "Dutch and British Exceptionalism." As the class description states:

Several reasons can be found to explain why Great Britain and the Netherlands did not follow the other major European powers of the seventeenth century in adopting absolutist rule. Chief among these were the presence of a relatively large middle class [prosperity], *with a vested interest in preserving independence from centralized authority, and national traditions of resistance dating from the English Civil War and the Dutch war for independence from Spain, respectively* [freedom].

This description clearly illustrates that Dutch and British had similar "national traditions" that created societies that were exceptional in their liberty and prosperity. These traditions were brought to the New World by the English who colonized the land. This is the story of the people who made it all possible. It is also a warning not to take the liberty and prosperity that we currently enjoy for granted. As this history shows, there are those who desire to deny their fellow man the liberty and prosperity the Anglo-Saxon system provides. They offer up alternatives that promise liberty and prosperity but inevitably produces poverty and servitude. As de Tocqueville wrote nearly 200 years ago:

Despotism often presents itself as the repairer of all the ills suffered, the supporter of just rights, the defender of the oppressed, and the founder of order. Peoples are lulled to sleep by the temporary prosperity it engenders, and when they wake up, they are wretched.

Chapter 2
Concepts

Famous 19th century historian John Motley wrote that "the so called revolutions of Holland, England, and America are all links of one chain." The chain Motley was referring to was the Saxon model of government and the prosperity and freedom it produces. In this book, we will examine the history of those three nations and how Saxon and Anglo-Saxon economic and political philosophy made them the freest and most prosperous nations, not only of their time, but in the history of mankind. From these "case studies" we will be able to see how the Saxon model of government does far more for society than any other ever devised by man. While the other systems and ideologies claim to create free and prosperous societies, only the Saxon model has a 500 plus track record of doing so.

Before proceeding, we need to understand a few terms and concepts,

dominium regale vs. dominium politicum et regale

During much of the history contained within these pages – and the history of man in general –kings were the primary leaders of nations. Therefore, it is important to understand that there was not one general form of kingship. That, just as today, there are variation in the way a leader can rule his people. Yet, when the term monarchy or king is mentioned, most people have the vision of an all-powerful absolute ruler of the Middle Ages. In fact, for many, monarchy has become synonymous with tyranny and absolutism. While this is a common belief, it is absolutely incorrect. In the 15th century John Fortescue, who is considered the first political scientist, observed that there are two basic forms of government that all governments fall into, regardless of the title of the leader. The first is *dominium regale,* in which "the king may rule his people by such laws as he makes himself and therefore he may set upon them taxes and other impositions, such as he wills himself, without their assent." The second is *dominium politicum et regale*. Under this model the "king may not rule his people by other laws than such as they assent to and therefore he may set upon them no impositions without their own assent."

In his book *On the Laws and Governance of England,* Fortescue noted that at that time (1471) *dominium regale* was the standard form of government throughout continental Europe. The Dutch and English, he wrote, had governments that operated in the *dominium politicum et regale* form. This gave those countries a very different form of monarchy. While the kings on the continent ruled in a way not that much different than Stalin, Hitler, Mao, or even Kim Dong Un, Dutch and English kings ruled not much different than the presidents and prime ministers of most modern day democracies. As British historian David Starkey points out, the position of the President of the United States and the Prime Minister of the United Kingdom have more power and authority than most English kings did. The only difference is that each person holds that power for a set period rather than life. As we will discover later in the book, there was no guarantee that an English king would hold his throne for life either.

The distinction between *dominium regale* and *dominium politicum et regale* will have a great impact on how the nations of Europe develop and its effects are still being felt to this day. Furthermore, it will determine the destinies of their colonies in the New World and beyond. In fact, much of the problems that still plague the modern world have their origins in the societies that each of these forms of government produces. One brings liberty and prosperity, while the other condemns the common people to servitude and poverty.

Saxon/Anglo-Saxon:

Saxons were the Germanic people who settled in what would become the Netherlands. After the fall of Rome, the ever intrepid Saxons migrated to the former Roman province of Britannia; where they became known as the Anglo-Saxons.

The Saxons quickly became the dominant power in what would become known in the Saxon language as *Aegla land* or, in modern English, England. This meant that there was very little to distinguish the Saxons who would eventually become the Dutch from the Anglo-Saxons who would come to found the nation-state of England. For this reason, I use both terms only to distinguish geographical location: the Saxons in Holland, the Anglo-Saxons in England. Politically and economically, both the Saxons and the Anglo-Saxons were individual-centric and there is so little difference between the two that I use the term interchangeably.

The Balance of Power

In his book, *The Riddle of the Modern World,* Dr. of Historical Anthropology Alan MacFarlane describes what factors allowed mankind to escape the internal and external predation that kept the common man in the state of perpetual servitude and poverty. Prior to the Modern Age, any wealth that could be used by an individual for the betterment of his condition was taken by the predation of kings (the state), priest (religion), lords, and over-powerful merchant guilds (economic). This usually took the form of "increasingly sharp stratification – castes and estates – and increasingly absolutist religion and government" which combined to destroy "personal liberty and thought." In other words, the more people were divided into separate and competing groups (stratification) the more vulnerable they were to the economic and political predation of the elites.

It would be this internal predation – or pillaging – that would deprive the common man the political freedom needed to break out of his seemingly perpetual state of poverty and subservience.

Yet, something very different was happening in northwest Europe, specifically in areas that would become England and the Dutch Republics. A new form of government based on the principles of limited government, personal liberty, private ownership of property (especially land) and the freedom to engage in economic activity was emerging from what were traditionally regarded as the backwaters of Europe. It would be this new form of government -- based on the decentralized consent of the people rather than centralized rule imposed by force -- that would transform the world and lead to the modern age, with all its conveniences and liberty, that today we take for granted.

At the center of this was the Saxon model and the balance it struck between the political, religious, and economic spheres of the society. Each one, independent and equal in power, would check the authority of the other two while pursuing its own agenda. This constant struggle of power checking power would result in any one sphere being unable to gain authority over the other two and society, in general. The product of this power struggle was an environment in which personal and economic freedom could flourish; resulting in a free and prosperous society.

Any unbalance of this equilibrium of power, either by the weakening of one sphere or the collaboration of two spheres against the third would produce an inequality between the three spheres. The result has and always will be tyranny and despotism. We see this with the uniting of the Roman State and the Roman Church, which resulted in the "most absolute monarchy known to man." Islamic fundamentalism, which also unites the political and religious spheres, is a modern example. Communism, fascism, socialism, Maoism, and any other form of Marxism, in which the political and economic spheres are united, are 20th century examples of this rule.

As much as we may disdain them, the power hungry politician, the greedy Wall Street banker, and the righteous pastor all have a role to play in preserving a free and prosperous society. In fact, they are essential to it. Remove or reduce the power of any one of the spheres sets the society on the path to despotism. As MacFarlane points out, "The secret to liberty was thus firstly a separation of spheres – economy from polity, religion from polity, religion from economy, and society from polity, religion, and economy."

Montesquieu wrote that "power should be a check on power" and how well a society achieves the balance between its powerful political, religious, and economic spheres will determine if it is an individual-centric or state-centric society.

Contractual Government

For most of man's history – and even to this day – the most common form of government is one in which those who have the power rule over those who do not. In most cases, the one with the biggest army enslaved the weak and defenseless. The duty of the common people was to serve the state, which in reality was an apparatus of the powerful. Most militaries were -- and still are in many parts of the world --used for the oppression of the nation's people as much as they were for defending from external threat. This is the top-down state-centered form of government that is prevalent throughout man's attempt to create an orderly society. The government's authority is sustained by force and compulsion. It is, as Mao Zedong put it, power "from the barrel of a gun".

The Saxons would start a model that would eventually evolve into the concept of contractual government. The Saxons would authorize selected members of their community to act on their behalf. The community would temporarily grant those selected certain powers and privileges while they were representing the interests of their community. The community had the right to revoke these powers and privileges whenever they deemed it necessary. This made the model a bottom-up form of government that made the government a servant of the people rather than the people the servants of the government. As we will see in the following chapters, this tradition would lead to contracts such as the Magna Carta, the Declaration of Rights, and the United States Constitution (including the Bill of Rights), which were used to grant and limit the power of those who govern. Many philosophers, including John Locke, Thomas Hobbs, and Jean-Jacques Rousseau, wrote extensively on what is commonly referred to as the Social Contract Theory. What is often overlooked is that they were not theorizing a new form of government, but were attempting to explain the world shattering changes they were witnessing at a time when the Saxon form of government was proving itself to be the "best created by the wit of man".

Individual-centric versus state-centric government

Whether it is Romanism, medieval absolutism, or the modern-day variants of Marxism, they all have one thing in common: they are all state-centric societies. This means that the state in the form of the government is the primary beneficiary and focus of the society. That the political sphere, in the form of the state, dominates the religious and economic spheres. The result is an ever increasing centralization of power. There is nothing of higher value than that of the state and no force strong enough to counter its authority. This creates a situation where the individual serves the state. In other words, state-centric government is a government of the state, by the state, and for the state.

While it is true that under the variations of Marxism the state does produce policies that are for the people, this is done mostly for the aggrandizement of the state itself. There are not any social reforms that have been implemented by a state-centric government that has not benefited the state more than the society as a whole. Every benefit that a state provides its citizens is accompanied with an expansion or the centralization of political power. In the end these "for the people" policies end up benefiting the government at the expense of members of the society.

Many see this centralization as the natural progression of good and effective government. What these progressives do not understand is that centralization of political power is the sign of bad, not good, government. Alexis de Tocqueville observed,

A centralized country is a country of imperfect and unprogressive cultivation...it is top-down and held together by physical force...the political institutions dominate the legal ones...it only serves to enervate the peoples that submit to it, because it constantly tends to diminish their civic spirit."

Those who favor increased centralization often do so in the name of equality. This was the argument of the communists, fascists, socialists, and progressives (aka Modern Liberals) of the 20th century. It is still the rallying cry for them in the 21st century. Yet, history tells us that centralization produces the opposite. That the more centralized a society becomes, the more inequality it produces. In time, as 18th century British essayist and statesman, William Young, points out, centralization results in "one district" or "great town" becoming "the sole achievement of ambition and executive authority, the extensive territory, the numerous people, will be quickly made to feel that they are in provincial subjection of the district or town."

This in turn, leads to an aristocracy, or ruling class, that "burthen the people" while "not being burdened themselves." They "make and enforce laws against others, which themselves are not subject to and it is a government which adds insolence to wrongs." It is, Young concludes, the "most hateful of all governments."

Individual-centric government is the opposite. It is a bottom-up political model and rules by the consent of the governed and not raw physical force. The law dominates the political. Hence, the principle of the rule of law. In individual-centric societies, nothing has a higher value than that of the individual. He is sovereign, inviolable, and has inalienable rights that no government has the power to grant nor deprive him of. Government serves the individual. Its main purpose is to create an environment in which the individual can prosper. This allows for a government that is for the people, by the people, and of the people. As a result, the power and reach of individual-centric governments are limited, individual liberty is sacrosanct, private property is uninfringeable. This unshackling of the individual, married with free-market (Anglo-Saxon) economics, creates a freedom and prosperity that is beyond the capability of state-centric government.

Natural versus Artificial Government

While it is true that on a societal level there is a tendency to create state-centric government, it is not the natural tendency of the individual. At the individual level, most people want to be left to themselves. They want to be able to live their lives with as little interference from others as possible. This is the natural tendency of all individuals; although, it can be suppressed by one's culture. This is why I say that individual-centric government is what is natural to man. It allows him to be the master of his own life and be captain of his own destiny. It also understands that man is not a perfect being and can have a tendency to doing harm for his own self interests. While recognizing that this fault in man can never be completely suppressed, individual-centric government creates a system that minimizes the impact such behavior can have on a society. Many proponents of state-centric government claim that their system is designed to suppress the negative tendencies of man by imposing an artificial system that controls his behavior. Unfortunately, as history has shown, the opposite is usually the result. The artificial system ends up suppressing the good tendencies of man while having little impact on his negative behavior. For this reason, all forms of state-centric government is artificial, foreign to the condition of all of mankind, and is ultimately destructive.

Anglo-Saxon Economic Model vs. the Continental Economic Model

The Anglo-Saxon model has an economic as well as the political aspects described above. The modern characteristics of this model are:

- Low government spending
- Low government presence in the economy
- Secure property rights
- Low taxation
- Low regulation
- Markets that focus on growth
- Highly developed contract law
- A general ease in starting and doing business

This is in contrast to the Continental system in which the economy is controlled or dominated by the state. Rather than growth, its primary focus is wealth distribution which, by necessity, demands high levels of taxation and regulation. Policies are often geared towards assisting the poor at the expense of the middle class, which, as the research in this book will show, helps neither.

Absolute versus Relative Poverty

Throughout this book I will be discussing the topic of poverty. But before we do this we need to recognize that there is a bit of sleight-of-hand when the subject of poverty is discussed in developed nations. When poverty is mentioned, people have the image of other people going without food, shelter, and the other basic necessities of life; which is absolute poverty. Unfortunately, this is not the poverty that the proponents of state-centric government refer to when they are talking about poverty. What they refer to is what is called "relative poverty", which has nothing with anyone going without the basic necessities of life. What it does have to do with is the "relative" poverty of those at the bottom of society when compared to those at the top. This is why people who do have all the necessities of life but lack such conveniences as a car, a color TV, a cell phone, etc. are considered to be impoverished. The difference between absolute and relative poverty is driven home by the story of a man from an impoverished country desiring to immigrate to America. When asked why he wanted to live in America, he replied, "Because I want to live where even the poor people are fat."

When I discuss poverty in this book it is about poverty in the truest sense of the word. When I write about prosperity it is not about everyone being financially equal. It is about a society being so wealthy that even "the poor people are fat." I do this because no society, not even those with state-centric government, has ever achieved the financial prosperity that the proponents of state-centric government say they can bring about. The irony (or hypocrisy) is that they condemn individual-centric government for not providing the type of prosperity that even their systems cannot provide. The sad truth is that not only can state-centric government fail to end relative prosperity, it actually ends up putting more people into absolute poverty. There is only one model that has a 500+ year proven track record of ending absolute poverty for all of its citizens and that is the individual-centric government that evolved from the basic Saxon principles of limited government, individual liberty, private property, and free market economics.

As mentioned above, over the last 150 years, there has been an explosion of political and economic philosophies; each claiming to be the solution. With so many promises and claims it can be nearly impossible to recognize which philosophy can do best for the society that embraces it. Fortunately, history can be a valuable teacher. It tells us that state-centric government can never produce the same results that individual-centric government does. It also tells us that, while there are many versions of state-centric government, there is only one version of individual-centric government. That version was stubbornly defended by barbaric German tribes -- specifically the Saxons -- against Roman authoritarianism and then transported to England after the fall of the Roman Empire. There, on that small, isolated, island-nation, it was allowed to grow and prosper, thus allowing the Anglo-Saxon based English-speaking countries to become the freest and most prosperous mankind has ever produced.

Part 1

The Saxons

Chapter 3
Rome vs. The Barbarians

If the history of Western civilization is taught, it is usually done so from the perspective that modern Western civilization has its origins in the city-states of Greece and the Republic of Rome. That Greece was the "cradle of democracy" and that Rome, which is portrayed as stretching throughout all of Western Europe and into its northern most province of Britannia, was the peak of civilization in ancient Europe. The victory of the barbarians over the armies of Rome caused the collapse of Roman civilization in the fifth century and all the achievements of Roman civilization ceased to exist. The once stable provinces of Rome soon found themselves dissolving into little fiefdoms ruled by petty nobles. Almost overnight, all the great advancements that the state of Rome had achieved the previous 1000 years were erased and all of Europe was thrust into the "dark ages."

For the next one thousand years, the narrative tells us, would be a period of intellectual darkness and economic regression for Europe. The feudal serf replaced the Roman citizen. Magic and mysticism displaced Roman science and philosophy. Trade and farming declined as Roman roads and aqueducts fell first into disuse and then disappeared altogether. Roman enforced peace (*Pax Romana*) was supplanted by centuries of conflict as the little Caesars fought for dominance within their regions. All of Western Europe became stagnant. Only the Renaissance, which was started in the 1400s by Venice merchants, would reignite European passion for knowledge and understanding, science and philosophy. This relighting of the conscious of man would mark the end of the dark ages and the beginning of what would become known as the modern age. It was during this time, the narrative points out, that we see the embryos of what would become the great nation-states of Europe.

From this narrative it appears that all of Western civilization comes from one main source; Rome. But is this accurate? Is Rome and its system of government at the foundation of all of Western civilization?

To great thinkers like Montesquieu, the answer would be an emphatic no. He saw that Europe was divided between two competing civilizations; the Roman civilization in the south and the Germanic to the north. Throughout the reign of the Roman Empire, these two rival social/political/economic systems would fight for dominance in Western Europe. This resulted in the wars continuously fought between the Roman Empire and the Germanic tribes of northern Europe (The Barbarians). While it is true that by Roman standards these people, with their paganism, bloodlust, and brutish manners, were uncivilized, they were not lawless or without a system of governance. As Montesquieu further wrote, "It is impossible to gain any insight into our political law unless we are *thoroughly* acquainted with the laws and manners of the German nations." [Italics are mine for emphasis]

Yet, not only are we not "thoroughly acquainted" with the Saxons, we are left completely ignorant of their history and system of government. Instead, modern educators and academics, contrary to hundreds of years of consistent and fact based history, push upon us a false narrative that glorifies the state while reducing the individual to one of many units that makes up "society."

As British historian David Starkey writes, Rome "was perhaps the purest and most absolute monarchy the world has ever seen. The emperor incorporated in his own person all the powers of the state: military, executive, judicial, and legislative...He was even regarded as a God himself...His person, his palace, his very treasure 'sacred'". The duty of the Roman citizen was to "obey and pay their taxes". Although the Roman Republic did have the appearance of representative democracy, this was superficial and throughout much of Rome's history the state was controlled by an oligarchy comprised of a few wealthy (and sometimes rival) families. Projects were all directed by the state and the labor more often than not was comprised of slaves rather than freemen participating in an open labor market. Even professionals such as accountants, teachers, and engineers were slaves. As Moses Finley points out in his book *The Ancient Economy,* Rome was one of only five slave societies in recorded history.

In theory there was private property, but in practice most property was owned by the influential families that comprised the oligarchy. Obligations to the state, especially military service, made it very difficult for individuals to effectively and profitably run farms. Over time, the elite families were able to accumulate large sections of land that would comprise huge estates known as *latifundias*. As a result, the average Roman was forced to dwell in urban centers comprised mostly of tenements; many of which were nothing more than slums. There were attempts to reform this system but these were easily defeated in the Senate, which, as previously noted, represented the interests of the elites rather than those of the individual citizen.

These the rich men employed in cultivating their ground of which they dispossessed the citizens. Caius Laelius, the intimate friend of Scipio, undertook to reform this abuse; but meeting with opposition from men of authority, and fearing a disturbance, he soon desisted, and received the name of the Wise or the Prudent, both which meanings belong to the Latin word Sapiens. -Plutarch Tiberius Gracchus

Just from these few observations it is clear that Roman society was state-centric. The government, in the form of the Emperor, was all-powerful and had no limits. The legal system, being dictated from the elite controlled Senate, was top-down. Private property was collectively owned by a few elite families that used the state to further their own interests. While there was a merchant class, which gave a semblance of a free market economy, the lack of a vibrant real estate market and the predominance of slave labor meant that the impact of such economic activity was very limited. More significantly, is the fact that the individual Roman citizen was subservient to the state with the sole dual duties of obeying and paying his taxes.

The longer a peoples were part of the Roman Empire the more the values of the absolute power of the state, subservience of the individual to the state, collective property rights, and state controlled economies became ingrained in their culture. "In Italy and what would to become France and Spain," as Starkey writes, "things continued pretty much as before. The cities with their bishops survived; 'senatorial' aristocrats continued to entertain each other in their opulent villas; the trade to the East remained open. The difference was that in place of the emperor, barbarian local leaders took over the imperial role. They divided it and localized it. But they kept all of the wealth, pomp and authority they could...a hybrid sub-Roman society continued to propagate Roman and Christian [Roman Church] ideas of politics...the new nobility retained the names of the senior military ranks -- *comes* or count and *dux* or duke -- as aristocratic titles."

As Rome collapsed, and the local nobility claimed unto themselves the authority of the former Roman Emperors, the people of Romanized Europe were more than willing to trade their liberty for security. As renown American historian John Motley noted, "the people had no rights at all and were glad to assign themselves as slaves to any noble who was strong enough to protect them." This is serfdom at its most fundamental level and the practice of trading liberty for security became ingrained into the cultures of Romanized Europe.

In his study of history, de Tocqueville observed that absolutism began with the "reintroduction of Roman law and the Roman Catholic religion."

Aided by Roman law and by its interpreters, the kings of the fourteenth and fifteenth centuries succeeded in founding absolute rule on the ruins of the free institutions of the Middle Ages...the singular availability of Roman law -- which was a slave-law -- was the true cause of the phenomenon [rise of absolutism]. The Roman law carried civil society [the state] to perfection, but it invariably degraded political society [freedom], because it was the work of a highly civilized thoroughly enslaved people. Kings naturally embraced it with enthusiasm, and established it wherever they could throughout Europe, its interpreters became their Ministers or their chief agents. Lawyers furnished them at need with legal warrant for violating the law. They have often done so since. Monarchs [and Presidents] who have trampled the laws have almost always found a lawyer ready to prove the lawfulness of their acts -- to establish learnedly that violence was just, and that the oppressed was in the wrong. In essence Europe lost its freedoms to a resurgent Roman civilization.

Soon all of Romanized Europe would be dotted with tiny kingdoms and principalities controlled by little Caesars. The most successful of these little Caesars would, in time, claim the Roman title of *Rex;* which in turn would evolve into the Spanish word *Rey,* Portuguese word *Rei,* and the French word *Roi*. The supremacy of Caesar was preserved through the principles of Divine Right, which made the king God's representative on earth, and Absolutism, which granted him absolute authority and power over everything within his domain, including the people. These two principles meant that the state, embodied by the king, was all powerful and was the center of all Romanized societies. It is significant to note that the English name 'king' originated from the Germanic term meaning 'war leader' and not the all-powerful.

Due to their small size, the governments of these kingdoms were able to establish a level of authority over their people that was not possible in the expansive Roman Empire. Over the centuries, as the kingdoms consolidated, governments were able to develop sophisticated state apparatuses [civil government] that continued to keep the people subjugated. The law continued to be top down with the Roman practice of codification being the foundation of their legal systems. In this system, ruling bodies--often comprised of elites--wrote laws that the masses were forced to abide by. As is the case with state-centric governments, these laws often benefitted the elites at the expense of the individual. It was not uncommon for lawmakers to exempt themselves from the same laws that they wrote and expected the average person to obey. This resulted in what has become known as an aristocracy, which British essayist William Young notes, "is the most hateful of all governments".

It is a government of privileges and of exemptions. It is a conspiracy of a certain number of individuals to burthen the people, and not to be burdened themselves. The aristocrats make and enforce laws against others, which themselves are not subject to and it is a government which adds insolence to wrongs, and wounds the spirit, whose body and substance it destroys. -William Young (1793)

Another myth that is widely accepted is that Christianity converted the pagan Romans to Jesus. This might have been true initially, but by the fall of Rome, Christianity had been fully co-opted by the state. The Roman church became more of an instrument of the state than of faith. As de Tocqueville warned, "where the Church is so thoroughly in the hands of the State as to become an instrument of government" despotism inevitably results. Following the example of the Roman church, "the Catholic clergy throughout Europe had become both a religious and political body." This marriage of church and state created an unbalance between the political, religious, and economic spheres and the individual was made to suffer. As political philosopher Adam Smith would write, "the reconstitution of the church of Rome may be considered as the most formidable combination that ever formed against the liberty, reason, and happiness of mankind."

The Roman economic system was only slightly modified, if not left intact. The collectivization of land under the Roman *latifundia* continued. It became the cornerstone of the *hacienda* system in Spain, the *estancia* in Portugal, and the *fanzenda* in France. With land being the primary wealth producing asset in pre-industrial age societies, this inevitably produced a society where the elites dominated both economically as well as politically. It is not surprising that the patron – peon system thrived in these countries. A patron was the title of a high person in Roman society and it remained so in most Roman-influenced societies. The patron was usually a large landholder who supplied a protected, self-sufficient village, supported the church, and provided the necessities of life for his peons, which were the common people of the village. In exchange, the patron expected obedience and loyalty. Low-level patrons had patrons of their own and likewise pledged obedience and loyalty to their patrons. This system continued up through society until it reached the principle patron: the King. This is state-centric government in its most fundamental form. At each level the individual, in exchange for protection and security, makes himself subservient to the state.

The result of the Roman system was the absolutist-peasant societies that became the norm throughout continental Europe and well into the 19th century (Spain would suffer authoritarian rule and a peasant style economy until the mid-1970s). Unfortunately, for the people of what would become Latin America, both France and Spain created colonial governments based on the same Roman-style rule. Minor, yet loyal, nobles would be appointed governors of the colonies and have all the authority of the King. This instilled in these cultures the Roman values of absolute power of the state, servitude of the individual, collective property rights, and state dominated economics. As I will show later in the book, this will greatly influence the development of the former colonies of Spain, France, and Portugal.

If we accept the standard narrative of the development of Western civilization, then all Western nations should have similar political and economic systems. But that is not the case because there was a competing system that resisted Roman authoritarianism and came to dominate northern Europe. This system originated with the Germanic tribes; specifically, for this book, the Saxons. This was fully recognized by the founders of United States, including the author of the Declaration of Independence, Thomas Jefferson. Jefferson would write, "their [the English settlers] Saxon ancestors had… possessed themselves of the island of Britain…and had established there that system of laws which has so long been the glory and protection of that country." Jefferson's admiration for the Saxons led him to argue that the national seal of United States should depict "Hengist and Horsa, the Saxon chiefs for whom we claim the honor of being defended, and whose political principles and form of government we have assumed." As president of the University of Virginia, Jefferson had the Anglo-Saxon play *Beowulf* performed in the original Anglo-Saxon language. Furthermore, like the Israelis would do nearly two centuries later with Hebrew, Jefferson wanted the Anglo-Saxon language taught in grammar schools so that future generations of Americans would learn of their liberty "in the tongue from whence it comes." This demonstrates that he understood that the political laws of the Saxons evolved to become the political laws of England and, 1300 years later, the political law of a new and unique nation known as the United States of America.

As we will see in the following chapters of this section, the Saxons had a very unique political system that was the antithesis to Roman authoritarianism. As much as Romans were state-centric, Saxons were individual-centric. The government was limited, the individual was supreme, the legal system was bottom-up, property was privately owned, and individuals were free to do business with whoever and however they wished as long as both parties did so voluntarily. As historian Thomas Grattan writes in his book *Holland: The History of the Netherlands* (1830), for the Saxons "the fall of Rome did not end civilization; it ended the struggle between liberty and conquest."

This fundamental ideological difference between state-centric Romanism and what would become known as individual-centric Anglo-Saxon-ism would politically, economically, and theologically divide Western Civilization for next sixteen centuries. Its exportation through colonization has taken it global and, as this book illustrates, it is the reason why the English-speaking countries have dominated the world for the last 400 years.

Chapter 4
The Saxon Model

In his book, *The History of the Netherlands,* Thomas Gratton details a fierce battle that was fought between the Romans and the Saxons in the 4th century. Fought with ax and sword, the battle was vicious and brutal. Throughout the day, neither side could strike a decisive blow. Eventually, though, the Romans were able to overcome their Saxon foes. As the Roman general toured the bloody battlefield, he saw dead and dying Roman soldiers mixed with dead and dying Saxon warriors. Gazing upon the carnage, he was driven to say that the Saxons fought "as if living without liberty is a curse."

The general's observation was more accurate than he could have imagined. Like the Dutch, the English, and the Americans who would follow, the Saxons "were," as Montesquieu notes, "certainly a free people...they put such restrictions on the authority of their kings, that they were properly only chiefs or generals. Thus theses kingdoms, although founded by force never endured the yoke of the conqueror." They were the original non-conformists, rebels, and individualists. Thus, they embraced and fiercely defended the principles of limited government, individual liberty, private property, and free-market economics. From these principles they produced a system of governance that has created the most freest and prosperous nations the world has ever seen.

According to Dr. Alan MacFarlane, professor of historical-anthropology at Cambridge University, a society must have four key elements to be free. Those elements are the private ownership of land, easy transmission of wealth, geographical mobility, and social mobility. History tells us that there is only one form of government that has a 500+ year track record of producing those four elements. That form of government is based on the Saxon principles of limited government, individual liberty, private property, and free-market economics. For over five centuries, the people who have lived in a society based on these principles have usually lived in the most free and prosperous nations of their times. No other system, no matter what they promise, has the same history of success that the Saxon system of government does.

In his survey of *English Constitution and Legal History* Colin Rhys-Lovell details what he saw as principal points of Anglo-Saxon law and government.

1. All decisions in the selection of leaders had to be with the consent of the people, preferably by full consensus, not just the majority.

2. The laws by which they were governed were considered natural laws given by divine dispensation, and were so well known by the people they did not have to be written down.

3. Power was disbursed among the people and never allowed to concentrate in any one person or group. Even in time of war, the authority granted to the leaders was

temporary and the power of the people to remove them was direct and simple.

4. Primary responsibility for resolving problems rested first of all with the individual, then the family, then the tribe or community, then the region, and finally, the nation.

5. They were organized into small, manageable groups where every adult had a voice and a vote. They divided the people into units of 10 families who elected a leader; then 50 families who elected the leader; then 100 families who elected a leader; and then thousand families who elected a leader.

6. They believed the rights of the individual were considered unalienable and could not be violated without risking the wrath of divine justice as well as civil retribution by the people's judges.

7. The system of justice was structured on the basis of severe punishment unless there was complete reparation to the person who had been wronged. There were only four crimes or offenses against the whole people [society]. These were treason, by betraying their own people; cowardice, by refusing to fight or failing to fight courageously; desertion; and homosexuality. All other offenses required reparation to the person who had been wronged.

8. They always attempted to solve problems on the level where the problem originated. If this was impossible they

went no higher than was absolutely necessary to get a remedy. Usually only the most complex problems involving the welfare of the whole people [society], or a large segment of the people, ever went to the leaders for solution.

As we can see, this is a blueprint for individual-centric government and, although his survey was specifically written for the Anglo-Saxons of England, it can justifiably be applied to the Saxons. As John Motley points out, "To all who speak the English language; the history of the great agony through which the Republic of Holland was ushered into life must have particular interest, for it is a portion of the records of the Anglo-Saxon['s] and is essentially the same, whether in Friesland, England, or Massachusetts."

This is supported by the writing of the Roman historian Tacitus. Two thousand years ago, he observed something quite extraordinary about the Germanic barbarians living to the north of the Roman Empire. He noted that they were in the habit of deciding their affairs through open-air clan meetings and that the chiefs governed not as autocrats, but by the consent of the people. They had to rely on the ability to inspire, rather than the power to compel. This meant that the people were not subjects, but free and equal participants in the administration of their affairs.

Within these assemblies resided the sovereignty of the people. The chieftains, unlike the leaders of Rome, were chosen usually by universal suffrage. Even once elected the chieftain's power was greatly limited. In the assembly he acted more as a chairman then a leader of the tribe. Like the leaders of today's modern democracies, the Saxon chieftain had to rely more on his ability to inspire and persuade rather than his power to order and compel. Only in times of war was the chieftain allocated authoritative power and these powers were relinquished at the end of hostilities. Even times of war the chieftain was not above the traditional customs and practices of the Saxon people. He was expected to share the same risks and deprivations as that of the lowest warrior. This is clearly highlighted in the Saxon tradition of sacrificing 10% of their warriors as a thank you to their gods for providing them a victory. The process of choosing those to be sacrifice was completely random and egalitarian. Each warrior, including the chieftain, would draw straws. Those who drew the short straws, including the chieftain, were sacrificed.

The assemblies were usually convened on the night of a full moon. During these meetings the assembly elected the village magistrate and decided upon all important matters. This meant that all state affairs were in the hands of this fierce democracy. It is these assemblies that set individual-centric Saxon government from that of the state-centric Romans. Not only was the Saxon government democratic, it was also republican. These assemblies form the core of Saxon government and will be duplicated by their descendants in both Holland and England. In England, as author Daniel Hannan writes in his book *Inventing Freedom,* the assemblies (known as *Witans*) would have several features in common with the modern parliaments of English-speaking countries.

1. Within these assemblies, sovereignty and legitimacy of the government was affirmed.

2. Their purpose was to ratify the most important decisions in the kingdom.

3. In time, the assemblies would meet on a consistent basis.

4. They served as guardians of the established law, willing, on occasion to lay down terms to the chieftain and, in time, kings.

It is awe-inspiring to think that the origins of the parliamentary system that governs most of the free world can be traced all the way back to the age of the Roman Empire; but not the Romans themselves as we are led to believe. The Romans could never envision such a system because it was a product of a culture that valued the sovereignty of the individual over the power and needs of the state.

Any form of government is only as good as the legal system it is based on. Today, nearly a third of the human race now lives in one form or another under the common law legal system that originated with the Saxons. De Tocqueville would observe, "the customs of the Saxons are interesting in themselves...their legal procedure is the oddest that ever existed." What distinguishes the Saxon system from the Roman or even the Napoleonic systems is that its laws are created by the people for all the people, including the leaders.

In Romanized Europe, the legal system is best described as a system where the law is created by the state for the people. This meant that the writers of the law, in most cases the elites who control the state, are able to create laws for people that they themselves are exempt from. A prime example of this is taxation. It was not an uncommon practice for the elites to create taxes for the people while exempting themselves from those very same taxes. Common law evolves outside the authority of the elites as judges decide cases based on previous law (i.e. precedence or a doctrine known as *stare decisis*) and is not determined by the rulings of a few powerful men.

Another way of reducing the authority or power of the elites was the creation of the jury system. Although the jury system of the Saxons and Anglo-Saxons was very primitive when compared to the system we have today, it did remove the authority of the judicial system out of the hands of the elites and into those of the common people. As de Tocqueville noted, "The jury is the most direct application of the principle of the sovereignty of the people." He further observed that since juries sat in judgment of their neighbors, they "teach men equity in practice" since he may one day be judged himself. For de Tocqueville, the jury "should be regarded as a free school which is always open and in which a juror always learns his rights."

Additionally, courts were dispersed and often at the local level. The more important cases were tried at the county level, while the more mundane cases were heard at a lower level of the 100 families. Over time it became clear that there were cases that were beyond the capacity of the county court. This gave rise to the development of the high court, whose judges would tour the county courts. These judges became known as "circuit judges."

As Daniel Hannan points out, common law have four additional properties that distinguish it from most civil law systems.

1. Common law lays particular emphasis on private ownership and free contracts. This conforms to the Saxon principles of private property and free-market economics.

2. Common law is based on the notion that anything not expressly prohibited is legal. This conforms to the Saxon principle of individual liberty. If it is not expressly

prohibited by law, then an individual can feel free to do it without first getting government permission.

3. The law is the property of everybody. The policeman was and is a citizen in uniform, not an agent of the state. In many English-speaking nations, law officers are directly accountable to the communities they serve, not the state that governs.

4. Since common law was a law that originates from the people, and not the state, there was a need for an ultimate popular tribunal to determine the law. This was the responsibility of the assemblies discussed above and led to the creation of the parliamentary system that is the foundation of representative democracy in English-speaking nations.

This meant that powerful men were never able to constitute a hereditary caste with legal privileges as they did in Romanized Europe. This avoided the Saxonized nations from developing, as William Young put it, "the most hateful of all governments; the aristocracy." This is because common law was a bottom up legal system rather than the top-down system that dominates Romanized Europe. No one person, even a king, is above or exempt from obeying the law.

A prime example of this is the case of Queen Edith. Nine hundred years ago, Edith was Queen of the Anglo-Saxon kingdom of Wessex. She had entrusted her horses to a man named Wudumann who also owed her six years of back rent. She wrote to the court of the 100 of Wedmore in Somerset asking for "a just ruling concerning Wudumann." There is no record of the final ruling in this case, but is hard to imagine an 11th century monarch having to go through the legal system in order to get one of her subjects to pay her the back rent he owed. This could only happen in an individual-centric culture that values the individual and the rule of law above the state and monarchal authority.

In 1922, Dean Alfange wrote the poem *My Creed*. This poem is so powerful, so profound, so inspiring that I have included it all my previous books; and I will do so again here. What is incredible about this poem, which was written nearly a hundred years ago and a thousand years after the Anglo-Saxons united England, is that it is just as applicable to the Saxons as it is to the Americans who would inherit their form of government several centuries after their conquest by the Norman tyrant William the Conqueror.

My Creed

I do not choose to be a common man.
It is my right to be uncommon...if I can.
I seek opportunity...not security.
I do not wish to be a kept citizen,
Humbled and dulled by having the state look after me.
I want to take the calculated risk;
To dream and to build,
To fail and to succeed.
I refuse to barter incentive for a dole.
I prefer the challenges of life to the guaranteed existence;
The thrill of fulfillment to the stale calm of utopia.
I will not trade freedom for beneficence
Nor my dignity for a handout.
I will never cower before any master
Nor bend to any threat.
It is my heritage to stand erect, proud and unafraid;
To think and act for myself,

Liberty & Prosperity

Enjoy the benefit of my creations
And to face the world boldly and say,
This I have done.

Chapter 5
The Opportunity Seekers

It is unclear exactly when the Saxons actually arrived on the scene in central Europe. There is no mention of them by Tacitus when he wrote *Germania* in 98 A.D., but they were mentioned less than a century later by the Ptolemy. In his work on the geography of the Greco-Roman world, Ptolemy mentions the Saxons inhabiting the country north of the lower Elbe; which is near the current border between Germany and the Czech Republic. One of the explanations for this is that the Saxons were not a specific people, race, or even a tribe. They were actually a confederation of various individual-centric tribes that formed an alliance to resist Roman state-centric authoritarianism. The warriors of these tribes carried a short sword called the *saex* (also spelt *saxe*), which quickly became a symbol of freedom and liberty. In time the Romans started calling "those who carry the *saex*" *Saxones.* In Old Dutch this became *Saksen,* which evolved into the English variant; Saxon.

In northern Germany, the name was applied to the all the low Germans on the Rhine, the Frisians and Batavi on the Dutch coast, as well as the Jutes and Angles of Denmark. As 18th-century historian Thomas Grattan points out, the name Saxon "comprehends all the tribes of the coast from the Rhine as far north as Denmark." Regardless of where they may have been first located in Germany, it is certain that Saxons migrated to other areas from that in which the main body occupied. During Roman times the Saxons migrated to the coast of modern-day Belgium and Northeastern France. More importantly, they occupied an area that would become known as the Netherlands. As author Daniel Hannan points out, the Saxons were always looking for new lands offering opportunity.

It was in what would become the Netherlands that the Saxons proved themselves to be enterprising as well as intrepid. When the Saxons arrived in the area they found a country inhabited by just a few uncivilized people. The country formed but one immense quagmire which was constantly inundated by the waters of the sea. The coast consisted of only sandbanks surrounded by slime as the land was alternately overflowed with seawater or left semi-dry. Trees were found further inland, but the soil was so marshy that the roots of the trees would rot to the point that a strong storm could level a whole forest. It would be during the storms that the sea had no limits and the rivers no banks. As the Roman expert on Germania, Pliny the elder, wrote in the mid-first century, "There the ocean pours in its flood twice every day, and produces a perpetual uncertainty whether the country may be considered as a part of the continent or of the sea. The wretched inhabitants take refuge on the sand hills, or little huts, which they construct on the summits of lofty stakes, whose elevation is comfortable to that of the highest tides. When the sea rises they appear like navigators; when he sea retires, they seem as though they had been shipwrecked. They subsisted on the fish left by the refluent waters, in which they catch in nets weaved of rushes or seaweed. Neither tree nor shrub is visible on the shores. The drink of the people is rainwater, which they preserve with great care; their fuel, a sort of turf, which they gather in form with the land." A third century visitor observed, the ground was so soggy that there was not "a spot of ground that did not yield under the footsteps of man".

As we will see, this is the land that the Saxons would turn within a millennia into one of the freest and most prosperous nations in the world. But first, they would have to resist Roman authoritarianism. Motley notes that every Roman Legion that entered into this inhospitable land "was forced to retreat disastrously, or to perish miserably." The Saxons, willing to trade their lives for their freedom, never allowed themselves to be conquered..

When the Romans were not trying to conquer the Saxons they were using them as mercenaries in their wars of conquest against other tribes comprised mostly of Gaelic and Celtic people. Once again the Saxon warrior established himself as someone to be reckoned with, feared, and respected. In fact, the Saxons became the only non-Roman warriors that the Romans considered their equals. The Roman commanders knew that they could count on the Saxons to fulfill their missions. This sentiment was echoed by the common Roman centurion who knew that they could trust the Saxon not to turn and run in the heat of battle. It was this respect for their Saxon enemy that led the Romans to take a more conciliatory approach to their attempts to subjugate the Saxons. When the Romans did defeat their liberty loving adversaries, they allowed the Saxons to remain relatively autonomous and, as long as they supplied warriors to the legions of Rome, they were exempt from paying the taxes Rome imposed on other conquered peoples.

One by one the neighboring tribes and allies of the Saxons traded their freedom for Roman favors. They traded their ancient language and customs by learning Latin and adopting the manners and customs of Rome. The moral effect being that even the most vigorous of peoples-- with the loss of their liberty – would become lethargic. Their zeal for life replaced by apathy. This was not the case for the Saxons. Even when the Romans managed to conquer their land the Saxons refused to become a conquered people. All that was needed was a charismatic leader to reignite the Saxon passion for liberty. One of the most famous leaders went by the Roman name Claudius Julius Civilis and he led a revolt that the Dutch celebrate to this day.

Claudius Civilis, whose Teutonic birth name has long been forgotten, was of Batavian nobility and, as was common among the nobility, he accepted the trappings of Roman civilization. He had a Roman education and was fluent in Latin. This, along with his schooling in the Saxon warrior traditions, positioned him well for service within the Roman legions. He became a mercenary for Rome and fought throughout the Empire and beyond. This allowed him to witness the degraded condition that state-centric government always produces. He observed that as government gained more power, it also became more corrupt. He saw the degenerating effect the dependence on government has on the character of the average citizen. He was alarmed by how quickly a once proud and independent people could be reduced to a condition where their survival rested on the generosity of politicians and debauchery was the only means of escaping their empty existence. More significantly for Claudius, he noted the impact the transition from an individual-centric to state-centric society had on the populaces of regions conquered by Rome. People who adopted the Latin language and the manners of Rome, no matter how famous they were for their bravery, eventually "lost their liberty, their energy, and their courage."

After 25 years of loyal service, he and his brother were falsely charged with conspiracy and sent to Rome in chains. His brother was executed, but Claudius was able to escape with his life. Having retained an unconquerable love for liberty and upon learning that Romans were taking young Batavians as slaves, Claudius dedicated himself to a nobler cause; the liberation of the Batavian people from the state-centric rule of Rome. In 69 A.D., by his courage, eloquence, and talent for political strategy, Claudius was able to create a confederation of tribes, including Celtic and Gallic as well as Saxon, to resist the Romans. Batavians serving as auxiliaries in the Roman legions revolted and joined Claudius; thus splitting the northern part of the Roman army.

Initially, what became known as the "Batavian Revolt", was successful with one victory after another. One by one, the pro-Roman rulers within the Netherlands were replaced. Rome responded by sending several legions each comprised of a few thousand soldiers under the command of Quintus Petillius Cerialis. In April 70 A.D., Cerialis defeated Claudius near what is today Nijmegan. Although defeated, Claudius was not ready to give up the struggle for liberty and vowed to carry on the fight. Unfortunately, his allies did not have the same passion for liberty. They claimed that their destruction was inevitable, "that one nation could not arrest the slavery which was destined for the whole world." "Who are they," they asked, "to contest the Holy Roman Empire?"

Sensing the defeatism, the Imperial commander Cerialis seized the moment by sending emissaries to the leaders of the various tribes allied with Claudius. In exchange for their oath of loyalty to Rome, the tribes would not be oppressed by having to pay tribute for taxes to Rome. The only demand that would be placed on them was that they would supply warriors who would bravely fight wherever the Roman eagle was carried into battle. From beyond the Rhine, Claudius watched as the Celtic followed by the Gallic tribes defected to the Roman side. Seeing that the weaker tribes had lost their passion for liberty, Claudius accepted the offer of negotiation from Cerialis. The Roman general, eager to bring a revolt to an end, granted Claudius a full pardon and reenlisted, once again, the brave soldier into the service of the Empire.

This marked the beginning of the end for the Batavians. The Romans would rename the region *Belgic Gaul*, which is the area that comprises most of modern-day Belgium. Under state-centric government, the independent character of the Batavians rapidly degenerated and by the time Tacitus did his study of the Germanic tribes 20 years later they were looked upon as the least brave and most subjugated of all the Germanic tribes in the Netherlands. It was said that "they were not a nation, but merely prey" and within 150 years the Batavians, having been conquered by various tribes, would cease to be a nation and a people.

In history, it is not only victories but also defeats that can shape the ethos of a nation. Just as Dunkirk did for the British in the Second World War and the Alamo did for Americans in the Mexican-American War, so did the failure of the Batavian Revolt do for the Dutch. The spectacle of a brave nation, inspired by the soul of one great man and rising against overwhelming state-centric despotism, would be preserved from one generation to another. Even the great Roman historian Tacitus documented the details of the revolt. He described the battles, the sieges, and the defeat of Claudius with a respect that he bestows on no other enemy of Rome. His admiration for the resolute spirit of Claudius, who only accepted defeat after being abandoned by his weaker willed allies, is evident throughout his narrative of the revolt. Later generations of Dutch would see the Batavian Revolt as a symbol of their traditional resistance to tyranny and authoritarianism. In the 17th and 18th centuries, Dutch writers would see the Batavian's as the "true" forefathers of the Dutch and their tradition of choosing individual-centric liberty over that of state-centric authoritarianism. Areas that were populated by the Dutch will often have streets, towns and cities named "Batavia." Even today, just as the French are sometimes referred to as "Gallic" and the Germans as "Teutonic", "Batavian" is a term sometimes used to describe Dutch people.

From this time forward, we can trace the progress of a totally new and distinct population that was different from the Saxon tribes of the north. Once the Batavians were annihilated, their land was taken over by the Belgic and Gallic tribes from the southwest. These people would remain allied with the Romans and in time would create a region that straddled the cultural boundary between Latin and Germanic Europe. Although it would remain part of the Netherlands well into the 19th century, the mixture of the two cultures would give the people of this region, now known as Belgium, a distinct identity separate from that of the Saxon dominated Netherlands.

Although the Batavians were defeated, the Saxon and Germanic tribes continued to resist state-centric Roman authoritarianism. For the next three centuries, the Romans would send legions of soldiers to suppress the Saxons of Northwest Europe and the Germanic tribes of central Europe. As the popular narrative tells it, it is these border conflicts and colonial wars that will lead to Rome's final collapse in the fourth century. As will see in a later chapter, the collapse of Rome would not have been possible without the internal rot that state-centric government always produces.

Chapter 6
The Collapse of Rome

One of the biggest deceptions that man inflicts on himself is the belief that the way things are in his lifetime is the natural and unchanging state of the world. We do this today, and they did it back when Rome reigned supreme. In his seminal work, *The Rise and Fall of the Roman Empire,* Gibbons observed that Rome hit its pinnacle in the second century A.D. and proceeded to decline over the next 300 years. This decline was obvious to the historians who had the benefit of hindsight, but even as late as 350 A.D. very few within Rome foresaw that, after 1000 years of world dominance, the Roman Empire would cease to exist. Nevertheless, by the end of the fifth century, Rome would have its last Emperor and the Western world would be thrown into chaos.

The most common narrative regarding the fall of Rome tells us that the principal factor that caused its collapse was the centuries of colonial wars waged against the Germanic tribes of Northwest Europe. A few accounts may casually mention the internecine fighting and internal strife as additional factors that weakened the Roman Empire from within. It is more likely that the internecine fighting and the internal strife had more to do with the collapse of Rome than the colonial wars it raged against the Germanic tribes. For although the colonial wars were a burden on the Roman state and economy, it was the rot created by state-centric government that weakened Rome from within.

An unavoidable consequence of state-centric-ism is the massive and overbearing government that it eventually produces. By definition, the state, in the form of the government, is the key player in societies that are state-centric. It's power is beyond that of any other element of society. Its reach can affect the lives of the lowest members of the society. It quickly becomes the primary vehicle for wealth, influence, and power. This destroys the balance of power needed in order for liberty and prosperity to flourish. As this happens, who controls the levers of government becomes critical. Politics come to dominate everyday life as factions compete with each other over who will control the government. Polarization of society becomes inevitable as opposing groups struggle to increase their control over the power of government while limiting that of their political enemies.

This is the rot created by state-centric government. In time, as the balance of power shifts to the political sphere, so does the necessity for factions to keep the levers of government in friendly hands. Politics stops being about serving the people and becomes more about the retention and increasing of power. Out of the desire and desperation for power, factions will start using tactics, strategies, and methods to undermine democratic institutions. Voter fraud, intimidation, ridicule, and demonization of the opposition supplant the once revered principles of fair elections, political tolerance, respect for people's personal views, and pluralism. An individual's political views, once respected and tolerated, now divides neighbors, coworkers, and even family members into opposing political camps to be exploited by power-hungry politicians. Cronyism and corruption become the norm, not the exception. As the society's body politic fractures, so does the society as a whole. It becomes weaker and, like someone with a weakened immune system, susceptible to outside threats.

It is this rot that, over a 300 year period, weakened from within the once mighty and powerful Roman Empire. Internal power struggles affected Rome to the point that it could no longer resist the incursions by bands of barbarians. Even the advanced technology and tactics of the Roman legions could not protect Rome from the primitive Germanic tribesmen. Once through the Empire's outer defenses, the barbarians found a rotted and dying carcass ready to be put out of its misery. And thus, the greatest empires the world has ever seen vanished from the face of the earth and ushered in what would become known as "The Dark Ages."

If, as Gibbons writes, the collapse of Rome came as a surprise to those living within the Empire, then it must have come as an unbelievable shock to those on the outside. In much of Western Europe, including the Netherlands and Southeast England, the collapse of Roman authoritarianism left a vacuum that needed to be filled. As we have seen, the former provinces of Rome broke apart into small little kingdoms and fiefdoms that vied with one another for control. In most areas of the former Empire, it was the people who had adopted the state-centric ways of the Romans that were in the best position to take advantage of the power vacuum created by the collapse. They were better organized and their top-down form of government allowed leaders, who had already taken on the airs of a Roman emperor, the authority to take control of the people and to exploit the situation for their own benefit.

In the Netherlands, it would be the Franks who would initially keep the Saxons under state-centric despotism. The Franks, who had emerged in the third century, occupied most of the land south of the Saxons and, like the Saxons, were the result of the consolidation of several smaller Germanic tribes. Unlike the Saxons, the Franks submitted to Roman rule and adopted its state-centric style of governance. Over time, a widening cultural divide grew between the Franks in the south and their Germanic cousins in the north. As the Franks became more Romanized, the "Vulgar Latin" of the Gauls would replace German as a primary language. This would eventually evolve into the French language just as the Low German of the Saxons would evolve into Dutch and English. In the four centuries following the fall of Rome, the Franks would greatly expand north into Saxon territory.

Frankish expansion, along with a warming of the climate, produced a mass northward migration of German-speaking people--mostly Saxons, Angles, and Jutes--into Holland. Most settled on the northern coast while others proceeded across the channel into England where they became known as the Anglo-Saxons. The newcomers that stayed in the northern Netherlands would eventually be referred to as "Frisians." Since the roots of the Frisians of Holland and the Anglo-Saxons of England were the same, their respective languages were very similar. Old Frisian is the most closely related language to Old English and many modern Frisian dialects are closely related to contemporary English. This is important because language is the means by which the values and principles of a society are transmitted from person to person and from generation to generation. The fact that Old Frisian is nearly identical to Old English explains why both the Dutch and the English developed individual-centric and balanced societies based on the values of limited government, individual rights, private property, and free market economics.

Over the next three centuries the Frisians resisted Frankish authoritarianism. It would not be until 785 A.D., when the Frankish king Charlemagne the Great would finally subjugate the Frisians. As John Motley wrote, "They [the Saxons] had already been once united, in their slavery to Rome. Eight centuries pass away, and they are again united, in their subjection to Charlemagne." Charlemagne is renowned for his military achievements but he was just as politically astute as he was martially capable. Having a deep respect for the independent and liberty minded character of the Frisians, Charlemagne resisted the urge to impose serfdom on his new subjects. As historian Thomas Grattan writes, Charlemagne agreed "first, in the freedom of every order of citizen; second, in the right of property-a right which admitted no authority of the sovereign to violate by confiscation, except in cases of downright treason; third, in the privilege of trial by none but native judges, and according to their national usages; fourth, in a very narrow limitation of military service which they owed to the King; fifth, and a hereditary title to feudal property, and direct line, on payment of certain dues or rents."

This meant that crown appointed military and judicial functionaries had to work within traditional Frisian customs, traditions, and laws. More significantly, Frisians retained ownership of their lands and the Franks never had the authority or power to revoke the ownership, even upon death of the owner. Instead, as according to Saxon tradition, the owner, upon paying what we would call today an 'inheritance tax', was able to bequeath the land to his heirs, thus preserving the fundamental Saxon principle of private ownership of property.

The significance of this agreement cannot be overstated. In time, this agreement would be, as Grattan points out, recognized as the Dutch 'Magna Carta'. "Their privileges secured, their property inviolable, their duties [taxes] limited, the Frisians were altogether free from the servitude which weighed down France. It will soon be seen that the special advantages produced a government nearly analogous to that which Magna Carta was the means of founding at a later period in England."

By the end of the 8th century, Charlemagne had brought most of Western Europe under his control. It was not lost on men such as Pope Leo III that, for the first time since the fall of Rome over three centuries earlier, a large part of the Western Roman Empire had been reconstituted by Charlemagne's conquests. With the goal of returning Roman style government to Western Europe, Pope Leo III crowned Charlemagne as the new Roman emperor on Christmas Day, 800 A.D. Emperor Charles I, as Charlemagne would now be known, would be the first of a long line of emperors who would lead the Holy Roman Empire until its final demise a thousand years later when it was dismantled by Napoleon in 1806.

For Western Europe, this unholy alliance of the church with the state would lead to the two most vile and oppressive doctrines of the Dark Ages; that of Divine Right and Absolute Rule. The doctrine of Divine Right was, as historian John Motley observed, "invented to sanction the system [of absolute rule]; superstition and ignorance gave currency to the delusion." Combined with absolute rule, this meant that the king was empowered by God and that his word was the word of God. This gave the king absolute power over all within his domain including the people. As a result, the common man did not even own his life because the king and his representatives, often minor nobles, had complete control over him, including life and death. To disobey a noble was to disobey God, to violate God's law. This meant that, "the people were now governed, the rulers appointed by an invisible hand. Edicts, issued by a power, as it were, supernatural, demanded implicit obedience. The people, acquiescing in their own annihilation, abdicate not only their political but their personal rights."

Motley goes on to write that by the 10th century, "the old Batavian and later Roman forms had faded away. An entire new polity has succeeded. No great popular assembly asserts its sovereignty, as in the ancient German epoch... the elective power had been lost under the Romans... the Franks pursued the same course... in Charlemagne's time the revolution was complete." People were property, and like all property within a realm they were owned by the nobility which made up the state. The noble was the master who told the peasant or serf how to live. Like animals, children were raised to be replacements for their parents when they died or were no longer useful. With the help of an army of priests, the common people became convinced that they were condemned by God to a life of servitude. During this period, as Motley jarringly sums it up, "The sword is the only symbol of law, the cross is a weapon of offense, the bishop is a pirate, every petty baron a bugler, while the people, alternately the prey of duke, prelate, and seignor [sic], shorn and butchered like sheep, esteem it happiness to sell themselves into slavery, or huddle beneath the castle walls of some little potentate, for the sake of wolfish protection." This would evolve into the prime characteristic of the peasant society, which would dominate western Europe well into the 19th century.

In the end, the Holy Roman Empire never did achieve the unity that Pope Leo III had dreamed it would. Although it would encompass most of modern-day France, Italy, Germany, the Netherlands, Belgium, Luxemburg, Switzerland, Austria, the Czech and Slovak Republics, Slovenia, and Poland, it was never more than a loose confederation of kingdoms, dukedoms, and principalities of various sizes and ethnicities. Each one semi-autonomous and whose obedience to the empire depended on the leadership abilities of the emperor and family ties. Just as Charlemagne remained the King of the Franks, an emperor was a king of his people first and emperor of the empire second. It was not uncommon for member states of the empire to disregard orders from the emperor or the pope. Member states often waged war against other members of the empire including the emperor's. In the end, the Holy Roman Empire became a dysfunctional body of feudal monarchs; most of them petty.

It would be family ties, and not the Holy Roman Empire, that would draw and redraw the map of Europe during the Middle Ages. It was during this period that the political (aka royal) family came to dominate European politics. Kingdoms were united through marriage and then divided as it was, upon the king's death, parceled out to his heirs. Changes in who controlled a territory and ruled a people was determined more by changes in the family than it was by military conquest. Although the degree of despotism would vary over time from kingdom to kingdom, often dictated by the person on the throne, they were all state-centric with peasants serving their all-powerful feudal lords. As John Motley points out, "it was a miserable people, with personal, but no civil rights whatever. Their condition, although better than servitude, was almost desperate. They were taxed beyond their ability, while priest and noble were exempt." The Dark Ages had cast its shadow over Europe.

Due to the semi-autonomy granted by Charlemagne, the Netherlands escaped much of the totalitarian effects of the Dark Ages. "Whatever the nominal sovereignty over them, this most

Republican tribe of Europeans [the northern Dutch], had never accepted feudalism... They created, not for all inhabitants, but for great numbers of them, the right, not to govern themselves but to be governed by law: they furnished a local administration of justice. They provided against arbitrary imprisonment... They held up a shield against arbitrary violence from above and sedition from within... They encourage peacemakers, punished peace breakers. (Motley) "

It was during this period that the individual-centric principles of the Saxons first demonstrated their unchallengeable ability in producing freedom and prosperity for not only the elites, but for the common man. In an historic transfer of commercial hegemony from the Mediterranean to the North Atlantic, the Netherlands, free from the state imposed restrictions and municipal protectionism that had kept medieval industry unprogressive, became the business capital of Europe. As historian William Durant wrote in his 11 volume historical epic *The Story of Civilization* "The harbor [of Antwerp] saw 500 ships enter or leave on any day, and 5000 traders trafficked on the [stock] exchange. A bill on Antwerp [financial exchange] was now the commonest form of international currency."

Motley was also astonished by Dutch prosperity. In reference to Antwerp he would write, "No city. except Paris, surpassed it in population, none approached it in commercial splendor. *Its government was very free."* It is clear from the last sentence that Motley recognized that the key to Dutch prosperity was due to local governments formed on the principles of limited authority, individual liberty, private property, and economic freedom. This becomes strikingly evident when we observe that the Dutch provinces generated half the annual income of Charles V, Emperor of the Holy Roman Empire (r. 1519-1558). This is quite impressive when we consider that at the time the Holy Roman Empire encompassed all of Western and Central Europe (minus France. Portugal, and England), as well as the Spanish Empire in the New World.

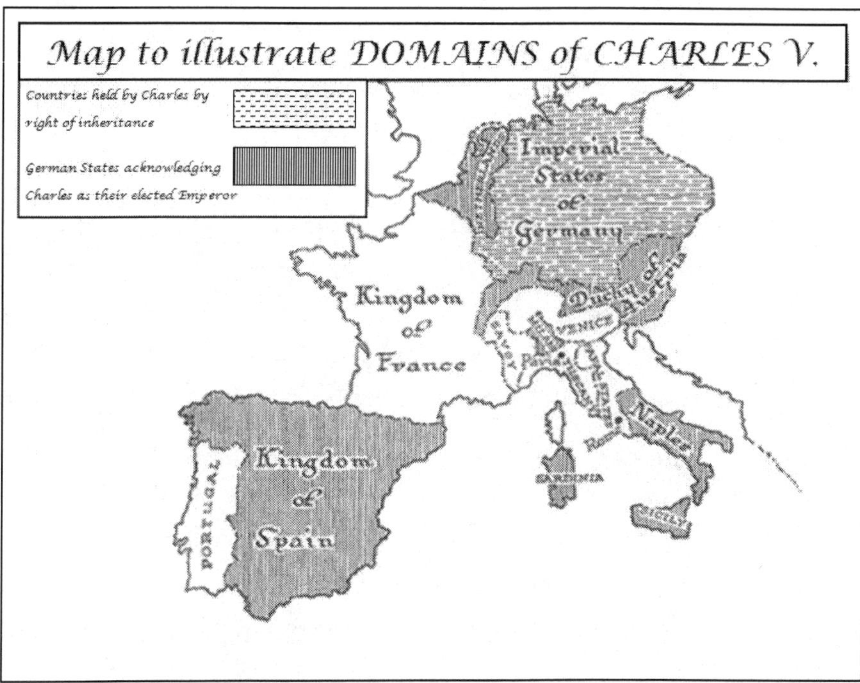

Yet, as autonomous as the Dutch were, their potential was hindered by being part of the state-centric and feudalistic Holy Roman Empire. It would require an 80 year war for independence before Saxon principles could be unleashed to usher in what is known as *The Dutch Golden Age*.

Part II

The Dutch

Chapter 7
Road to War

History demonstrates that two diametrically opposed systems cannot permanently coexist within one society. Over time one, usually the most oppressive and unbalanced, will eventually subjugate the other. This is especially true of state-centric systems, which puts the state above all else and demands that everyone within their realm submit themselves to the needs of the state. Even in decentralized and dysfunctional states such as the Holy Roman and Spanish empires, it would eventually attempt to stifle any individual-centric sentiment within its control. Although it would take several centuries to transpire, the conflict between the individual-centric Saxonized Dutch and the state-centric Romanized Spanish was inevitable.

As John Motley writes, "The democratic instincts" of the ancient Saxons would "survive" in the Dutch. "Their love of freedom, readiness to strike and bleed at any moment in her cause, manly resistance to despotism, however overshadowing, would be the leading characteristic" of the of the people that occupied the area that would become known as the Netherlands. This would lead 14th century French chronicler, Jean Froissart, to comment in the language of the time that the Dutch "were a most unreasonable race for not recognizing the authority and power of the great lords."

Froissart's observation is more significant than just being a mere criticism of Dutch character. We need to remember that the Roman Empire was seen as the apex of man's development; the height of civilization. For the political elites and the educated class, the collapse of Rome -- and the civil government it created -- set humanity back a thousand years. They made it their goal to recreate Roman state-centric-ism. This, they believed, would establish the civil government [state dominance] required to create the ordered, authoritarian society necessary to end what they saw as the political chaos of the Dark Ages. The sole purpose of the Holy Roman Empire was an attempt to do just that. Therefore, serfdom was not seen in the negative light which it currently is. In the Middle Ages it was seen by the top thinkers of the time as being the way the civilized world should be and the future of mankind. In other words, it -- and not freedom -- was progressive.

The Dutch, on the other hand, were seen to be hanging onto the archaic values of the savage people who resisted being civilized by the Romans; and may have even caused their downfall. They were the "barbarians"- a word that even in modern parlance is used to describe people who are uncivilized, primitive, atrocious, savage, and, yes, unreasonable. To the political elites and educated class, their resistance to the prevailing political wisdom of the age -- centered on absolutism, authoritarianism, and serfdom -- was considered regressive and provincial.

In the 16th century these two diametrically opposed ideologies will collide in what historian Will Durant calls "one of the great dramas in the history of freedom."

As mentioned in the previous chapter, the Frisians and most of what would become the Netherlands became part of the Holy Roman Empire when Charlemagne was crowned its first Emperor. Through a series of marriages, purchases, and wars the 17 provinces that make up the modern nations of Belgium, Luxembourg, and the Netherlands would come under the control of the Habsburg family. During that time, the Dutch would find themselves being the subjects of various autocratic kingdoms including the authoritarian Austrian Empire and, when Spanish King Charles I became Charles V Emperor the Holy Roman Empire in 1519, the despotic Kingdom of Spain.

Charles' authority was constitutionally limited by his sworn pledge to observe the charters and local laws of the Dutch cities and provinces, which each had their own governments and courts controlled by the local nobility. But, as Charles' empire grew, he became more imperious. The Spanish imposed an overall government called the Estates General of the Netherlands and it had its own crown appointed officials and courts. Through this government, in violation to the agreement signed by Charlemagne, Spanish officials overruled Dutch nobility, dismissed local officials, and blatantly ignored their traditional liberties. Charles then went on to station Spanish troops within Dutch cities and severely suppressed any opposition to his international policies. As Thomas Grattan writes, Charles V would focus "a jealous eye on the institutions of those provinces which place limits to his power and... would soon degenerate into a usurping master in the north."

An example of Charles' tyrannical nature was demonstrated when the people of Ghent, suspecting an improper or improvident application of the funds they had furnished for previous campaigns, voted not to grant Charles the military funds he requested for a new campaign against France. Charles saw this as a challenge to his authority and reacted with unrelenting force. He immediately marched his army to the city and demanded entry. Taken by surprise, the city leaders had no option but to allow Charles to enter. Once inside the city walls, Charles punished the city with extreme severity. In addition to the requested funds, he made the city pay an additional indemnity to guarantee future compliance. He then went on to order the beheading of 27 leaders of the locally elected government and replaced them with Imperial appointees who abolished the traditional liberties of the municipality. Finally, as a reminder to the people of Ghent of his authority, Charles had a citadel constructed nearby to house a garrison of Spanish troops ready to suppress any opposition. While this is an extreme example, it does show Charles' willingness to violate the constitutional limits of his power in order to get what he wanted from the Dutch people.

Although actions like these would lead to an ever increasing amount of anti-Spanish sentiment within the Dutch provinces, they did not initially lead to the desire to obtain Dutch independence. At the time, the Dutch were becoming a very wealthy and prosperous people. Unaware, as noted previously, that the Dutch provinces were generating over half of the income of the Spanish Empire, the Dutch people mistakenly attributed their good fortune to being part of the most powerful and wealthy empire in Europe, if not the world. To sacrifice a few liberties in order to maintain the prosperity they had achieved while being part of the Spanish Empire was a trade-off they were willing to accept.

It would only be after the provinces gained independence that they would discover that it was not their association with an authoritarian, state-centric regime that made them prosperous, but the values they inherited from their Saxon forefathers. In the end, it would require use of the Inquisition as a means to oppress the teachings of a monk by the name of Martin Luther to create a situation that was so intolerable to the Dutch that, inspired by their Protestant leaders, they saw no alternative but rise in arms against their Spanish masters.

It is impossible to understate the role that the Protestant Reformation played in bringing about the 80 year war that would eventually result in the independence of the Dutch people. By the 16th century, as Grattan noted, "the ecclesiastical power became greater and greater, and was quite as arbitrary and enormous as that of the nobility." The cross had become a symbol of oppression rather than salvation. Through the preaching of divine right the church gave God's blessing to every monarch sitting on a throne regardless of whether he was good or bad, libertarian or oppressive, humane or brutal. The sale of indulgences to the nobility meant that for a price a nobleman could be brutal and inhumane here on earth but still be guaranteed a place in heaven. Meanwhile, even the slightest rebellious thought that a commoner may have against a tyrannical king would condemn him for eternity to the fiery pits of hell.

John Motley's use of the term "pirates" in describing the bishops of the time was not very far off the mark. In 1430, a German contemporary of Martin Luther would write, "Greed reigns supreme in the Roman court [the Vatican] and day by day finds new devices for extorting money." Furthermore, it was not uncommon for the church, with its large number of literate priests, to provide administrative services to the nobility. This often included the writing, copying, and storing of legal documents including deeds to property. Many bishops became extremely wealthy by replacing a legitimate property deed with a fraudulent one that conveyed ownership to a nobleman or even to themselves. In his book *The History of the Popes*, German historian Ludwig von Pastor would write:

A deep-rooted corruption had taken possession of nearly all the officials of the Curia... The inordinate number of gratuities and exactions passed all bounds. Moreover, on all sides deeds were dishonestly manipulated, and even falsified, by the officials. No wonder that there arose from all parts of Christendom the loudest complaints about the corruption and financial extortions of the papal officials.

As a tool of suppression, the victims of these thefts were usually people who were out-of-favor of both the nobility and the church since both institutions protected their own. This resulted in a cronyism that only an unbalanced state-centric system can produce.

The Dutch, like their Saxon predecessors, were as resistant to state-centric religion as they were to state-centered government. Over 1000 years earlier, their Saxon forbearers resisted the authoritarian religion of the Romans and, to the Dutch of the 16th century, the church currently based in Rome was no better. The Dutch people resented it's overbearing authoritarianism, it's promulgation of the concept of divine right, and the rampant corruption that afflicted the entire church body. This made them extremely vulnerable to the teachings of Martin Luther and would make the Netherlands one of the two most powerful Protestant nations in Europe (the other, not coincidentally, being England).

Initially, Protestantism would arrive in the Netherlands in the form of the Anabaptists from Switzerland. These were people who "adopted a Puritan severity of morals and simplicity of manners and dress... Condemned all government... Rejected military service... They were Tolstoyan anarchists three centuries before

Tolstory (Durant)." They rejected all materialism except for the basic necessities and set up communistic societies where all goods, and in some cases even wives, were considered communal property. This they believed would prepare them for the kingdom of heaven where "communism would be automatic and universal." Finally, they were apocalyptic and believed that Christ's return was near. "Then all the ungodly - in this case all but Anabaptists - would be swept away by the sword of the Lord and the elect would live in glory and a terrestrial paradise without laws or marriage, and abounding in all good things (Durant)."

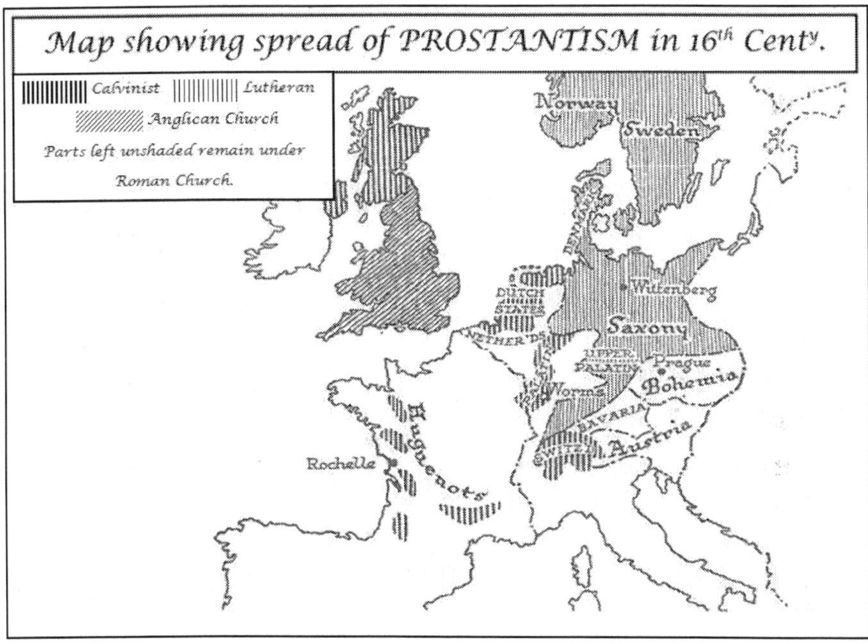

Just as communism is repugnant to most English-speakers today, Anabaptism had little appeal to the Dutch people who still considered their traditional right to private property and economic freedom inviolable. It would take Protestantism which saw the making of wealth as a virtue and not a sin to win over the Dutch people. And that Protestantism came in the form of Calvinism.

Calvinism had a lot of appeal to the average Dutch person. It was individualistic in nature; each person had a private relationship with God. It preached that the moral and legal acquisition of wealth was not a sin, but a virtue for how can you take care of others if you do not have the means to even take care of yourself? For the first time, the concept of a "calling in life" was applied to more than just serving the church. People learned that they were on this planet to fulfill a purpose that God had created for them. They would discover this purpose through hard work, self-improvement, and a never ending desire to learn. In time, this will become known as "the Protestant work ethic", but it originated with the Calvinist and, as we will see in a future chapter, would allow the Dutch, the English, and then the Americans to become the dominant powers of their time. More importantly, it would -- by ending the unholy alliance that had developed between the state and the Catholic church -- reestablish the balance needed for liberty and prosperity to thrive. As we will see, this would have historical implications that are still felt to this day.

With Spain being the most rigid and powerful of all the Catholic nations, Charles felt it his sacred duty to extinguish the heresy of Protestantism. Initially, with the Dutch rejection of Anabaptism, he did not see Protestantism as being a serious threat in the Netherlands. Other then placing a few placards admonishing the Dutch to resist the heresy of Luther, he did very little to stop the incursion of Protestantism into the Spanish Netherlands. Instead, as the King of Spain, he focused on exterminating the pockets of Islam that remained within his kingdom. As Protestantism spread throughout the Holy Roman Empire, he as Emperor was duty-bound to suppress the heresy of Luther wherever it was being preached. This resulted in a protracted holy war against the German principalities that converted to Lutheranism. During the same period, Charles found himself fighting an imperial war against his fellow Catholic monarch Francis I King of France. The pressure of these continuous wars would break Charles' health and in 1556 he voluntarily, at the age of 56, abdicated his throne.

Charles' son became Philip II King of Spain and Spain's relationship with the Dutch went from bad to worse. Having initially negotiated, in exchange for revenue, the removal of all of Spanish troops from Dutch territory, it appeared that an environment of cooperation had been created between him and the Dutch leaders. Yet, even before the last Spanish soldier left for Spain, Philip created eleven new bishoprics.

These bishoprics, charged with ending spread of Protestantism, meant that all the abuse of power and barbarism of the Spanish Inquisition was now being unleashed onto the liberty-minded and religiously tolerant Dutch. As Durant describes it,

Councils [created by the bishoprics] were to ferret out and arrest all persons suspected of opposing the Catholic Church or the Spanish government, to try them privately, and to ultimately punished the convicted without tenderness or delay [often by being burnt alive at the stake]. Agents were sent out to spy; informers were encouraged to betray their relatives, their enemies, their friends. Emigration was forbidden; shipmaster's aiding emigration were to be hanged. Every town that failed to stop or punish rebellion was held guilty, and its officials were imprisoned or fined. Thousands of arrest were made; and one morning some 1500 persons were seized in their beds and carried off to jail. Trials were summary. Condemnations to death were sometimes voted upon in groups of thirty, forty, or fifty at a time. In one month (January 1568) eighty-four residents of Valenciennes were executed. Soon there was hardly a family that did not mourn a member arrested or killed... Scarcely anyone in the Netherlands dared to protest; the slightest criticism would have meant arrest.

Leading men who spoke out against such abuse of power were forced to flee or face the Inquisition themselves. One of those men was William of Nassau, the Prince of Orange who was the richest and ablest of the great landowners. Under the protection of the Lutheran princes of Germany, he formed an army to once and for all give the Dutch their freedom. Little did he know that it would be eighty long and bloody years before the dream of freedom he had for his people would be realized.

Chapter 8

The Struggle for Independence

When John Motley wrote that, "The so-called revolutions of Holland, England, and America are all links in one chain." he was referring to all three being parts of the struggle between Saxon inspired individual freedom and Roman inspired state-centric authoritarianism. But the similarities between the Dutch War of Independence and that of the Americans 200 years later go far deeper than just a struggle for freedom. Like the Americans, the Dutch were a prosperous colony of one of the most powerful nations in Europe, if not the world. Although the provinces were wealthy, most of that wealth had gone into the coffers of the mother country and they did not have the financial means to field an army. What army they could form was created mostly from local poorly equipped and trained militia, German mercenaries, and French Protestants known as Huguenots. As a result, they had to rely on friendly foreign powers for aid, which came mainly from the

Protestant principalities of Germany and, as in the American Revolution, France.

From the conflict would emerge a George Washington like figure named William of Nassau, Prince of Orange. William, as previously mentioned, was one of the wealthiest landowners in Holland. Although religion would play a big part in the war, William was neither Catholic nor Calvinist, which was the dominant Protestant sect at the time. He could be at best called an Erasmusian. Having a natural aversion to extremes he, like Erasmus, saw the dangers that the rigid doctrines of both Catholic and Calvinism posed to liberty. Instead, he sought a middle ground, including religious tolerance, which led some to claim he was an atheist. Regardless of the critique of his religious beliefs, the Dutch provinces -- which was equally split between Catholics in the south and Protestants in the north -- needed William to form a coalition that could resist the military might of the Spanish Empire. Additionally, his religious tolerance appealed to the Lutheran German princes whose support he desperately needed. Furthermore, it would allow him to work closely with his French allies who, although Catholic, were more than anxious to use the situation to damage an imperial rival. More importantly, while not a great military leader, William was a great leader of men. He knew who to select to lead his armies and how to inspire all Dutchmen, regardless of religion, to the cause of liberty.

It is hard to imagine that, without William, the struggle for Dutch freedom would have started much less been successful. Unfortunately, William will never see a free and independent Netherlands, he would be assassinated before the end of the conflict. "Having sacrificed nearly all of his belongings in promotion of the revolt, he left his twelve children almost penniless (Durant)." The sacrifice of his time, wealth, and ultimately his life for the cause of liberty did not go unnoticed by the Dutch people. He was buried in the city of Delft with the honor of going down in history as "Father of His Country."

Initially, William's primary adversary would be the very capable and experienced military commander Fernando Alvarez de Toledo, Duke of Alva. In response to Dutch resistance to the brutal methods of the Inquisition, King Philip charged Alva to lead a select force of 10,000 highly trained and well-equipped Spanish troops back into the Netherlands. Phillips orders to Alva were quite clear: crush the Protestant rebels without mercy. On August 22, 1567, Alva's army entered the city of Brussels and he immediately garrisoned the larger towns with his Spanish troops. With his troops occupying the provinces, he moved his command to the citadel near Antwerp and proclaimed himself Regent and Governor General of all the Netherlands. When secured in his position, he prepared to cleanse the Netherlands of all heresy. He invited the Calvinist leaders Egmont and Horn to dinner where, upon finishing the meal, they were promptly arrested. William, who was in hiding in Germany, was declared an "outlaw whom anyone might kill with legal impunity." It appeared as if the fight for Dutch independence was over before it had a chance to get started.

William realized that if the Dutch were ever to be a free and independent people, now was the time. He immediately proceeded to form an army and requested that his brother Louis do the same. He knew that only trained and experienced soldiers would be able to defeat the Spanish troops of Alva; which meant hiring expensive mercenaries. He asked for aid from the Lutheran princes of Germany and the Protestant queen of England, Elizabeth. The princes, skeptic of his success, gave only small amounts while Elizabeth, fearing war with Spain, gave none at all. In the end, it would be the Dutch themselves who would finance the initial part of Williams war for Dutch independence. Funds came from Antwerp, Amsterdam, Leiden, Haarlem, and Flushing. Yet, this was still not enough to field an army and William was forced to sell all his jewelry, tapestries, and furniture.

William's plan was to invade the Netherlands with three simultaneous attacks. "A force of Huguenots from France was to attack Artois in the Southwest; Count van Hoogstraaten was to lead his men against Maastricht in the South; Louis of Nassau [William's brother] was to enter Friesland from Germany in the Northeast. The Huguenot and Hoogstraaten invasions were repulsed, but Louis won a victory over the Spanish soldiery at Heiligerlee (May 23, 1568)." In order to release the 3000 troops that were guarding Egmont and Horn, Alva ordered their execution on June 5. With these reinforcements he attacked and overwhelmed Louis' weakened army at Jemmingen on July 21, killing over 7000 men. William responded by personally leading 25,000 men into Brabant in order to meet Alva in a decisive battle. Although outnumbered, Alva's force was better disciplined and he was able use delaying actions to draw out the campaign; eventually exhausting William's funds. Unable to pay his mercenaries, William retreated into France where the army was disbanded. Dressed as a peasant, he then made his way back into Germany where he moved from one town to another to avoid assassination. "With these disastrous campaigns began the "80 Years' War," which was raged with unprecedented perseverance by the Netherlands till their final triumph in 1648. (Durant)"

Keeping an army in the field is expensive and after several months of campaigning Alva was just as penniless as William. Philip was able to arrange with some Genoese bankers to send Alva 450,000 ducats by sea. The vessels were intercepted by English privateers and forced into Plymouth harbor. Although Queen Elizabeth had shied away from sending William financial aid, she was willing, in the name of neutrality, to keep Phillip's money. Soon afterwards, a group of Calvinists calling themselves "Beggars of the Sea" seized control of eighteen vessels. Receiving a commission from William, these vessels were able to ensure that Alva could no longer receive supplies through northern Dutch ports. This meant that Alva was dependent on supplies arriving overland from Spain, thus restricting his activities to southern Netherlands. This provided a sufficient sense of security for the principle cities in the northern provinces of Holland, Zeeland, Gelderland, and Friesland to give their allegiance to William and promise to supply him for the duration of the war. This change of fortune in the struggle for Dutch liberty inspired Philip van Marnix to compose "Wilhelmus", which would become the national anthem of the Netherlands and is today the oldest national anthem in the world.

With William firmly secure in the north and Alva entrenched in the south, the war settled into what could best be called a stalemate. Both sides made attacks into the other's territory only to find their resources, especially financial, inadequate to obtain any meaningful advantage. In fact, it took on the characteristics of a sectarian civil war rather than one against a colonial oppressor. Wars such as these tend to bring out the worst in men and this war was no different. As Motley would write:

On more than one occasion men were seen hanging… their own brothers, who had been taken prisoners in the enemy ranks… A Spaniard had ceased to be human in their [the Dutch] eyes. On one occasion a surgeon at Veer cut the heart from a Spanish prisoner, nailed it on a vessel's prow, and invited the townsmen to come and fasten their teeth in it, which many did with savage satisfaction.

As heinous as the above may sound, it paled in comparison to what was known as the "Spanish fury." Alva tasked his son Don Federigo Alverez de Toledo with the job of punishing the cities that had declared for William or had surrendered to him. The first city to feel the Spanish fury was Michelin. Having surrendered to the Spanish with scarcely any resistance, the town's leading citizens including priests and Catholics begged for the town to be spared. But Alva wanted the city to be made an example for the rest. For three days Don Federigo's troops "sacked homes, monasteries, and churches, stole the jewels and costly robes of religious statuary, trampled consecrated wafers under foot, butchered men and violated women, Catholic or Protestant." In hopes to avoid the fury, the townspeople of Little Naardin greeted the conquering Spaniards with tables full of food. After the soldiers had their fill of food and drink they killed every person in the town. The worst was reserved for the Calvinist stronghold of Haarlem. The 4000 strong garrison put up resolute resistance but after a seven-month siege were reduced to eating weeds and leather. On July 11, 1573 the city surrendered. Of the original 4000 only 1600 survived the siege only to be put to death by Alvarez's forces. Four hundred of the city's leading citizens were executed and the rest spared only upon agreeing to pay a ransom of 250,000 guilders.

The siege of Haarlem was very expensive in both lives and treasure for the Spanish. During the seven-month siege over 12,000 Spanish soldiers died due to disease or wounds. The financial cost of maintaining a siege of the city the size of Haarlem for that period of time cost more than King Philip could afford to pay. Furthermore, the atrocities made Alva as unpopular with Catholics as it did with Protestants. The Bishop of Namur estimated that Alva had done more harm to Catholicism in seven years than Luther and

Calvinism had done in a generation. The result was that more Dutch, both Catholic and Protestant, saw the religious tolerance of William and Dutch independence preferable to the tyranny of Catholic Spain. Sensing his monarch's displeasure, Alva resigned and, on December 18, 1573, he returned to Spain.

William's new adversary would be the former Viceroy of Milan, Don Luis de Requesens the new governor of the Netherlands. Don Luis was shocked by the number and morale of the rebels. "Before my arrival," he wrote to the King, "I did not understand how they could maintain such considerable fleets, while your Majesty could not support a single one. It appears, however, that men who are fighting for their lives, their firesides, their property, and their false religion -- for their own cause, in short -- are contented to receive rations only, without receiving pay." Understanding the severity of the situation, Don Luis asked Philip to allow him to grant a general amnesty to all but persisting heretics, to allow these to emigrate, and to abolish the 10% sales tax.

William correctly saw this as nothing more than a tactic to drive Protestantism out of the Netherlands. For him, nothing short of full freedom of worship, the restoration of the provinces' traditional privileges and liberties, and the withdrawal of all Spaniards from civil and military post would be acceptable. The war would continue but at great personal cost to William. On April 13, 1574, he would lose both his brothers, Louis (age 36) and Henry (age 24) in the battle of Mook.

Several years of warfare, including the loss of revenue from his Dutch colonies, left Philip bankrupt and nowhere close to ending the stalemate that was draining Spanish blood and treasure. To make matters worse, less than three years after his arrival, Don Luis died during the siege of Zierikzee. Scrambling to find a replacement, Philip ordered his half-brother Don Juan of Austria to take control of the Netherlands. It would take Don Juan several critical months to arrive in the provinces. During that time the representatives of Holland and Zealand signed the Act of Pacification, which gave William supreme command on land and sea, the power of appointment to all political post, and if needed, the right to put the provinces under the protection of a sympathetic foreign prince. In an appeal to other provinces to join the struggle against the Spaniards, William demonstrated his religious tolerance by promising liberty of conscience and worship to all the Dutch people, regardless of whether they were Protestant or Catholic.

This appeal may not have been as successful as it was if not for the atrocities of the leaderless Spanish soldiers. On November 4, 1576, they seized Antwerp and committed the worst atrocities in Netherland history; including the years under Nazi occupation during World War II. All through the night the Spaniards plundered the city leaving no home untouched. In search of treasure, "parents were tortured in their children's presence, infants were slain in their mother's arms, wives were flogged to death before their husbands eyes (Durant)." For two days the soldiers, overcome with bloodlust, slaughtered men, women, and children regardless of their religion and razed thousands of buildings. In the end, over 7000 citizens of Antwerp perished.

The timeliness of this event could not have been better for William. At that very moment an assembly of representatives from the southern provinces were in Brussels debating the Act of Pacification and William's appeal to resist Spanish rule. The seven Catholic dominant provinces were reluctant to join what they saw as a declaration of war against the King and it appeared that they would refuse William's offer. But then the news of Antwerp arrived and with the ratification of the Pacification of Ghent on November

28, the southern provinces joined William in the struggle for Dutch independence. They would reaffirm their dedication to the struggle a year later when all the provinces except Namur joined the Union of Brussels.

With William having unified Catholic and Protestant Netherlands, the war for Dutch independence appeared all but over. Unfortunately, the first victim of a holy war is religious tolerance and as soon as it was established, the Union started to be torn apart by sectarian violence. The Calvinist saw the Catholic use of symbols and images as idol worship and refused to believe that they would disavow their allegiance to Spain and Rome. Upon gaining control of the provincial assembly in Holland, the Calvinists immediately voided William's promise of liberty of conscience and worship as Catholic services were outlawed. This alarmed many of the Catholics in the south and they immediately opened the city gates when the most able general of the age, the Duke of Parma, arrived with 20,000 well-trained Spanish troops. William was dismayed by what he was seeing. Everything he had worked and sacrificed for had now been torn apart by religious intolerance. Yet, to the Calvinist only a nonbeliever could be tolerant of a false religion and many openly condemned William as an atheist.

Alessandro Farnese, the Duke of Parma, is recognized by historians as one of the great military leaders of his time. Much of that reputation would be made in the southern provinces of the Netherlands. Not only did he surpass Alva in military skill, he was also equal to William in the art of negotiation and the talent for inspiration. "The battle for the Netherlands," Durant writes, "now became a duel between the Duke of Parma's diplomacy and arms, supported by Catholic funds and hopes, and that heroic perseverance of the Prince of Orange, financed by Dutch merchants and helped and hindered by the fanaticism of his friends."

Parma's arrival immediately changed the military and political situation in the Netherlands. Secure under the protection of Parma and his army, four of the southernmost provinces formed the League of Arras on January 5, 1579. The objective of the league was to protect the Catholic religion and the property of its adherents. No other religion except Catholicism could be practiced within the League and the privileges of the provinces restored as long as they recognized Spanish sovereignty. Two weeks after the formation of the League of Arras, the northernmost--and most Protestant--provinces of Holland, Zeeland, Groningen, Utrecht, and Gelderland formed the Union of Utrecht. Trapped between the League and the Union where the remaining religiously mixed provinces, many of whose assemblies were controlled by prominent local Calvinist.

Through political astuteness, military might, and the coffers of King Philip Parma was able to bring six of the eight colonies into the League. One by one, the Calvinist lost the vital and anti-Catholic cities of Brussels, Ghent, and Ypres. Only at the strategic city of Maastricht would William's forces make a stand. This required Parma to lay siege to the city for four months before he would be able to enter its gates victoriously. Immediately upon taking control of the city, he had 6000 men women and children massacred. Of the original 30,000 souls that inhabited the city, less than 400 would survive the siege. Previously religiously mixed, Parma now repopulated the city with Catholics from Walloon. Driven by a well justified fear, many Protestants fled north. This mass exodus would result in the relocation of half the population of Antwerp, three quarters of the populations of the cities of Bruges and Ghent, and the entire populations of Nieuwpoort and Dunkerque to Holland.

The depopulation of Protestants from the south, gave the Catholics unchallenged control of the lower half of the Low Countries.

Although the division of the seventeen provinces into two separate states resulted in a Catholic dominated south and Protestants controlled north, it would be the land's natural waterways that would determine the final borders of the two regions. The last provinces of Friesland and Overijssel were protected by a series of rivers, waterways, and dykes that the Spanish forces could not overcome. Out of the reach of Parma, both of these provinces eventually joined the Union. Neither side being able to overcome the watery obstacles, the military part of the war stagnated and these borders would remain throughout the rest of the conflict.

The loss of ten of the seventeen provinces was a blow to the cause of Dutch independence and to William's prestige. Many began to question whether he was the right leader. Some staunch Calvinist opined that the loss of the provinces to Parma was God's punishment for William's tolerance of "false religions" and his absence at religious services led many to believe he was really an atheist. Sensing William's drop in popularity among the Dutch, Philip seized the moment to promulgate a ban against the Prince of Orange. On March 15, 1581, Philip issued a proclamation declaring:

Therefore... for all his [William's] evil doings as chief disturber of the public peace, and as a public pest, we outlaw him forever, and forbid all our subjects to associate with him or communicate with him in public or in secret, or to administer to him victuals, drink, fire, or other necessaries. We declare him an enemy of the human race and give his property to all who may seize it. In order this sooner to remove our people from his tyranny and oppression, we promise, on the word of our King and as God's servant, that if one of our subjects be found so generous of heart... That he shall find means of executing this decree and ridding us of the said pest, either by delivering him to us dead or alive, or by depriving him at once of life, we will give him and his heirs landed property or money, as he will, to the amount of 25,000 gold crowns. If he has committed any crime, of any kind whatsoever, we will pardon him. If he'd be not noble we will ennoble him.

Yet, despite his drop in popularity, William was still popular in the northern seven provinces and he was made stadholder of Holland and Zealand on July 24, 1581. Two days later representatives of Holland, Zeeland, Gelderland, Utrecht, Flanders, and Brabant signed at The Hague a document that rivals that of America's Declaration of Independence and England's Declaration of Rights. Predating the English document by 100 years and the American equivalent by 200 years, the Act of Adjuration, proclaimed that a ruler who treats his subjects as slaves and destroys their liberties should no longer be accounted their legitimate sovereign and may lawfully be disposed. Thus denouncing their allegiance to the King of Spain, the Dutch had proclaimed their independence with a promise by William that he would "hold fast" in the struggle for Dutch self-government.

Meanwhile, ardent Catholics were inspired by Philip's proclamation. As defenders of their faith, they saw it as their duty to exterminate the outlawed heretic William. Additionally, the chance at earning earthly rewards such as title and wealth made the holy deed enticing to many lukewarm believers. One such individual was Jean Jaureguy. Armed with a pistol he made his way to the Prince of Orange and shot him in the head. Jaureguy was immediately killed; fully content that his place in heaven was assured by his dispatch of William into the fiery depths of hell. Unfortunately for the would be assassin, William was not instantly killed. For weeks he seemed to be on the verge of dying. Only the around the clock care he received from his wife Charlotte kept him from slipping into the abyss. Miraculously, he recovered. Sadly, Charlotte would die of exhaustion.

Over the next few years, there would be several unsuccessful attempts on William's life. It is a testament to the Dutch that even after such attempts on the life of their leader that they resisted mob rule by upholding the principle of the rule of law and due process. In one case, after an attempted poisoning, two conspirators were arrested. One committed suicide while in jail, but the other was given a trial. Upon being found guilty, the offender was sentenced to quartering. This was accomplished by tying each of the four limbs to a different horse and spurring them in different directions. While barbaric by modern standards, this was the customary penalty throughout Europe for high treason. The main difference is that in most countries of the period, the suspect would not have the benefit of due process and a trial.

To William's supporters, his miraculous recovery and the failure of multiple assassination attempts were signs that God was on their side and that their leader was divinely protected. This would all come to an end on July 18, 1584. William was in the town of Delft providing aid to the poor when he was approached by an impoverished young Calvinist seeking William's charity. The beggar was really a young man from Burgundy named Balthasar Gerard. By exploiting William's commitment to helping the impoverished citizens of the Netherlands, Gerard was able to get close enough to shoot William three times. As he collapsed mortally wounded to the ground, William was heard to cry out, "My God, have pity on my soul...have pity on these poor people." Gerard was immediately arrested and after a trial by the city magistrates was sentenced to death. As promised, his parents received the reward offered by Phillip and for the next fifty years Spanish and Dutch Catholics unsuccessfully appealed to have him declared a saint.

William was buried in Delft with the high honor of going down in history as the "father of his country." He had lost his brothers and his wife to the cause of Dutch liberty and freedom. Having personally financed much of the struggle for Dutch independence, he was nearly as destitute as Gerard pretended to be; leaving his twelve children almost penniless. It would have been almost out of character for him not to have made the ultimate sacrifice for the people and nation he loved so much.

In familiar terms, the loss of William had the same effect as the loss of Churchill would have had on Britain in World War II or Lincoln during the American Civil War. William's dream of a united and free Netherlands comprising of all 17 provinces died with him. Although the war would continue for another 64 years and would eventually engulf most of western Europe, the Union was never able to mount any serious campaign against the League. Likewise, safe behind their water defenses and with their harbors protected by a well-armed fleet, the League ceased to pose any serious threat to the Union. Only with signing of the Peace of Westphalia in 1648 would the seven northern Dutch provinces officially gain independence from Spain. The southern ten provinces would remain part of the Spanish Empire for the next 200 years when, under the Treaty of Utrecht, it would become Belgium.

William would have been proud of the nation and principles for which he sacrificed so much. Within a hundred years, the newly formed United Dutch Provinces -- established on the individual-centric principles of the Saxons -- would go from being the backwoods colony of a state-centric empire to being the freest and most wealthy country in the world.

Chapter 9
The Dutch Century

In today's relatively free world it is easy to forget that the natural tendency of humans is to seek safety in numbers by trading individual freedom for the perceived security promised by collectivization and centralization. Throughout history, this tendency resulted in the lot of the common man being one of servitude, slavery, poverty, and hunger while their leaders ruled with the power and authority of gods. Now, after a more than a millennium of struggle against Roman authoritarianism and Spanish absolutism, the Dutch were establishing one of the first nation-states founded on the Saxon principles of limited government, individual self-governance, private property, and economic liberty. This would be no less an experiment in the ability of the common man to rule himself than the American revolution would be nearly two centuries later. And, like the American experiment, it would astound the world by creating what is known as the *Dutch Golden Age*.

During this period (1580-1670), the United Dutch Republic would become the freest and most prosperous nation on earth. It would hold "commercial leadership in Europe" and "their wealth per capita was greater than that of any other country in the world"(Durant). Dutch financial ingenuity would create financial institutions that today are found in only the most modern financial centers; a thriving stock market upon which shares from the world's first joint-stock companies (corporations) were traded, currency exchanges to facilitate international trade, lending banks to finance both domestic and foreign commercial activity, and insurance to protect assets. By the first quarter of the 17th century, Amsterdam would be the financial capital of the world.

The Bank of Amsterdam alone had assets totaling what would be, in 2014 dollars, over $700,000,000; could settle accounts into the millions of dollars in a single hour; and, much like the dollar is today, the Dutch *rijksdaalder* became the currency of international commerce. No other nation at the time had such organizational and financial capacity. This made the United Dutch Republic the only place in the world capable of lending the quantity of funds that governments worldwide required. This was especially true in times of war when governments required more money than could be raised domestically without establishing confiscatory and unpopular levels of taxation.

Dutch financing was also required for peaceful endeavors. When, in 1803, another newly formed republic across the Atlantic needed money to purchase property from Napoleon's France, it sent a representative named John Adams to the Netherlands to arrange the needed loan. When Adams approached the Dutch bankers, he did so with apprehension. He could not comprehend how wealthy the Dutch were and was confused by the Dutch bankers reaction when he told them what he considered an astronomical sum; the bankers laughed and, basically, opened their checkbooks. This is an example of Dutch financial power, for if it were not for the private bankers of the Dutch Republic, the United States would never have been able to conclude the Louisiana Purchase.

Dutch ascendancy of the world's finances made the Republic the unchallenged master of international trade during the 16th and 17th century. Within a quarter of a century of de facto independence, the Netherlands had 160,000 sailors manning a merchant fleet of over 16,000 vessels each capable of carrying 57 tons of cargo. This was more than the entire merchant fleets of Spain, France, and England combined. Of the twenty thousand ships conducting maritime trade within European waters in 1665, fifteen thousand of them flew the orange, white and blue flag of the Dutch Republic. With such dominance, the Dutch had a near complete monopoly on world trade. By 1600, Dutch merchantmen were carrying cargo to and from Italy, the Ottoman Empire, Persia, and India. In the early part of the 17th century, the Dutch expanded that trade to Japan (1610) and Siam (1613) while establishing control of the Moluccas, Formosa, and, eventually, all of Indonesia. They established the colony of New Amsterdam in North America and the Cape Colony in South Africa. This is quite impressive when we consider the fact that the United Dutch Republic, just slightly larger than the state of Maryland and half the size of South Carolina, would dominate world trade well into the mid-1700s. It is no coincidence that the people who would unseat the intrepid Dutch were from the only other Saxon nation; England.

An independent and thriving economic sphere, based on the private ownership of property and the economic freedom to engage in commerce, resulted in the wealth being shared with even the lowest Dutchmen. This does not mean that there wasn't economic inequality or that there wasn't even any poverty. What it does mean is that the Dutch poor were a smaller segment of society. As Adam Smith noted in the *Wealth of Nations* (1776), Holland "in proportion to the extent of the land and the number of inhabitants was by far the richest country in Europe." It was "far richer than England" and the "wages of labour are said to be higher in Holland." This prosperity, along with a decentralized form of government, would give the Netherlands the unique distinction of having the largest middle class in Europe. Even in Amsterdam, with all its moneyed elites (bankers, financers, etc.), the middle class would come to dominate both numerically and politically. This resulted in the average Dutchman having a standard of living far greater than that of his equivalent living under a state-centric government. In a 2005 lecture on Dutch exceptionalism, Yale University professor John Merriman noted that the Netherlands was "the most prosperous country for ordinary people anywhere" and, "without question, had the most sophisticated charitable institutions" in the world.

The condition of the population was prosperous. There were but few poor, and those did not seek but were sought by the almoners [charity representatives]: the schools were excellent and cheap. It was difficult to find a child of sufficient age who could not read, write, and speak, at least, two languages.

As the above quote from John Motley's *The History of the Netherlands* (1854) illustrates, the Dutch were not only prosperous, but also very educated. They had the highest literacy rate of all of Europe and, as Durant writes, with schools in every village, the Dutch nearly "wiped out illiteracy." Often charged by their contemporary rivals, and modern Marxists, as being nothing more that "uneducated and unsophisticated shopkeepers interested only in money", Dutch businessmen were extremely knowledgeable and cultured. They were just as versed in classic literature, art, and music as they were in balancing a ledger. Many, upon retiring from business, would dedicate themselves and their fortunes to politics, music, literature, art, and other scholarly pursuits. It was not uncommon for them to open their homes to artists, composers, philosophers, and scientists. This combination of freedom and prosperity would make the Netherlands an international refuge for many of the great thinkers of the age and Amsterdam the intellectual capital of Europe. In the words of Descartes, who spent much of his life in the Dutch Republic, "There is no country in which freedom is more complete, security greater, crime rarer, the simplicity of ancient manners more perfect than here."

The combination of literacy and prosperity resulted in the Netherlands having the most printing presses, publishing houses, newspapers, and bookstores in the world. While England had two publishing centers (London and Oxford) and Paris and Lyons provided books to French aristocrats, the Netherlands had Amsterdam, Rotterdam, Leiden, Utrecht, and the Hague printing books in Latin, Greek, German, English, and Hebrew as well as in Dutch. In Amsterdam alone there were over 400 businesses printing, publishing, and selling books. Through numerous libraries, the poorest individuals had access to books, which, in the rest of Europe, could only be found in homes of wealthy aristocrats.

At a time when state controlled press was the norm, the Dutch press was completely free. In fact, it would be the first time in the history of man that a society would have a press completely free of state control. This freedom to speak freely resulted in Dutch papers, such as *The Amsterdam Gazette*, becoming highly prized and read throughout Western Europe. French and Spanish monarchs, being favorite targets, repeatedly demanded that the offending papers be suppressed. Accustomed to the power that state-centric absolutism provided them, they were dismayed to find that the Dutch government had no authority over the nation's press.

If a picture is worth a thousand words, then the paintings of the period speaks volumes as to the difference between the standard of living in individual-centric Netherlands and that in state-centric nations. In state-centric nations, portraits are almost exclusively of royalty, nobles, top political and religious leaders, and other members of the aristocracy. In paintings done by Dutch painters, such as Rembrandt, the subject was more often than not of a setting of or a person from the middle class. This is not because Dutch artists were more social conscience than their Spanish or French contemporaries, but because the average Dutchmane, secure in the ownership of property and free to fully participate in the economy, had the wealth to actually commission artists to paint him and his family. Dutch paintings from this period are snapshots of the lives of the average Dutch family. They lived in small, yet, comfortable homes playing games, eating and drinking merrily, having pets, and wearing comfortable refined clothes.

As Dr. Alan MacFarlane writes, "Holland exemplified the advantages of a balance. It had discovered that a liberal course – separating and balancing, encouraging political and religious liberty, decentralizing power, avoiding extreme stratification, all encouraged a rapid growth of wealth so that a tiny country with such a virtuous structure could defeat the greatest empire in the West."

While this level of decentralization allowed the Dutch republics to prosper, it would also be their Achilles' heel. As mentioned earlier, the seven provinces that made up the United Dutch Republic were actually autonomous republics tied together in a loose federation that was not too dissimilar than the United States under the Articles of Confederation. While the States-General was the general assembly at the federal level, it had very little authority since most government functions remained at the provincial State level. Even when the States-General did vote on an issue, the decision had to be unanimous in order for it to pass. This gave even the smallest province the power to veto any bill it did not like.

The Republic's neighbors, who preferred taking wealth rather than creating it for themselves, coveted the wealth the Dutch had produced. The federal government's lack of ability to respond to these external threats made it susceptible to predation from these states, including the rising English. This fatal flaw became apparent during the Anglo-Dutch wars of the 17th and 18th century. These wars, fought primarily on water, would witness some the largest navel battles in history. While decentralization provided the Dutch with the resources to build ships equal to the quality and quantity of the English, it put them at a grave strategic disadvantage.

During this period, it was common for provincial militias led by local commanders to make up most of a nation's military forces. In Saxon-based societies, decentralization of the states military power acted as a check on the authority of the central government. Unfortunately for the Dutch, they took it to the extreme by applying it to their naval forces. The result was not unlike what the Confederacy faced during the American Civil War. The national government, not having direct control over its military forces, had to rely on the generosity of the provincial governments in order to put to sea a fleet large enough to challenge the English. Even at sea, the decentralization caused problems. Although there was an overall commander, the individual ships operated under the authority of their provincial navy. This often led to incidences where a provincial admiral would act independent of the national commander, often at crucial times with critical results.

Even though the navies were equally matched in the quantity and quality of their ships, the English navy was designed on the national level. The Admiralty had complete control at all levels of the fleet. If a commander disregarded an order, he could be relieved or even court martialed. This cohesion gave the English navy the advantage it needed to defeat their Dutch rivals. Thus allowing England to replace the Dutch Republics as ruler of the sea and eventually the superpower of the world. In America, it would result in the Dutch colony of New Holland becoming the English colony of New York.

It is interesting to note that even with its decentralized command system, the tiny Dutch Republics were able to defend themselves from their larger centralized neighbors. They were able to maintain their independence from all powerful absolutist Spain even though the Spanish controlled the ten Dutch Catholic provinces to the south. Even authoritarian France, which had the largest military in Europe could not overcome the strength created by the Saxon form of government.

As we will see in the next few chapters, it would be the English Saxons who would eventually dethrone the Dutch as the world's financial and military superpower.

Part III

The English

Chapter 10
Ængla-land

When people think of the great turning points in English history they often think of the Magna Carta or, if they are very knowledgeable on the subject, the Battle of Hastings and the resulting Norman conquest of 1066. But it is the Saxon conquest of the former Roman province of Britannia in the fifth and sixth centuries that would have consequences not only for England itself, but for all of humanity. The fact is that there would not be an England if Rome had not collapsed, thus creating a situation that allowed the Saxons to occupy Britannia. For it would be the Saxons themselves who would eventually create the world's first nation-state; England. It would be Saxon principles upon which the rights of Englishman, and eventually human rights, would be founded on. This fact was not lost on the descendants of these people who were, over 1000 years later, establishing a new country in a new world. It is not a coincidence that both Thomas Jefferson and Benjamin

Franklin wanted on the reverse of The Seal of United States of America an image depicting the Saxon brothers Hengist and Horsa.

As previously noted, on the continent Roman influence lived way beyond the fall of the Empire. Roman customs, manners, and language would remain to be the foundations of the nation-states that would eventually rise out the Empire's ashes. Even the Germanic tribes that brought about the fall of Rome would adopt Latin, thus making it the *lingua franca* of most of Western Europe. The great Frankish king, Charlemagne, modeled his government on that of Emperor Constantine -- as would Napoleon's France, Mussolini's Italy, and Hitler's Germany. But the fall of Rome would be very different for its northern most province: Britannia.

"Uniquely in western Europe," as David Starkey points out, "there was a fresh start [in Britannia]. For along with their new language, the Anglo-Saxons brought a new society, new gods, and a new, very different set of political values. And from these, in time, they would create a nation and an empire that would rival Rome. A version of their tongue would replace Latin as the *lingua franca*, English common law would challenge Roman law as the dominant legal system, and they would devise, in free market economics, a new form of business that would transform human wealth and welfare. Most importantly, they would create a new politics that depended on participation and consent, rather than the top-down autocracy of Rome."

When the Romans invaded the land of the "Brythons" -- or painted ones -- they found a land suffering from decades of intertribal conflict. This allowed the Romans to focus on one single dominant tribe, the Catuvellauni. Once defeated, the Romans took over all of the Catuvellauni's territory in the southeast. Rather than fight the other tribes, the Romans sought settlements with the chieftains. In exchange for compliance, the Romans permitted the chieftains to remain the nominal leaders of their tribes. The result was that, within 30 years, direct Roman rule covered most of southern Britain and was being aggressively extended into modern Scotland. As Starkey points out, "Romans did not conquer Britain" but won by conducting the "smallest of small colonial wars." There would not be another king in Britain until the Romans left.

Over the next 300 years Britannia became a fully integrated part of the Roman system. As what happened in most of conquered Europe, the elites quickly became Romanized. They eagerly embraced the Roman language of Latin, the toga, hot and cold bath, and the habit of eating while reclining on couches. As Tacitus observed, "they called it civilization when it was but a part of their servitude." With temperatures being warmer than they are now, Britannia became known for its vineyards and wines. Romanized Britons filled the ranks of the Emperor's armies and fought under his standards throughout the empire; with quite a few rising to leadership positions. Others became administrators and bureaucrats, serving Rome wherever the Emperor desired.

Yet, the common Briton remained unchanged by the Roman style that the elites so quickly embraced. Unlike the other conquered people of the Empire, the average Briton never considered himself to be a Roman citizen or to be the heirs of the culture and politics of the Empire of Rome. For them, they were natives who were subjects of Rome and the Romanized elites that governed the island. They definitely were not Roman and never fully embraced Roman authoritarianism. It would be these Britons, who would now be conquered by a people who would become known as the Anglo-Saxons.

For nearly four centuries, Romans governed and administered Britannia. Its governors, administrators, bureaucrats, and civil servants were drawn from all over the Empire. The British elites were more Roman than Briton and had very little in common with the Emperor's British subjects. The majority of the Britons were farmers, skilled laborers, merchants, and traders. Dependent on Rome for protection, they had lost the martial ardor that their ancestors once possessed. The Britons, especially in the south, were feeble and incapable of defending themselves. As historian Cyril Johnson observed, "they had known peace too long." So when the last Roman legion left the province of Britannia in 409 A.D., it created a power vacuum that the Britons were incapable and unprepared to fill. Worse yet, no longer having the Roman legions to protect them from the barbaric tribes that inhabited the territory just outside of Britannia's borders, the Britons were now fully exposed to the raiding, raping, and pillaging that the Celtic and Gaelic tribes to the north and west thrived on.

Out of desperation the Britons made one of the biggest miscalculations in human history. They employed the Saxons, many from the Netherlands, as mercenaries to protect them from the tribes that were tormenting them. As Starkey writes, "Proportionally, it was the largest immigration that Britain has ever known. Perhaps 200,000 people flooded into a native population which by then had been reduced by the raids, famine and disease to less than two million. Moreover, as most of the immigrants were men, it quickly turned from an immigration into a conquest. In the areas of densest Anglo-Saxon settlement, in the East and the Midlands [of England], DNA evidence shows that up to 90% of the native male population was displaced -- they were driven west or killed -- and their women, their villages and their farms taken over by the incomers. This was ethnic cleansing at its most savagely effective."

The Kingdoms of Anglo-Saxon England

From chroniclers of the time, we know that the Saxon invasion began in 449 A.D. when Hengist and Horsa, two Saxon chieftain brothers were invited to Kent by a British king to help defend his realm from barbarian raiders. After occupying Kent, they went on to settle in what would become known as Sussex, which means the land of the Southern Saxons. Upon hearing of the rich land that England had to offer, more Saxons soon followed. Initially they followed the south coast westwards, occupying all the land west of Hampshire. Named Wessex, this land would eventually be the birthplace of the nation known as England. At the same time that the conquest of the south was being completed, the move north up the east coast began. The East Saxons occupied Essex; while the Angles from Denmark settled in what they called East Anglia.

More Angles arrived to occupy the less hospitable land of northern England and southern Scotland. This land they called Northumbria and with its occupation the Germanic tribes, collectively known as the Anglo-Saxons, had occupied all of the former Roman province of Britannia except its interior. Named Mercia, this final territory would eventually be settled by the Angles from Northumbria and East Anglia in approximately 680 A.D. One hundred and fifty years after the arrival of Hengist and Horsa.

Upon the native people, the Anglo-Saxons imposed a new language: Old English. As this lexical chart of German shows, both Dutch and English have their origins in the low German of the Saxons. For many centuries after the Anglo-Saxon takeover of Britannia, those speaking Old English could easily converse with their Saxon brothers across the channel. This would establish a link, especially the principles upon which Saxon societies are based, between these two peoples that would make the Dutch and the

English-speaking peoples to live in the freest and most prosperous nations the world has ever seen.

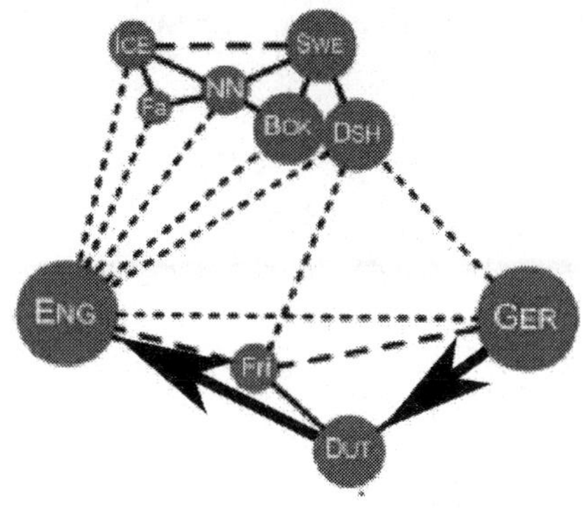

Although the Anglo-Saxons occupied all of what was the Roman province of Britannia, it would take nearly four more centuries before the similar, yet rival, kingdoms united to become England. Initially, it was Northumbria under Edwin. Under his leadership, the Northumbrians were able to drive the Picts out of the Scottish lowlands and establish the town of Edwin's Burgh -- known today as Edinburgh, the capital of Scotland. Having defeated his enemies to the north, Edwin immediately turned south and quickly brought East Anglia, Mercia, and Wessex under his sovereignty. For the first time since the Fall of Rome, the whole province of Britannia was nearly under the rule of one monarch and Edwin could proclaim the proud title of Bretwalda, which meant overlord of Britain.

But this, as most of the early attempts of unification would be short lived. The Mercian king, Penda, bristled at the authority of Edwin and resumed hostilities as soon as he was able. Edwin was killed in battle and his kingdom overrun by the Mercians. The Northumbrians fought back and a bloody stalemate ensued. Penda would die before he could witness his dream of a united Ænglaland under Mercian domination. It would be his son Offa who would fulfill his father's ambitions.

Offa was one of the most brilliant kings of his time. Even the great Charlemagne considered him an equal. In return, Offa was very impressed by the Frankish King's resurrection of the Roman model of government but appears to never have attempted to replicate it in Britannia. Maybe he understood that, even as powerful and skilled that he was, he could never get the liberty minded Anglo-Saxons to submit to such a system. In the end, the Anglo-Saxon system of government would prove itself up to the task of uniting Britannia. Under Offa's leadership Mercia would become more and more powerful. Northumbria was defeated in 726 and the power of Wessex was broken soon after. Less than a century after Edwin took Northumbria to the pinnacle of Anglo-Saxon power, the Mercian king Offa was now the Bretwalda of the Britain. Much of the power that a medieval leader had was based on his charisma, ability, ambition, and ruthlessness. Upon the death of the king, these personal traits usually died with him. It was very rare for the heir of the throne to maintain the same authority of his predecessor. This was the case with Offa and, upon his death, Mercian power soon began to wane.

It was now Wessex's turn to shine. Under the capable leadership of King Egbert, Wessex was able to defeat the Mercians, led by King Beornwulf, at the battle of Ellandun in 825. Inspired by the defeat, the East Anglians rose up against Mercian domination and killed Beornwulf when he attempted to suppress the rebellion. Egbert then sent his son, Æthelwulf to attack the remaining southeastern provinces of the Merican Empire. Seen by many as a liberator, Æthelwulf quickly occupied Sussex, Kent, and Essex. Four years later, Egbert would conquer Mercia itself and then move on to defeat the Northumbrians. This made Egbert the new Bretwalda and, under the dominance of Wessex, Britain would remain united longer than it was under Edwin and Offa. More importantly, it is said that it was while Egbert was Bretwalda that he gave the united nation the name Ængla-land, or England. For the first time since the last Roman left Britannia, the island was unified under a government that not only gave it a settled and permanent shape, but also a name that represented that unity.

This unity would not have been possible without a unifying religion. While Christianity was converting many, an equal number still followed the old pagan religion of the one-eyed Woden (also known as Oden), his wife Frig, and their son Thor. Their influence is still reflected in the names we currently use for the days of the week; Wednesday for Wodenday, Friday for Frigday, Thursday for Thorday, and Tuesday for the one-handed god of law and martial glory, Tyr. Valhalla was where warriors who died in battle went to spend eternity fighting, feasting, drinking, and carousing with young maidens. The earth was considered the middle ground, trapped between heaven and hell. At night, evil spirits would roam the world in search of any unfortunate soul caught out in the darkness. The gods controlled one's fate and to lose their favor would bring misfortune and even death.

Edwin was one of the first kings to abandon this dark and mystic religion for Christianity. Soon all of Northumbria followed. Yet, Penda had no time for the nailed-God of the Christians. He considered their chanting and praying to be foolish. To a warrior like Penda, Christianity was the religion of the weak and this was one of his motivations for resisting Edwin's dominance on the island. Upon his father's death, Offa eagerly accepted Christ and, like Northumbrians did with Edwin, most Mercians, as well many in Wessex, followed Offa's example and embraced Christianity. By the time Egbert established himself as Bretwalda, the new nation of Ængla-land was predominately Christian.

Along with the political and religious, we also see the beginning of the economic sphere. More coinage from this period has been found in England than in any other part of Europe. Offa alone struck millions of coins of various varieties. Some similar to the coinage of the Romans with the portrait of Offa in place of Caesar. Others had depictions of the Kings of Israel as they appeared in Anglo-Saxon manuscripts. Regardless of the imagery, this was not a rebirth of the state controlled economy of the Roman. The sheer quantity of coinage indicates that the Anglo-Saxons of this period had a thriving free-market economy that had no rival on the continent. Additionally, we see emergence of the yeoman farmer who would eventually become the backbone of both English and American liberty.

With the settlement of political and religious matters and the emergence of the economic sphere, the Anglo-Saxons appeared well on their way to establishing Ængla-land. But an external threat would nearly destroy the idea of a united Anglo-Saxon Ængla-land before it even had a chance to be born. This threat would come from the most feared people of the age; the Vikings.

Chapter 11
Wessex Stands Alone

History teaches us that there are, economically speaking, two types of people; those who create wealth and those who take it. This is the cause of the predation that, as the great thinkers such as Montesquieu and Adam Smith tells us, has plagued humanity since the beginning of time. Although the Saxons had taken wealth – as they did when they invaded Britannia – they were very capable of creating wealth. They turned the swampland of the Netherlands into one of the most prosperous parts of Europe and did the same in England. In fact, by the time of Offa (757-796), Anglo-Saxon England had become very wealthy and may have even surpassed the wealth of Roman Britain. This made the Anglo-Saxons perfect targets for the most predatory peoples of the age: the Vikings.

In the fourth and fifth centuries the Saxon were the scourge of Europe. Able seafarers, they struck fear into anyone living close to a coastline. By the late eighth century, their principles had made the Saxons of the Netherlands and the Anglo-Saxons of Britain so wealthy that they had long given up plundering as a means of acquiring wealth. Their Germanic cousins in Denmark and Norway, collectively known as the 'Vikings' soon took their place as the most dreaded peoples of their age. Like the term 'Saxon', 'Viking' was a label used to describe the people who raided northwest Europe throughout the much of the last half of the first millennia. They encompassed several groups of Germanic peoples scattered throughout Demark and Norway. To the Anglo-Saxons, they were collectively known as "Danes", "Norsemen" or "Northmen". Although Germanic cousins of the Saxon, they exhibited a savagery beyond anything the Saxons were capable of, who were quite savage in their own right. Initially, they kept to themselves but as Charlemagne expanded his Frankish Empire eastward, the Germanic people of the area were driven to the sea. Having taken to boats, they soon discovered that plundering was an easy way to gain wealth. As historian Cyril Robinson wrote, Charlemagne had shaken a "hornet's nest" and soon afterwards no coastline, from northwest Europe to the Mediterranean to even the yet to be discovered lands to the west were safe from the raiders.

The first Viking raid occurred during Offa's reign. A small party landed in Portland and killed the king's reeve, the highest royal official they could find. Shortly afterwards, in 792, the Vikings raided Lindisfarne, a monastic church located on an island just off the coast of Northumbria. Being pagans, they tortured and murdered the priest and monks of the monastery before fleeing with their booty. The savagery of the attack sent a shockwave throughout the western world. Upon hearing the news of the raid, a chronicler of Charlemagne's court would write, "Never before has such terror appeared in Britain as we have now suffered from a pagan race…the heathens poured out blood of saints around the alter, and trampled on the bodies of saints in the temple of God, like dung in the streets." Unfortunately this was only the beginning.

As the center of Christianity in Northumbria, the church in Lindisfarne was extremely wealthy. Within its walls was a vast treasure of gold and silver crosses, gem encrusted religious icons, and plates made of precious metals. This is the type of wealth that the Vikings sought. It was portable and could be easily divided among the members of the raid. The fact that it belonged to a rival religion only made the plundering even more pleasurable. The Vikings hated the Christians. To them, like the pagan king Panda, it was a religion of the weak. The timidity of the monks and priest -- with their constant praying and chanting -- and their fear of dying, enraged the Vikings beyond simple bloodlust. Christianity was the biggest rival of the warrior paganism of the Vikings whose dark beliefs extolled the virtues of being slain by a foe in combat. In fact, to die other than with a sword or other weapon in hand would sentence a Viking to their version of eternal hell. So the Viking raids initially focused on churches and monasteries where they never tired of devising ways to make the death of their victims as slow and painful as possible. Skinning or roasting over a long period of time appears to have been one of their favorite methods of dealing with priest and monks. Of course, nuns provided a source of entertainment that ensured that the sisters experienced an earthly hell before getting to heaven.

As word of easy plunder spread among the Norsemen and Danes, the raids became larger and would often take the form of a military operation. With shields lining their sides, a dragon's head or other fear-provoking ornament on the prows, and multiple poles striking the sea as they raced toward the beach, the longboats, each carrying up to 150 warriors, would strike terror into all who saw them. Once on the beach, the Vikings would establish a base from which the warriors would scour the countryside for horses. Only when sufficient mounts were acquired would the raiding begin. While churches and monasteries, with their portable wealth, were primary targets, the estates of wealthy noblemen were not exempt from the raiders' attention. The weakness of the Viking raids was that they could not afford to suffer casualties. Everyman was needed to help row their longboats back home so they would concentrate their focus on soft targets and leave as soon as they encountered serious resistance.

To rectify this limitation, the Vikings started to establish permanent settlements. By the reign of Æthelwulf (839-856), the scattered raids had turned into an ever expanding conquest. By 878, Northumbria was under Viking rule, temporarily ending the Christianity started by Edwin two centuries before. The Vikings quickly overran East Anglia, where they cruelly killed its Christian king, Edmund, by tying him to a tree and shooting him with arrows. It is said that he had over 25 arrows pierce his body before he succumbed to the mercy of death. The church, seeing Edmund as a martyr, bestowed sainthood on him and the modern Suffolk town, St. Edmundsbury, marks the location of his final resting place. This destroyed the unity achieved by Egbert. England was effectively cut in two with the kingdoms of Northumbria and East Anglia being under 'Danelaw." Caught between the Danish to the north and east and the Anglo-Saxons to the southwest, Mercia found itself torn apart as rival armies fought each other for dominance. Neither Christian, nor pagan was safe - their fate dependent on the fortunes of the fighting armies. Christians killed the wearers of Thor's Hammer just as often as the Vikings did those wearing the cross of Christ.

At the time of Æthelwulf's death in 856, Wessex was the only Anglo-Saxon kingdom powerful enough to check the Viking takeover of the entire island. In succession, each of his three eldest sons -- Æthelbald (r. 856-860), Æthelberht (r. 860-865), and Æthelred I (r. 865-871) -- would die resisting the Danes. All their efforts would prove disastrous for Wessex and by 870 the Danes were threatening its capitol at Winchester. Wessex appeared to be doomed and the vision of an Anglo-Saxon England was going to die with it.

It was at this pivotal point that the Saxon system proved not only its superiority, but displayed the ability to change the course of history.

In 871, when Wessex was facing it darkest hour, Æthelred I died without an heir old enough to be crowned king. On the continent, the principle of divine right meant that the king's eldest son, regardless of age, was God's chosen heir to the throne. If the heir was too young to be crowned king, a prince-regent would be selected to act in the king's place until the heir was old enough to reign in his own right. Even in the best of times, such situations could cause a successional crisis as various political factions fought to have their man named prince-regent. Quite often, the internecine fighting would result in a civil war. If a prince-regent satisfactory to all could be found, his temporary status and limited authority would reduce his effectiveness as a leader, especially in time of war. Coming at a time when Wessex was already on its knees, this practice would have resulted in the complete destruction of the last Anglo-Saxon realm on the island.

Fortunately for Wessex, the Anglo-Saxons still retained the Saxon tradition of electing their kings. As covered in a previous chapter, upon the death of a king, the Witan (a proto-parliamentary body) would select his replacement. The king could nominate his successor but the Witan was not obligated to honor his request and it was not a given that the king's son, regardless of age, would automatically inherit the throne. This continued the Saxon principle that the king was in theory, if not always in practice, a servant of the people. Even if a king became powerful enough to overlord his people, his tyranny would end upon his death and his people would be free to choose a more congenial leader. More significantly, this mechanism of succession gave the Anglo-Saxons the ability to avoid having an incompetent or foolish king on the throne. In 871, this custom would save Wessex.

In one of the most forgotten, yet, significant decisions in history, the Witan chose Alfred.

Although Alfred was Æthelwulf's youngest son, he, at the age of 23, was ill prepared to lead a nation, especially in a life and death struggle. As the youngest son, there was no expectation of Alfred ever being a king -- even under the Saxon system -- and he was educated instead for the priesthood. Since childhood he suffered from various maladies including intestinal problems and seizures that many historians believe were caused by epilepsy. It is said that he even suffered an attack during the feast celebrating his marriage.

As unlikely a candidate as Alfred was, he did have some very exceptional qualities for the time. Having studied for the priesthood, Alfred was literate in at least Old English and would also become completely fluent in Latin. This was very rare during a time when most monarchs – in England and on the continent – were completely illiterate. Their words transcribed by an army of monks ready to take down their every word. With this ability, he was able to study history, especially military history, and learn how to lead an army. Fighting alongside his brothers against the Danes added the practical experience to the knowledge he had gained from the books.

Even though he was plagued by various maladies, Alfred developed a reputation of being a highly competitive sportsman. He was an excellent horseman and was more than proficient at sword craft. This, along with his habit of leading from the front, earned him the title of warrior king. More importantly, Alfred had that special quality that drove men to follow him. Like Churchill during the darkest days of World War II, Alfred was able to keep the faith of the people even while Wessex -- the last independent Saxon kingdom – appeared to be doomed to the same fate that had befallen her Saxon neighbors; complete and brutal subjugation by the Vikings.

Alfred's ability to retain the faith of his people was a consequence of his own faith in God; which may have stemmed from the pilgrimage he took with his father. When Alfred was six, his father decided to go to Rome. He took young Alfred along and they stayed in the Holy City for a year, during which time the future savior of Wessex developed a deep devotion to God and a keen interest in history. As Alfred grew into manhood, so did his devotion. He believed in God's ability to effect events on earth and he saw his undiagnosed maladies as a sign of God's displeasure. His lifelong quest for God's approval drove him to constantly strive to be a better man, a better king, and, most importantly a better Christian. Robinson would write that Alfred "was none of your Christian monarchs who went to mass in the morning and bullies their subjects in the afternoon." His faith "was deep, practical, and many." Wherever he went, he carried a book of psalms and prayer. He attended mass daily and surrounded himself with a small army of bishops and monks to pray on his behalf. These religious men would also act as advisors; although, not always providing the best advice.

It would be this faith that would provide Alfred with the strength and courage that would be needed to see him through the dark days that would mark the first years of his reign.

Taking advantage of the confusion that the change of leadership causes, the Danes struck Wessex within a month of Alfred becoming king. Alfred, caught unprepared, took a small force to meet the larger Dane army. The two forces met at Wilton, where Alfred was thoroughly defeated. This put the Dane army within striking distance of where the Witan was meeting in Wimborne. Having no forces to resist the Dane advance, Alfred sought to buy time by suing for peace. Providentially, word reached the Dane commander that the Northumbrians were revolting against their Viking overlords. Acknowledging that his forces were needed elsewhere, the Dane commander agreed to withdraw his forces from Wessex in exchange for a large sum of money. Alfred, seeing that this would give him the much needed time to reconstitute his forces, readily agreed.

It would take the better part of a year for the Danes to suppress the Northumbrians in a struggle that would spill into Mercia. The independent spirit of Northumbria was broken and they no longer posed a threat to the Danes. Mercia would find itself divided between areas under outright Dane domination and those under a puppet Christian king who, completely controlled by the Danes, was a king in name only. Only thc kingdom of Wessex stood between the Danes and their total conquest of the island. Now, with the total subjugation of Mercia, the Danes had a completely new invasion route through which it could attack Wessex. This is exactly what Guthrum, the greatest Viking warlord of the time, did.

Striking south, Guthrum drove his army across Wessex all the way to the coastal town of Wareham. He then turned west and took Exeter. For three years, Guthrum terrorized Wessex as his army marched the length and breadth of the kingdom; pillaging and burning as they went. Once Alfred had mustered enough men, he surrounded the Danes at Wareham and Exeter. The Danes, trapped between Alfred and the sea, sued for peace. Why Alfred agreed is unclear but the most likely reason is that he did not have a force large enough to defeat the Danes in an outright battle or to maintain a long-term siege. Either way, it is now obvious that the Danes request for a truce was done in bad faith. That very evening the Danes broke the truce and escaped to Gloucester where they set up their winter quarters.

Alfred followed and set his headquarters in the royal lodge in Chippenham. It appeared that both armies had settled in for the winter and that no combat would take place until after the spring thaw. But, on January 6, 879, Guthrum attacked Chippenham without warning. The date was chosen wisely for it was the last day (the twelfth day) of the Christian feast celebrating Christmas. Alfred, taken by complete surprise, was in his lodge celebrating the birth of his king and savior as the Danes approached. His army was spread thin with most of them having returned home for the holy season and the winter conditions made it impossible for Alfred to assemble a force large enough to contain the Danes. Alfred had no choice but to flee.

With a small band of men who -- in number -- were nothing more than a royal bodyguard, Alfred fled south and east through the Somerset bogs (or fens). Knowing that their numbers were too small to offer any serious resistance, the royal troops avoided population centers. Keeping to the forests and swampland, the small force eventually arrived at the confluences of the Rivers Parrett and Tone in Somerset. The convergence of the two rivers created an island upon which a very few could hold off many. The rivers provided clean water and enough fish to feed everyone. The island itself was lightly inhabited by people who lived in complete isolation. None knew who Alfred was or of the Dane hoard that was searching for him. It was on this island that Alfred, living in near anonymity, decided to make his stand.

This was the low point of Alfred's life. During his short reign, he had been thoroughly outmaneuvered and defeated by the Danes. His kingdom had been reduced to a nearly uninhabited island in the Somerset swamps; Guthrum had complete control of the heartland of the kingdom. Alfred's military was effectively nothing more than the handful of loyal men who were serving as his bodyguard. Wessex itself was in a complete panic. Nobles fled; leaving the common folk to the mercies of the invaders. It appeared that Wessex, the last Anglo-Saxon kingdom, was going the way of Northumbria, East Anglia, and Mercia. The future would belong to Daneland; not England.

This is where Alfred's deep faith in God proved to be practical. Like his maladies, Alfred saw his defeats as a sign that God was displeased with him. This forced the young king to reflect on his situation. As he would later write,

In the midst of prosperity the mind is elated, and in prosperity a man forgets himself. In hardship he is forced to reflect on himself, even though he is unwilling.

It was during one of these reflective times that a tale that would become part of Alfred's legend was born. While escaping the cold, Alfred took shelter in the hovel of one of the inhabitants of the island. The old woman who occupied it was baking cakes over its fire. Unaware of who Alfred was, she ordered him to watch the cakes while she attended to her other chores. Shortly afterwards, Alfred slipped into one of his contemplative states; completely forgetting the cakes. When the old woman returned, the cakes were completely burnt. She immediately berated the king for his laziness and lack of attention. Recognizing that he had failed in his responsibility to ensure the cakes did not burn, Alfred meekly accepted the tongue lashing. It is not known if this event actually occurred but it spread throughout Wessex as proof that Alfred was a king of the common people. As Starkey writes, "it points to the closeness of monarch and people which would be the salvation of Wessex."

Chapter 12
Alfred the Great

And so it was. As the tale of Alfred's burning of the cakes spread throughout Wessex, Anglo-Saxon soldiers and warriors made the dangerous trek to join their king on his island. First they came in pairs and then in small groups. Soon whole units led by noblemen began to arrive. It was not long until Alfred had the manpower to strengthen his position by constructing a fort from which he launched raids against the Danes. As his army grew, so did his confidence that all was not lost. Relying on his extreme intellect, faith in God, and knowledge of history, Alfred was soon developing a plan that would forever banish the Danes from Wessex.

The key to the success of Alfred's plan was the political structure that Wessex inherited from the Saxons. The kingdom of Wessex was comprised of five shires (known as counties after the Norman conquest of 1066): Devon, Dorset, Wiltshire, Hampshire, and Somerset – in which Alfred's island was located. Each shire was further divided into what was called 'Hundreds' since each one, in theory, contained a hundred families. Each shire had its own assembly comprised of representatives of the Hundreds. These assemblies would meet twice a year to pass laws, levy taxes, and raise troops as needed. Later known as courts, these assemblies would try both civil and criminal cases. In time, these courts would hear sworn testimony related to property rights and inheritances. This would be the genesis of the jury system.

Relying upon the decentralization of the Wessex government, Alfred sent messengers throughout all of his kingdom. Besides going to the halls of e noblemen, who would provide the army its leadership, they also went to the meetings of the common folk outside their shire courts. Several weeks after Easter, everything was ready and Alfred gave the signal. Led by Alfred, the army left its island sanctuary and marched east to a place called Egbert's Stone. There they were met by "all the people of Somersetshire, Wiltshire, and Hampshire." It is unclear why the other two shires did not send troops but Dorset had suffered the most from the Dane invasion and Devon had a coastline to defend. For those at the stone, seeing their king brought many to tears. As one witness wrote, "when they saw the King, receiving him not surprisingly as if one was restored to life after suffering such great tribulations, they were filled with immense joy."

Knowing that Guthrum and his Vikings were camped at his old estate in Chippenham, Alfred and his new army, estimated to be between 2500 to 4,000 strong, left the next morning in hope of catching the Vikings by surprise. Unfortunately for Alfred, Guthrum had already received reports of the approaching Wessaxon army. In order to block Alfred's approach, Guthrum immediately moved most of his army to Ethendun (now called Edington). After two days of marching, the army of Wessex came into contact with Guthrum's Viking army on a hilltop near Edington. This was to be a battle that would decide whether

Alfred's dream of a united and Saxon England would live or be forever shattered by the Viking battle axe. Guthrum knew that in order for his conquest of Wessex – and the Dane domination of the isle – to succeed, he would have to kill Alfred as soon as possible. For Alfred and his men, victory would mean the difference between liberty and slavery. For, if Guthrum won, Viking domination of Wessex and England would be complete. This would be a winner takes all situation. Therefore, the battle was particularly savage:

Fighting fiercely with a compact shield wall against the entire Viking army, [Alfred] persevered resolutely for a long time. At length he gained the victory through God's will [and} destroyed the Vikings with great slaughter. – Cyril Robinson

Alfred won a complete victory and thoroughly routed the Danes. In a panic and with Alfred right on their heels, the Danes fled back to their fortified position at Chappinham. This was medieval warfare at is most brutal and no mercy was given. Filled with bloodlust, the Wessaxons ruthlessly killed any Viking unfortunate enough not to be able to keep up with the main Viking force.

At Chappinham, Alfred laid siege to Guthrum's stronghold. In the panic, the Wessaxons were able to capture all the Viking livestock and horses. Alfred then ordered the surrounding countryside to be stripped of all provisions that Viking raiding parties might find. After two weeks, the Vikings were "thoroughly terrified by hunger, cold and fear and in the end by despair." Recognizing the futility of his situation, Guthrum sued for peace. This time the Viking leader was in no position to equivocate. He promised to withdraw all his forces from Wessex and, as a sign of his sincerity, allowed himself and thirty of his chief men to be baptized. To symbolize the completeness of Alfred's victory, he became Guthrum's godfather and gave the Viking warlord the Christian name of Æthelstan. It was not lost on anyone that the baptism would take place less than four miles from the island upon which Alfred suffered his darkest moment.

The battle of Ethandun (also known as the battle of Edington) was a turning point in Alfred's life. It established his reputation as a great warrior king. Through his leadership (often at the front of his army), Wessex was not only saved, but would have fifteen years of peace. Additionally, the resulting Treaty of Wedmore established a fixed border between Ængla-land and Daneland. Running diagonally through the Midlands from London to Chester, the dividing line would cut the former Roman province of Britannia in half. Alfred had complete control of all of southwest England including Kent, Sussex, and the western part of Mercia while the Danes controlled Northumbria, East Anglia, Essex, and the eastern part of Mercia. Although Wessex was saved, the struggle between Anglo-Saxon and Dane was not over and the future of England still hung in the balance.

From past experience, Alfred knew that Guthrum's guarantees guaranteed nothing. Not knowing if and when another Viking invasion would occur, Alfred immediately set out to restore the government of Wessex. The Viking invasion exposed the weakness of the fyrd, or militia, system that was at the heart of Wessex defenses. It took too long for men from all across the kingdom to assemble as a force large enough to challenge the invaders. Additionally, it was comprised of men who were farmers, ironsmiths, herders, first and soldiers second. This had disastrous consequences when the Wessaxon army met the Vikings who considered martial prowess to be the primary responsibility of manhood. To rectify this, Alfred created a mounted quick reaction force that could quickly counter an invasion. This force, led by nobles, were manned by retained men who came as close to being professional soldiers as Wessex could muster.

Of course, this mobile force could not cover the entire kingdom and an area that was invaded would be on its own until the force could arrive. As a solution, Alfred devised the plan of fortified burhs. These were thirty fortified towns along rivers and the old Roman roads. Each town was encircled by a wooden palisade that was protected by a garrison of trained men. Upon sighting or warning of a Viking attack, the people would gather all their belongings, especially their livestock, and seek protection within the walls. The result was that the Vikings would find themselves riding about countryside that was bereft of people and, more importantly, provisions. It also resulted in nobles, feeling safe behind their walls, not surrendering to the invaders as soon as they saw them.

With the combination of the mobile force and the fortified burhs, Alfred created what modern strategist call a 'defense in depth' system, which was extremely revolutionary for its time. It was also extremely effective against the Vikings. It is telling that many of these burhs developed into towns that still exist to this day. With each garrison averaging approximately 900 men (depending on the size of the town), the burhs had the power to strike as well as defend. Such a threat could not be bypassed and an outright assault, if successful, would result in an unacceptable loss in men. The only alternative was to lay siege to the burh in hopes that its provisions and will to resist ended before Alfred's quick reaction force could arrive. As a result, Alfred had neutralized the two advantages that had been the key to Viking military success: mobility and surprise.

The other advantage that the Vikings had was that they could attack Wessex from the sea. This meant that Alfred had to detail much needed manpower to guarding the coast, as well as the inland waterways. As a counter, Alfred ordered the construction of a dozen warships that he designed himself. These boats would serve as England's first navy. With sixty oars, each ship was bigger than their Viking counterparts and could carry more men. This was fine out in the open sea, but proved to be a disadvantage in the rivers and estuaries where most sea battles occurred. In one such battle Alfred's new fleet encountered six Viking boats at the mouth of an undisclosed river. The boats of the Wessex navy were able to destroy two Viking boats before the tide went out, leaving friend and foe stuck. As the tide returned, the lighter Viking boats became unstuck and started floating downriver. The Wessaxons, still marooned on their boats, had no choice but to watch the Vikings as they escaped into the sunset.

Yet, even with these disadvantages, Wessex proved to be a formidable challenge when the Vikings returned in 894. The Viking attack took place on two fronts. First, a seaborne force from France landed in Kent. This was followed by an attack by the Danelaw Vikings who struck from the northeast. As in the previous invasions, the Vikings brought all the martial ardor they could muster. Each and every battle was fought with the brutal zeal of bloodlust. If not for Alfred's military reforms, Wessex could have found itself in a situation not too dissimilar than it did in the dark days of 879. Alfred's navy performed admirably as it engaged Viking boats in open water. The burh system resulted in the Viking forces wondering aimlessly in a land empty of people and food. Any sieges they attempted were broken by the arrival of Alfred's quick reaction force. The decisive victory came when the Wessaxons caught a Viking force by surprise on the Thames River just south of London. Placing booms across the river, the Wessaxons captured the entire Viking fleet.

The Vikings learned their lesson and did not attempt another attack on England while Alfred was alive.

Besides being a warrior king, Alfred was also a scholar who recognized the value of education. Literacy was very important to him and he required that his noblemen also be literate. Having a nobility that could read and write gave Alfred the ability to write orders that were directly delivered to and read by his nobles. This removed any chance of the orders being miscommunicated by an intermediary. It would also be another way in which Anglo-Saxon England would distinguish itself from the Romanized continent. For Alfred, being literate in Anglo-Saxon was not enough. He knew that the greatest works of the ages were in Latin and he wanted the ability to read them for himself. His friend and biographer, a monk named Asser, added to Alfred's legend by claiming that the king taught himself to read and write Latin in one day. It is more probable that the monks who surrounded him taught him the language they knew so will. What is not questioned is the fact that Alfred spent many nights translating Boethius' *Consolation of Philosophy*, Pope Gregory's *Pastoral Care*, Orosius' *Universal History*, and Bede's *Ecclesiastical History of England* into English so that they were available to any literate person. This, Alfred believed, was the natural progression of literature. As he would write:

I recalled how the Law was first composed in the Hebrew language, and thereafter, when the Greeks learned it, they translated it all into their own language, and all other books as well. And so to the Romans, after they had mastered them, translated all through learned interpreters into their own language…Therefore, it seems better to me…that we too should turn into the language we all understand certain books which are the most necessary for all men to know.

This was quite impressive in an age when most monarchs were completely illiterate and had to rely on monks as scribes. More significantly, as Will Durant observed in *The Story of Civilization*, "this early instance of the readiness in which Englishmen used English instead of Latin for works of history and theology " set it apart from "the continent [which] still blushed to write such dignities in the 'vulgar' speech." This would ensure that English, and not Latin, would become the de jure and well as the de facto language of England.

Alfred's passion for education did not stop with the nobility. For Alfred, the need for general education was urgent. In most of his kingdom, monks and priest were the only people capable of reading and writing; and they did most of it exclusively in Latin. "There is not one south of the Thames," Alfred would write, "who could render the Epistle out of Latin into English." To rectify this deficiency, he allocated an eighth of his annual income to the construction and maintenance of schools that would teach English, and even Latin, to anyone who desired to become literate in those languages. He also established a network of libraries that would remove the great literary works of the ages from being the exclusive purview of the wealthy. Besides translating the great works into English, Alfred also put in writing the oral histories of the Anglo-Saxons and "set men to compile the history of his country" of Ængla-land. This recording of the island's history, which is part of the Anglo-Saxon Chronicles, would continue until the Norman Conquest in 1066. As Robinson would write, "Without it, we should know little of these distant times."

He was also very much concerned about the welfare of the poor. He dedicated an equal amount to their welfare as he did to education. He built hospitals that would take care of them when they were sick and pantries that would feed them when they were hungry. These institutions were run by the various religious orders that were present in every town and burh, ensuring that even those in the most remote parts of the kingdom had access to this succor. His laws would protect even the lowest slave from arbitrary punishment. Even if the slave did not have full enjoyment of all his freedoms, he did have the protection of a primitive form of due process; which was more than the common man had on the continent. His laws limited the number of hours a slave could be worked and, by allowing them to keep anything they produced on their own behalf, basic property rights.

By having a literate population, Alfred was able -- for the first time in English history – to put its laws in writing. No longer would the law be what a man said it was, but what the law itself said. It would be a mistake to compare this to the codification of Roman law on the continent. The bottom up legal system of the Saxons was preserved and it would serve as the foundation of English common law that limits the power of the government as much as it preserves the liberty of the common man. More importantly, once in writing, a law took on a permanent status. It was readily available to whoever wanted or needed to use it. Thus, thanks to Alfred, England became a land of law, rather than men. Married with the Hundred courts and the jury system, the Wessex legal structure would evolve into modern jurisprudence which eventually made the English-speaking countries the freest in the world.

These changes would make Wessex the most powerful and prosperous kingdom on the island. Within fifty years of his death in 901, all of the former Anglo-Saxon kingdoms, including those in Danelaw, would be united. The Danes themselves would join the Anglo-Saxons to become one people, known as the English. This would result in the isles developing as an independent nation rather than a colony of Scandinavia. Thus, united by language, religion, and, for the first time since the fall of Rome, as a single political entity, the nation of England was born!

Alfred did great things for his people and, when we stop to remember that Alfred was a king in the 9th century, his accomplishments become even more noteworthy. In an age when most rulers kept their subjects in a state of ignorant servitude, Alfred was intent on his people being free both physically and mentally. Rather than exploiting them for all he could squeeze from them, Alfred chose to invest in their defense, well-being, and education. By modern standards these accomplishments appear to be very primitive, but, as Durant writes, "his moral qualities – his piety, his unassuming rectitude, temperance, patience, courtesy, devotion to his people, anxiety to further education – he offered to the English nation a model and stimulus that it gratefully received." Furthermore, it is within this primitive medieval arrangement that we find the genesis of our own modern political and legal system.

It is not an overstatement to say that if it were not for Alfred, the world we live in would be very different. The Vikings were a brutish and uneducated people. Rape, murder, and pillage were their preferred activities. Their religion was dark and celebrated dying more than living. In time, they would have been conquered by the ever growing Romanized powers on the continent. The isolated Saxons in the Netherlands would have also been subdued. There would not have been an island nation in which the principles of limited government, individual liberty, private property, and free market economics could mature and flourish. The Saxon system of government would have been lost to humanity forever.

Robinson would write: "Some men in history have been great in war: others in peace. Few have been equally great in both. Alfred was the exception." This would make the 'first King of the English' one of the greatest. His accomplishments rivaled that of Charlemagne, just on a smaller geographical scale. Yet, his impact on the yet to come modern world would be far greater than that of Charlemagne. The nation he set the foundation for would become the world's first nation-state, be the first to break the cycle of predation that kept (and still keeps) most of the world from entering the modern age, would be one of the first industrialized nation, and would, through its empire and its progenies – including the United States – create what would become known as 'the free world." It is no surprise that Alfred would be the only king in English history to be bestowed the title of "the Great." In the words of Voltaire:

I do not think there ever was in the world a man more worthy of the regard of posterity than Alfred the Great.

Chapter 13
The Manchurian Candidate

The Anglo-Saxons held Alfred in such awe, they assumed that anyone with his blood must be equally endowed with his exceptional strength, wisdom, piety, and courage. As the struggle between the Anglo-Saxons and the Vikings continued beyond the his death, it appeared that the faith in Afred's bloodline was well placed. His son Edward (r. 901-924) would overcome all Viking resistance in the north; his grandson Æthelstan (r. 924-939) would subdue their most determined effort to revolt against Anglo-Saxon rule; and his great-grandson Edgar (r.959-975) would succeed in turning Vikings into Englishmen. Whereas Edward's and Æthelstan's victories were military, Edgar's was political. By taking a course of reconciliation, he united the Anglo-Saxons and Vikings into one. Under Edgar, the Vikings – who had become just as settled as the Anglo-Saxons – joined the Witan, became archbishops, and married into noble Anglo-Saxon families. Thus they became equal members of English society and with their assimilation Alfred's dream of a united England became a reality. It was not without truth when Edgar had the coins minted during his reign with the Latin phrase *Edgar Rex Anglo(rum)*, Edgar, king of the English.

After a short reign by Edgar's eldest son -- who met a very premature death under suspicious circumstances -- his youngest son Æthelred became king. Æthelred II had one of the longest reigns in English history. It was also the most disastrous. In the 990s, the Norseman from Norway returned. Allied with the Kingdom of Denmark, the new Vikings attacked and pillaged the eastern shore of England. When Alfred died, he left a very advanced and genius strategy for handling such incursions. His England could readily respond to any threat. Since then the English had become wealthy and soft, making them perfect targets for their predatory neighbors. What was worse Æthelred II was not Alfred. His response was slow and feeble. This earned him the moniker of "Æthelred the Unready." His ill-fated reign ended when the great Viking pirate, Olaf Trygvasson, and the Danish King Sweyn conquered England in 1013.

Yet, the Anglo-Saxon principles of Alfred's Ængla-Land would prove themselves resilient and over the next thousand years live to bring freedom and prosperity to the modern world.

Six months after the conquest, King Sweyn suddenly died. His son, Cnut, became King of all of England and Denmark. At first it appeared that Alfred's vision would be short lived. Cnut (r. 1016-1035) ruled England with the same ruthlessness that his Viking predecessors did. But in time his approach to the English softened. He soon came to respect the system started by Alfred. He recognized that he could achieve more working within the established system than he could by using brute force. Therefore, he adopted the Saxon principle of ruling by consent over that of power. As Robinson would write, "Cnut never used his power to ill-treat or humble England: he ruled her rather as an Englishman than a Dane, and by whatever means sought to gain the loyalty of his Saxon subjects." "Cnut," history tells us, "started his reign as a Dane, but died as an Englishman."

The Saxon tradition of the Witan electing the king turned out to be one of the most resilient. Within seven years of Cnut's death in 1035, both if his son's would reign in succession and die without either leaving an heir. Instead of selecting someone from Cnut's line, the Witan returned to the line of Alfred by choosing Edgar's grandson, Edward. *The Anglo-Saxon Chronicles* tell us that this choice was very popular among the English people, "Before [Cnut's son Harthacnut] was buried, all the people chose Edward as king in London…[that] they received him as king was natural."

The fact that Edward was able to peaceably regain the crown for the House of Wessex (Alfred's line) is a testament to the strength of the Saxon system. Even in the best of times, such a rapid succession of monarchs leaving no clear heir to the throne would cause a crisis. The fact that Cnut's line inherited the throne through the violent actions of Sweyn only compounded the situation. Civil war seemed inevitable. Only the Saxon tradition of the Witan selecting the king prevented bloodshed. Even under tough and chaotic conditions, the Saxon system proved itself capable of providing a stable, organized, and bloodless transition of government. It was only due to the intervention of an outside force that the death of Edward would result in bloodshed.

In the past, the Witan had selected wisely, as in the case of Alfred. This was not the case with Edward. After 26 years of Danish rule, the Witan thought they were finally returning the throne to an Englishman. They never realized that what they were actually getting was a Norman in disguise. Edward's mother was Norman and when Sweyn dethroned Edward's father, Æthelred II, young

Edward went into exile in Normandy. He would stay there for the entire reign of Cnut and his sons. He was nearly forty when he returned to England to be king. Although Edward may have been born in England, he became "Norman in speech, Norman in habits and sympathies, and Norman in the whole temper of his mind."(Robinson)

Once Edward was seated on the throne he immediately surrounded himself with Norman friends. Normans would often visit him in Winchester which was the royal seat of Wessex. He gave them high offices within the government. He replaced the English Archbishop of Canterbury and the Archbishop of London with Norman priests. These actions gave the Normans great influence on the political and religious life of the English. This struck fear into the hearts of the English people, and rightly so. Although the Normans were originally Vikings who settled in the northwest part of modern France, they had become Romanized by French influences. As Robinson writes, the Normans "adopt[ed] the French language, French institutions [Roman law, government], French architecture, and French ways of life." Their authoritarian ways were antithetic to that of the free Anglo-Saxons.

The Norman Duke, William, had already established himself as one of the foremost figures of the period. He was a very ambitious man who had expanded his empire through the conquest of most of his neighbors. But the one prize he coveted the most was England; and in the pro-Norman Edward he found the perfect tool to subdue the island nation. Looking far ahead, he realized that he could use Edward to Normanize England through peaceful penetration of its politics and culture. Once achieved all William would need would be for Edward to name him heir to the throne, which Edward was more than willing to do. Upon Edward's death, William would have England without ever raising a sword. Or so he thought.

Being Romanized, both William and Edward failed to understand the process by which a man became king of Anglo-Saxon England. They thought all they needed for William to become King of England was for Edward to say so. The fact is that, even though Edward wore the crown, he could not pass it on to whomever he wanted. That was the responsibility of the Witan, which in theory embodied the sentiments of the English people; who were rightfully terrified of William. So when Edward and William conspired to turn England into a province of the Norman Empire, "it was [Edward's] so-called subjects – in particular the great earls – who stood between the shameful scheme and its execution. For they were Englishmen to the core, and had little intention of parting with their native [Saxon] liberties without a struggle." (Robinson)

Harold Goodwin, the Earl of Wessex, was the greatest of them all. Along with his southern province, and through his sons Harold and Sweyn, he controlled almost all of the eastern counties and those of the southwest midlands. Only in Mercia and Northumbria did he lack any authority. Additionally, his daughter was married to Edward. Thus, he was not only the head of half of England, but was also the father-in-law to the king. This made him a man to be reckoned with.

Goodwin was not the type to accept the treachery that was being planned by William and Edward. Soon a battle of wills developed between the English earl and the Norman duke. This came to a head when Edward's French brother-in-law, Count Eustace of Boulogne, was returning home after visiting Edward. The unpopularity of the French was already high when Eustace attempted to force the people of Dover to provide housing for him and his knights. Such an action was perfectly acceptable in France, but violated the basic

Anglo-Saxon principle of a man's home being his castle. A knight was killed when a householder resisted this violation of his rights. A brawl between the French knights and English townsfolk ensued. In the end, twenty members of the town and nineteen knights were killed. William demanded that Edward order Goodwin to punish the town. Goodwin, who was secretly delighted that his people would stand up for their rights as Englishmen -- especially in face of Norman tyranny -- refused. Edward, embarrassed by his lack of authority over the powerful earl, summoned the Witan to bring Goodwin to account for his actions. This placed England on the verge of a civil war and sensing that the people were not ready to take on the king, Goodwin and his family fled into exile.

Edward had won a major political victory and was confident that he had once and for all rid himself of his most powerful opponent. To celebrate, he invited William to come to England. In a show of force designed to intimidate the English, William arrived with a small army that looked more like an occupying force than a royal bodyguard. After initial ceremonial festivities, Edward and William had a private meeting. It is not known what they discussed when they met, but historians believe that it was at this time when Edward formally named William as his heir to the throne. Through this action, Edward was ensuring the future of England would be Norman, not Anglo-Saxon.

To the English people, it appeared that Edward was handing England over to the Normans and popular opinion switched to Goodwin. Goodwin promptly returned to reclaim his position as the Earl of Wessex and, once again, Edward summoned the Witan. This time Goodwin appeared to proclaim his innocence of all charges. Edward and his Norman advisors soon realized that the Witan, exercising its authority to check executive power, was going to side with Goodwin. Edward reluctantly accepted Goodwin's plea and he and his sons were officially returned their earldoms.

This did not satisfy Goodwin or the Witan. In a move that would have been impossible in Romanized Europe, the Witan sanctioned Edward. The Witan ruled that Edward's Norman advisors had "chiefly made the discord between Earl Goodwin and the king" and had "instituted bad laws, and judged unrighteous judgments, and brought bad counsel into this land." As a result, all of Edward's Norman advisors, minus his household servants who took the oath to be "true to him and all his people", were forced to leave the country. As Starkey notes, "Even in the language of opposition, it would seem, the foundations of English politics were laid in Anglo-Saxon England."

This shattered William's long term plan to take England through "peaceful penetration." If he wanted England, he would have to take it by force.

Chapter 14
The Norman Conquest

Upon the death of an English king, the Witan is called to select a replacement. Although it was usually the person with the strongest claim to the crown, the Witan had the freedom to select a better candidate. When Edward died he had no son and his closest next of kin was still just a boy, far too young to become king in those troubled times. This left the throne open to other candidates. Edward's promise to give the throne to William, the Duke of Normandy, gave the Norman duke a strong claim to the crown. Additionally, through Edward's Norman mother, William and the now dead king were first cousins. This gave William a familiar claim as well as a legal one.

The other claimant was Goodwin's son, Harold, who had become the Earl of Wessex upon Goodwin's death in 1053. Through family connections Harold effectively controlled all of England except Mercia. Although he had power, he had no family connection to the deceased king. Normally, this would have excluded him from consideration but he had three points in his favor: he was powerful, he was residing in England, and he was not William.

Therefore, to William's displeasure, the Witan selected Harold as the new King of England. The year was 1066.

Feeling he was deprived of what was rightfully his, William set out on taking by force what had become his obsession. Harold knew William was coming but first he had to fight off an unexpected threat in the north. Tostig, the Earl of Northumbria and Harold's brother, in an act treachery, convinced the King of Norway, Hardrada, that the new English king was weak and his position on the throne vulnerable. All Hardrada had to do was invade. And invade Hardrada did. With an armada of over 300 ships, Hardrada landed in Northumbria and quickly defeated the fyrds of Northumbria and Mercia.

Harold, whose forces were already on a war footing in anticipation of an invasion by William, immediately set out to meet Hardrada in the north. Harold was taking a huge risk in moving north with most of his forces. If William should land while the English army was in the north, he would be able to march on London with little resistance. The crown would be lost without a fight. But Harold believed he had no choice. He could not sit in the south while Hardrada was tearing up the north. Plus, if William did land with Hardrada still in the north, Harold would be forced to fight two foes at once. Harold's best chance was to quickly defeat Hardrada with hope of returning south before William invaded.

The two forces met seven miles east of York at Stamford Bridge. The speed in which Harold's forces marched caught Hardrada and his Norwegians completely by surprise. Harold won a decisive victory over the Norwegian king who, along with Tostig, was killed. What was initially a route, soon turned into a massacre as the English forces chased down the fleeing Norwegians. Of the 300 ships that brought the invading force to Northumbria, only 25 were needed to take the survivors back to Norway. It would be the most decisive and complete victory that the English would win over the Norsemen.

Harold ordered that a feast to celebrate the victory be held in three days. It was at this feast that he received word that William had landed at Pevensey and had occupied the old Roman fort of *Anderida*. Harold made the 200 mile journey from York to London in four days and, in an incredible feat of endurance, his army arrived five days later. In the meantime, William had repositioned his army to the more strategic town of Hastings where he built a wooden fortress. The stage was set for one of the most significant battles in history.

Harold and William were evenly matched with approximately 25,000 soldiers each. But Harold's army was heavily dependent on infantry drawn from the fyrds, or militia, of the local counties. Only his household guards could be counted as professional soldiers. William, on the other hand, had professional soldiers who were veterans of William's many military campaigns on the continent. Besides infantry, William also had archers and a force of highly trained cavalry comprised of knights from the nobility of France. As a warlord, William also ensured that his force had the newest and best equipment available. His soldiers had chainmail armor that covered them from head to waist. Helmets protected their head from all but the most direct hits. It was, as Robinson writes, "a testing issue between the old system and the new, between a system that relied on infantry and a system that relied on horse."

The battle started on the morning of 14 October, 1066 and raged all day. Initially, the Normans could not break the English shield wall. Even the vaunted knights on their chargers could not penetrate the English line. At one point, a rumor started to spread throughout the Norman forces that William has fallen in battle. To prevent a collapse of his army, William had to ride among his troops with his helmet off. At one point, William observed that the undisciplined fyrd broke ranks to pursue the Normans as they withdrew from a failed assault on the English lines. Although the fyrd was recalled in time to avoid a complete catastrophe, the weakness of the English forces had been exposed.

Not being able to break the English shield wall, William devised a plan that would exploit the lack of discipline of the fyrd. He ordered another assault by his knights, but this time, rather than press the attack, they were to draw the fyrd out of their protected defensive positions. The plan worked perfectly. The fyrd was drawn out and were either eliminated or fled in panic. Very few were able to make it back to the safety of their lines. With the collapse of the fyrd, Harold's house guards were doomed. They fought valiantly, but first Harold's brothers, the Earls Leofwin and Gyrth, were killed. Then Harold's eye was pierced by a Norman arrow. Seeing their king down, the last of his surviving house guards fled. Norman knights then set upon Harold's corpse. One cut off his head, another his arms, and yet another his legs. In fact, Harold would be dismembered to the point that he was completely unrecognizable. Only with the assistance of his mistress was his corpse identified.

"The result," as David Starkey writes, "was the death of one world and the birth of a new. Anglo-Saxon England had been a nation-state, in which ruler and ruled spoke the same language. This now ceased and, for the next four centuries, England was administered in Latin and governed in French. Anglo-Saxon instead become the patois of the poor and dispossessed."

Winning a battle is not the same as winning all of England. That would take William several years and result in an act of brutal oppression that would "shock an unshockable age."

The 11th century was a time when elites, even the king, fought alongside the common soldiers they commanded. When a side was victorious, as Alfred was, the king would gain the reputation of being a warrior king. If they were defeated, the nobility would often die with their king. This was the result of the battle of Hastings. The loss of the Wessex nobility was so complete that all resistance to William in the south collapsed. The Wessex nobility that did survive quickly fled into exile. The one family strong enough to stand up to William, the Goodwins, was completely decimated; never again to rise.

Eight centuries later, de Tocqueville observed that "He who desires in liberty any thing other than [liberty] itself is born to be a servant…they let it be snatched from their hands without resistance in fear of risking by an effort the very well-being [prosperity], which they owe to it." This is exactly what the Anglo-Saxons allowed to happen.

Once William had Wessex and London, the conquest was all but over. The English had lost their center of national resistance and could not produce a leader who could rally the troops on a national level. More tragically, with the Danish invasion and subsequent string of Danish kings, the English had lost the feeling of nationalism that the Anglo-Saxon kings has developed in the previous two centuries. In their prosperity, they lost who they were and forgot the principles which had allowed them to become so free and prosperous. As Robinson harshly notes:

The day of the Saxons were over; they were already a people in decay, slow of speech, indolent in habit, dull of wits...ready to sell their liberty for bread or to buy off an enemy with gold, and so besotted with ignorance and vice that 'they would eat (says the Anglo-Saxon Chronicles) until they were surfeited and drink till they were sick.' For such a people slavery was hardly an unnatural fate...It is a pitiful sight to watch a people, great and vigorous in its day, bowing thus meekly to the conquest of a foreign prince.

The north was a different story. Although some of their fyrds did fight Hardrada at Stemford Bridge, they were not present at the battle of Hastings. Their nobility was still intact enough to offer some form of organized resistance. Additionally, the north was still dominated by descendants of the Vikings and they had maintained, albeit at a reduced level, the willingness to fight for their liberty. They were savagely independent and, of equal importance, had in the Danish king an ally.

The revolt against William began in 1068 when a Danish fleet of 30 ships arrived in Northumbria. Feeling empowered by the presence of the Danes, the Northumbrians took the town of York and slaughtered its Norman garrison. In a direct challenge to William, they declared Edward's son, Edgar, the rightful king of England. William's reaction was swift and brutal. First, he came to terms with the Danes who accepted gold for the promise to leave. With lightning speed, he marched and attacked the Northumbrians who now stood alone in York. At the sight of his army, the Northumbrians fyrd abandoned their leaders and fled. William knew that terror was an effective weapon and he ransacked and burned all of York. This was followed by what has gone down in history as the "Harrying of the North."

The devastation William wrought on the north was complete and brutal. "From the Ouse to the Tyne," Robinson writes, "[William] undertook deliberately to blot out man and all his works. Villages were fired wholesale, their inhabitants either massacred or starved.

Churches were left in ruin, farms in ashes. Not even the fields were spared." Thousands – men, women, and children – would perish as a result of William's brutal actions. The chronicler, Orderic Vitalis estimated that the number to be as high as 100,000. Written 55 years after the event, the accuracy of that number is debatable. What is not debatable is that a survey conducted in 1086, showed that the north had only 25% of the population it had prior to the harrying. As William would proudly proclaim:

I have persecuted its native inhabitants beyond all reason. Whether gentle or simple, I have cruelly oppressed them; Many I unjustly disinherited; Innumerable multitudes, especially in the county of York, perished through me by famine or the sword.

Ominously, the 1086 survey lists "village after village" with the term wasta, or 'waste'. "The whole country was a desert, and recovery was so that the better part of five centuries elapsed before proper cultivation was restored. Meanwhile the lesson had not been lost on England. She saw now, if she did not see before, that her new master was not one to trifle with. There were no more revolts." (Robinson)

To establish his military dominance, William set out on an extensive program of castle building. The first two, which were constructed in Dover and Hastings, had the military purpose of protecting William's communication line to Normandy. The rest, that still dot the English countryside and includes London, were built as a symbol of William's power over the English. As Starkey notes, "Anglo-Saxon England had seen nothing like them. The burhs, or fortified towns, were designed to protect the people. The [Norman} castles were there to intimidate them. And they did...set in a tree-denuded landscape, each was the symbol of a profoundly alien military occupation."

With military dominance firmly established, the predation continued unabated. *Implementing the practices of the continent William* proclaimed himself owner of all the land and everything within it, including the people. He reinforced this proclamation by commissioning a survey that would inventory everyone and everything within his realm. This was more than a simple census. This was an owner taking stock of everything he possessed. This survey of England was so complete that "there was not one single hide [a parcel of land], nor yard of land, nay, moreover," as the Chronicles tell us, "even an ox, nor a cow, nor a swine was there left, that was not set down" in the book. The English called it the *Domesday* (or Doomsday) book because "not the last day of judgement could be so thorough."

As owner of all the land, William then proceeded to distribute it to his Norman allies. Private ownership of land was eliminated with William keeping 25%, which included most of the forests from which the English traditionally obtained their food. As an award for its support of William's subjugation of the English people, 25% was allocated to the Church in Rome. The rest of the property was distributed among William's loyal supporters and trusted servants, which numbered less than 20 individuals. This meant that land was consolidated in the hands of a very few elites. William then introduced serfdom into what was a relatively free society. From that moment on common people were placed into servitude on noble estates now controlled by Normans. Within a few years most of the Saxon nobles and landed gentry found themselves destitute. The subjugation was so complete that within one year, "It was," Henry of Huntingdon observed, "an insult to be called English."

In 1774, Thomas Jefferson felt it noteworthy to mention the action of the Normans and its impact on the Saxons. As he summed up the period,

Our Saxon ancestors held their land, as they did their personal property, in absolute dominion…William, the Norman, first introduced that system [of feudalism]…The lands of those who fell at the battle of Hastings, and in the subsequent insurrections of his reign, formed a considerable proportion of the lands of the whole kingdom. These he granted out, subject to feudal duties, as did he also those of a great number of his new subjects, who, by persuasion or threats, were induced to surrender them for that purpose. These, therefore by express laws,…were made liable to the same military duties as if they had been feuds; and the Norman lawyers soon found means to saddle them [the Saxon subjects] also with all the other feudal burthens.

Having military and economic dominance of England would be at best a temporary achievement. In order to maintain long-term control of the English people, William needed to have power over the Church. With the Pope's permission and assistance (he sent two legates to assist), William held a council to 'reform' the English church. By the end of the meetings, all but two of England's bishops were Norman. Of the two Englishmen that retained their bishoprics: one, Wulfstan of Worcester, became a saint and the other, Siward of Rochester, was senile. As another reward to the Roman Church, William reinstated the mandatory tithing to maintain the Church. This tithing, which had been voluntary prior to the conquest, was nothing more than a religious tax through which the Roman Church shared in the plundering of the English people.

Law under William was personal and autocratic, rather than legal or constitutional. "He issued no great codes of laws...held no theory of royal prerogative...he simply ruled as a strongman, whose slightest word must be obeyed." As we have seen with the Harrying of the North, his punishment was swift and brutal. A prime example were the "Forest Law." With this law, William created large game preserves over which he had exclusive jurisdiction. As the Anglo-Saxon Chronicle makes clear, "He [William] made many dear-parks, and he established laws therewith; so that whosoever slew a hart, or a hind, should be deprived of his eyesight." William's brutality did not stop at "depriving" a person of his eyesight. When starving Englishmen were caught "poaching" in the "King's Forest" -- which were the traditional hunting grounds of the English -- the punishment was having their hands and feet cut off so that they could live out the rest of their lives as human worms.

Similar laws were common in Romanized France and were done purely for the benefit of the elites. But, in Anglo-Saxon England, these laws appear to be entirely unknown and their importation "were hated, above all, because they were perceived to be arbitrary. They were a product merely of the king's will and they served only his pleasure. In other words, they were 'un-English'." (Starkey)

The un-Englishness of the Norman Conquest would have dire consequences for the common Englishman who was accustomed to the relative freedom of Anglo-Saxon England. As Robinson would write:

For the small men of England, peasants, farmers, craftsmen, and the rest, this change was the beginning of different and less happy times...the new master was not what the old had been: he had not been brought up among the villagers; he did not even understand their speech; he cared little or nothing for their welfare, but considered mainly what profit he could draw from them.

In 1066, it appeared that the flame of freedom was forever extinguished under the "Norman yoke." But thanks to the effort of Alfred to document the history of the Anglo-Saxons, primarily in *The Chronicles*, the Anglo-Saxon model based on the principles of limited government, individual freedom, private property rights, and free market economics would not he lost. They would continue to live in the hearts and minds of a free peoples. As historian Hugh Trevor-Roper notes, "Even the rude fact of the Norman Conquest had not interrupted this good old Anglo-Saxon tradition [of liberty]."

Within a century and a half, these principles would reassert themselves in a document that would one day become the basis of the free world.

Chapter 15
Magna Carta

For many, such as British parliamentarian and author Daniel Hannan, the signing of the Magna Carta represents "an event of truly planetary significance." A time when the English people rose up against Norman tyranny to reestablish the freedoms and liberties of their Anglo-Saxon forefathers. A moment, that would eventually guarantee the rights of all "freeborn Englishmen" from the tyranny of absolute and arbitrary rule. An event that, up until the last century, was celebrated as a reminder that the rights of the individual was superior to the needs of the state and that no man, not even a king, was above the law.

Within the faded text of the Magna Cart, we see – after a century and a half of Norman tyranny – a recommitment of the English people to their traditional Anglo-Saxon values. More significantly, we see the emergence of the three independent and competing spheres necessary for a free and prosperous society; in the court of King John we have the state exerting near absolutist power, the barons representing the interest of the money class, and, in the

Archbishop of Canterbury an independent minded church that, three centuries before Reformation, was willing to side against the king in London and the Pope in Rome.

This would not have happened if not for the inept and tyrannical King John I who, in 1199, inherited all of the Angevin Empire. This empire stretched from Scotland to the Pyrenees and was the largest landmass in Europe under a single ruler; dwarfing the state of France. Being one of the most impoverished kingdoms of the empire, England was seen as the backwater of the Empire. The Norman kings very seldom visited the kingdom, preferring to make their homes in Anjou or one of their other wealth producing kingdoms on the continent. This left England to be governed by Barons and magistrates who were wise enough to know how far they could push the king's Anglo-Saxon subjects. More importantly, it gave the Barons a level of autonomy and self-rule that would leave much of the people's Anglo-Saxon values, at least at the local level, intact.

Unfortunately for John, he did not have the military, nor political, skills of his Norman predecessors. Within a few short years, he would lose most of his inheritance in costly wars against his nemesis Philip II, King of France. The loss of nearly all of his continental holdings resulted in John having no alternative but to retreat to the one safe kingdom he had left: England. The prestige of John -- and England -- declined with every battlefield loss John suffered. In England, his loss of land earned him the ignominious moniker of "John the Lackland".

Unfortunately, Phillip II was not the only continental leader John had to contend with. His other nemesis, Pope Innocent III, would force John to lose effective ownership of England itself. The conflict began over the appointment of the archbishop of Canterbury. The ever insecure John, ignoring the traditional rights of the monks of

Canterbury, appointed a weak individual who would be in effect nothing more than his puppet. In response, the monks elected one of their own to the position and sent him to Rome for Innocent's approval. Innocent, rather than take sides in the dispute between the King and monks, appointed an English-born cardinal Stephan Langston to be the archbishop.

Langston was a perfect choice and, as we shall see, would become one of the key players in the struggle for individual freedom. Unfortunately, while the monks were satisfied, John stubbornly resisted the appointment. Innocent placed all of England under an Interdict, which meant that no religious ceremonies including mass, wedding, or baptism were performed. The dead, regardless of status, were carried out of town to be buried without any prayers or rites in roadside ditches. John, believing he was no longer obligated to respect the Church or the Pope, confiscated church property; resulting in his excommunication.

Philip of France knew that John was obsessed with reclaiming the ancestral land he had lost. This meant that Philip always had to maintain constant vigilance for any attempt by John against his newly acquired kingdoms. Philip saw John's excommunication as an opportunity to eliminate this threat by conquering the last of John's kingdoms; England and Ireland. With this in mind, Philip petitioned the Pope for permission to invade England, remove its excommunicated king, and return the kingdom to fold of the Roman Church.

In contrast to John's political ineptitude, Innocent's political prowess would make him one of the greatest medieval popes. He wisely understood that an England ruled by a weakened and even excommunicated king was preferable to a Philip with no rival. He had no false illusions that an empowered Philip, despite his pleas of fidelity to the Church, would be just as uncontrollable as John was. The reality was that Pope Innocent needed a king in England to act as a counterbalance to Philip.

Yet, Philip's offer was not without its usefulness. Innocent made sure that John became aware of Philip's offer in hopes that it would drive the English king to seek the protection of Rome. True to his nature, John underestimated his value to the Pope as a counterbalance to Philip and immediately sought reconciliation with Rome. In a desperate bid to avoid a church-sanctioned invasion by his nemesis, John not only gave absolute authority of the kingdom to the Pope, but also accepted Stephan Langston as the Archbishop of Canterbury. He agreed to compensate Rome for all the church property confiscated and, in an extreme move, signed a charter in which John recognized the Pope as his overlord. This committed John to pay Rome a large annual cash tribute, which was akin to John giving Innocent ownership of England and then leasing it back from him for an unsustainable annual fee.

With his international adventures ending in disaster, an astute leader would attempt to be more successful in his domestic affairs. Unfortunately for England, John was not astute and the financial situation caused by his losses on the continent would tragically impact his domestic policies.

Having spent every penny he had on fruitless wars on the continent, the funds to pay this annual fee would have to come from John's tax revenue; which – with the loss of the Angevin empire – meant whatever income he could squeeze out of his already impoverished English subjects. The burden of the taxes fell on the barons who had titles to the baronial estates. They, in turn, had to exact as much out of their serfs as possible. This made John very unpopular at all levels of English society.

Yet, this did not concern John. On the contrary, he once again turned a desirous gaze to the provinces he had lost to Philip.

John was playing a high stakes game. If he was successful, his reputation would be restored both at home and abroad. Furthermore, he would able to use the additional tax revenue from the newly reacquired provinces to pay the Papal fee, thus reducing the unpopular taxes that he was imposing on his English subjects. With his reputation restored, he could reign as a triumphant monarch and, more importantly, he would be able to justify his confiscatory taxing as a measure than had to be taken for the glory of England.

As Starkey writes, "There was only one way for John to reestablish his authority; to reconquer his lost lands in France…All the cash which had been wrung from his people and coerced from the barons had been amassed for [this] one purpose. If the diced rolled in his favor and he won a great victory in France all would be well." Wars require money and this strategy required that demand even more taxes. John had already taken the taxing of his subjects to an unheard level. Starkey writes, "From 1206 he [King John] began sucking the country dry. Taxes reached unprecedented levels. Jews were persecuted. The barons were squeezed hard and those who fell into debt to the crown were deprived of land and hounded into exile. The wealth of the nation, exacted by increasingly arbitrary means, was hoarded in royal castles."

But, if he lost, he could lose it all, including the English crown.

On 27 July 1214 the English and French armies met at Bouvines, which today sits along France's border with Belgium. As first, it appeared that John would have his great victory. The English army ruled the battlefield for most of the day. Philip came so close to defeat that, in the heat of battle, he was thrown from his horse. But then the French rallied. In a last ditch effort, they struck with all the might they could muster. Believing that the battle was all but won, the English, especially John, was taken off guard by the strength and ferocity of the attack. The English forces were decimated. Philip had snatched a decisive victory right out of John's hands. John had taxed the English people to the point of near starvation and now had blown it all on another fruitless military expedition; this time losing the entire wealth of England.

John returned home to a bankrupt England. His treasury was empty. In fact, he was no better off financially than many of his subject. But John was not one to let reality deter him. In a continuing demonstration of his lack of political skill, John demanded even more "scutage" in order to refill the treasury that his policies had left barren.

Over the last decade and a half, the barons had been drained dry by John's never ending need for revenue. In order to pay the taxes demanded of them, they had to squeeze every penny out of their serfs. Even the nicest and kindest of barons was forced to starve his people who had traded their liberty for his protection. Yet, he could not protect them from the king, and England became as oppressive as any modern day authoritarian state.

The one thing that John had in his favor is that the barons disliked each other as much as they did the king. John made use of this constant feuding by creating antagonisms between the rival factions. As king, it was his duty to settle disputes between barons and did so with the sole purpose of keeping the barons at each other's throats. It was the classic divide and rule tactic, which has been and always will be the mark of a failed leader.

John's defeat at the Battle of Bouvine and his demand for more revenue was the last straw for the barons. John had proven himself an inept and irresponsible ruler and the barons knew that they could not wrest anymore out of their already suffering serfs. It needs to be remembered that under the Normans, private ownership of property was virtually non-existent. Even the land "owned" by the Barons was granted to them by the king. If a baron failed to pay his taxes, the king could take the property without any due process.

Traditionally, this was reserved as punishment for disloyalty and the barons became accustomed to owing several years -- even decades -- of back taxes. In times of war, the king would often forgive all or part of the debt in lieu of the barons supplying troops and material. The barons expected the same would occur now. Instead John, in desperate need of funds, saw no reason why the barons should not have to pay their taxes when due. In a break with tradition, John threatened to revoke the grants of any baron incapable of paying his taxes. There was not one baron in England who was not in danger of losing his estate.

Once again John had overplayed his hand. The barons knew that with the treasury empty, John had no way of imposing his will on them. Now he was at their mercy. Realizing that they had to unite or perish, the barons put their differences aside. They met at the burial site of Saint Edmund, the East Anglican king gruesomely killed by the Vikings in 869, ostensibly to pay tribute to the martyr. Possibly inspired by the courage of the Saxon king, the barons quickly decided that "never again would a king be able to behave as John has done."

In January 1215, the barons went to London and presented John with a list of their demands. John asked for time to review the demands. The barons granted this request and a meeting was set for April in Northampton. The ever duplicitous John used the time to hire foreign mercenaries and convinced the Pope to condemn the rebellious barons. Secure behind his mercenaries and with the support of the Pope, John felt no need to keep his appointment in Northampton.

It is at this time that the choice of Stephan Langston as archbishop of Canterbury became so providential. Langston was an Englishman and, as such, was trained within the English church. Although officially part of the Roman church, the English church never accepted Rome having complete authority over the affairs of England. In direct contradiction to the Pope, Langston sided with the barons. As historian Cyril Robinson would write, "Langston was a man of high courage and large ideas...He understood the barons' grievances and saw that they were right. So when he backed them, the authority of his name and office won the entire nation to their cause."

With popular opinion on their side, the barons responded with surprising resolve. Having breached the trust of his subjects, the barons believed it completely in their rights to renounce their loyalty to the king. They marched on London, which openly welcomed them. Civil war seemed all but inevitable. Then, at the last moment, John agreed to meet with the barons. They chose a field known as Runnymede since its terrain prohibited the deployment of an army. The barons, who had come fully armed, presented their demands which King John reluctantly granted. The agreement became known as the *Magna Carta,* the Great Charter.

Yet, today, the signing of the Magna Carta is nearly forgotten. The primary reasons for this is the claim by revisionist academics and historians that the Magna Carta is nothing more than a myth. That the document did very little for the rights of the common man. That it was nothing more than a struggle between the King of England and the barons who made up England's wealthy ruling class. They point to the fact that the majority of the barons themselves were

Norman and had no interest in the traditional rights of the Anglo-Saxons. That the few rights granted in the Magna Carta to the common people were weak, completely ignored, and discarded before the English people were able to benefit from them. It is, they argue, a fairytale that no longer deserves to be honored. As a result of this revisionist history -- inspired by what Cambridge Professor Dr. Alan MacFarlane called "vulgar Marxist interpretations "-- one of the pivotal points in the age-old struggle against absolute tyranny has been erased from the cultural consciousness of the very people who created it.

It is telling that the legend of Robin Hood would be born during the reign of John. Unlike the modern version, the original Robin Hood was not a social justice warrior who "stole from the rich and gave to the poor." On the contrary, Robin Hood was an Anglo-Saxon Englishman who could no longer stand by as arbitrary government and high taxes starved his people. So Hood, a former Crusader (as the tale goes), decided to steal from an oppressive government (represented by the Sheriff of Nottingham) and a corrupt church (represented by the Bishop of Hereford) the money that was unjustly and cruelly extorted from the common people. He then returned the newly liberated funds back to people who were the victims of John's confiscatory taxes and arbitrary use of power.

This portrait of John being an exceptionally bad and evil king persisted into the early 19th century when Eleanor Farjeon penned this popular poem:

John, John, bad King John
Shamed the throne that he sat on;
Not a scruple, not a straw,
Cared this monarch for the law;
Promises he daily broke;

None could trust a word he spoke;
So the Barons brought a Deed;
Down to rushy Runnymede,
Magna Carta was it hight,
Charter of the People's Right,
Framed and fashioned to correct
Kings who act with disrespect -
And with stern and solemn air,
Pointing to the parchment there,
"Sign! Sign! Sign!" they said
"Sign, King John, or resign instead!"

With such a historical judgment of his actions, it is hard believe that anyone could see John as a good king. Yet, this is what revisionist historians are now doing. As Starkey writes, "A new generation of historians have come along who argue that, on the contrary [to the historical view], John was a 'good thing', or at any rate a good administrator. He was unusually interested in the mechanics of government, which he pursued with an often obsessive interest."

To revisionist historians there is no higher purpose for a government than for it to create order and stability. Viewing history through this state-centered prism, it comes as no surprise that many modern academics have come to see John as a good king. For modern academic historians, it is not whether a government is oppressive or not that matters, but whether the government is efficient in how it governs the people. And there is no better example than John.

We have already seen how John pressed the barons for every penny he could extract from them, but his attempt to exploit England was not limited to the barons. In a gross violation of the Anglo-Saxon principle of privacy, John created a bureaucratic apparatus that rivals those of the totalitarian states of the modern age. Armed with the king's authority, thousands of agents swarmed the English countryside with the goal of counting every man, woman, and child. This was more than just a census. Along with people, John's agents counted livestock, arable and non-arable acreage, tools, furnishing, and anything else a freeman could own. They even counted every waterhole, pond, and lake on a property. All with the intent to tax everything -- even the water -- his already overburdened subjects owned.

This went way beyond William's Domesday Book, whose purpose was to document what the king owned. John's mistrustfulness of his subjects bordered on paranoia and his obsession with record keeping made him the "Big Brother" of the Middle Ages. Through his agents, he was able to get people to spy on their neighbors and even family members. Through the tax code he was able to punish anyone who he perceived as being a threat to his authority.

Like the Patriots of the American Revolution, revisionist historians paint the barons as rich men who resisted the authority of the state because they did not want to pay their taxes. This Marxist-based view of history ignores the observations of the 15th century political philosopher John Fortescue. Fortesque noted that the more power a king has to tax his subjects, the poorer his subjects will be and the less freedom they will have. This makes taxes, and not the guillotine or the bayonet, the most effective tool of the tyrant. He also noted that the opposite was also true. When the government's power to tax is limited, the people prosper. This is at the heart of the Anglo-Saxon model of government and why it produces free and prosperous societies.

The other misrepresentation that the revisionist makes is that -- since the barons had Norman surnames -- the struggle that led up to the Magna Carta was nothing more than a quarrel between the Norman nobility and their Norman king. That the English commoner had a very small role, if any. The reality was very much different. Although the barons had Norman last names, they were culturally more Anglo-Saxon than they were Norman. By the 12th century, many of the barons had parents, grandparents, and great-grandparents who were English. As children, they learned the stories of great Anglo-Saxons such as Alfred and the Saxon principle of limited government raged in their hearts. They, like their Saxon forefathers, believed that liberty was a birthright of all Englishmen and that no man had the authority to deny them of it. Over the century and a half since the Conquest, the Norman's in England became a very distinct people far different than their Norman cousins on the continent. The Anglo-Normans, as they are now known, had gone "native".

More significantly, in an age when authoritarianism and absolutism came to dominate Europe, the English regarded their Great Charter as something very unique and extremely special. It reinforced the idea that they were a free people; destined to free themselves from the yoke of tyranny. As de Tocqueville points out, only a people dedicated to the philosophy of individual freedom, limited government, representative democracy, and the rule of law could produce such a document in the thirteenth century. This is what he called the "magic" of the Magna Carta.

They [the English] see the whole English Constitution in it; the two houses; ministerial responsibility; taxation by vote and a thousand other things that are no more there than in the Bible... [Yet] from then onwards a great many men marched under the standard of the great charter without knowing or caring what it had enacted.

This 'magic' is illustrated in an event that occurred over 400 years after the signing of the Magna Carta. The year was 1647 and England found itself on the precipice. The civil war that had been raging for the last five years had left the nation on the verge of a military dictatorship that promised to do what William the Conqueror never could; the destruction of Anglo-Saxon based liberty. That August, the Parliamentary forces that started the war defending traditional English liberties found itself victorious and in control of London. Like Washington's army at the end of the American war for independence, the Parliamentary soldiers were unpaid and angry at the mistreatment they had received from their political leaders. As they approached the capital, it quickly became apparent to the soldiers that they were now the only organized force in all of England and, more importantly, they had London. The army was about to become a vengeful mob.

Realizing the threat that 'their' army now posed, Parliament appointed the army's commander, Lord Thomas Fairfax, to the position of constable of the Tower of London, which put him in charge of the wealth of England. Fairfax's first act was to have England's greatest treasure brought to him. "It was not crown nor a scepter," as Daniel Hannan writes, "but a desiccated piece of parchment carrying barely legible Latin writing."

Fairfax held up the 432 year old copy of the Magna Carta for all his soldiers to see and said with veneration, "This is that which we have fought for and by God's help we must maintain it".

Events like the Magna Carta had the power of being a self-fulfilling prophecy. The principles that it came to symbolize would become the foundation of freedom of every English-speaking nation. The ideas it represented would create such monumental documents as the Declaration of Rights of 1688, the Declaration of

Independence, and the Constitution of the United States. Documents that are at the heart of what we consider today to be fundamental human rights and have been the cornerstone to all the freedom that has made the English-speaking countries the freest and most prosperous nations in the history of mankind.

Chapter 16
The English Civil War

When Lord Fairfax held up the Magna Carta before his rebellious soldiers, very few had any knowledge of what was written on that 435 year old piece of parchment. As de Tocqueville noted, it did not matter. What was important were the ideas, values, and principles it represented to the average Englishman. By calling it to be preserved, Lord Fairfax was reminding them of the Anglo-Saxon traditions that made them freeman with traditional rights and liberties. Rights and liberties that the soldiers believed so valuable that they were willing to raise arms against their king when he threatened to take them away. Now, with the Magna Carta in hand, Fairfax was warning his troops not to become the tyrant that they despised; King Charles I.

It would be, on 2 February 1626, at Westminster Abbey where Charles I would have the crown of England placed upon his head. For most of the Stuart kings, a king's divine right to rule was an intellectual exercise, something worthy of debate but an issue not worth losing the crown over. For Charles, his divine right to rule was an emotional, as well as a religious, principle. And when it came to principles, there was no king more unbending than Charles. Being exceptionally stubborn, even for a king, Charles was incapable of questioning whether a principle he was defending could be wrong. In fact, in his mind, he could do no wrong. Even to his last days, he could not admit that he had ever erred during his reign as king. Historian Cyril Robinson would note, that if Charles had a creed, it would read, "I believe in kings being heaven's chief instrument for the world's good, who, being by God himself appointed to their post, can make no surrender of it and can do no wrong; more especially do I believe in Charles Stuart, called by divine grace to set upon the English throne to govern the stiff-necked people of this unworthy island."

This attitude would not sit well with the English people and, in less than 25 years, it would cause Charles to not only to have the crown removed from his head, but his head severed from his body.

The Magna Carta established that Parliament had the right to share in the governance of the island nation. This did not mean that Parliament was able to govern in its own right, but that the king must consult it and get its approval on certain actions, such as taxation. This is the origins of the concept of "no taxation without representation" which would become a common rallying cry throughout the English-speaking world. It resulted in the English parliament having real power and not just a debating society as they were in the rest of the world. Furthermore, the English Parliament was not comprised of the privilege class. The members were small squires and yeoman farmers from the country, merchants and craftsmen from the towns, the class of folk who made England what she was. These were practical men who had little patience for academic discussions that produced nothing.

More significantly, they were free Englishmen who were willing to pledge their lives, fortunes and sacred honor in defense of that freedom.

Today, when we think of the weapons of tyranny such as the guillotine, the bayonet, or even the rifle, we fail to recognize that throughout history the most effective weapon of them all is the government's power to tax. Through the power to tax, a tyrant can punish his enemies and reward his friends. He can impoverish opposition while using the plundered money to buy support. This is why there has traditionally been a deep aversion and opposition to taxes in English-speaking cultures. In more than one case, that opposition has ended in bloody conflict. The English Civil War is one of those conflicts.

Once again it would be taxes and ill-fated military adventures that would pit king against Parliament. Just as the United States would establish in its system of government 125 years later, Parliament controlled the purse strings of the English government. It was the customary at the time for governing body to grant the king a block sum of funds which he could use as he saw fit to administer the affairs of the nation. After two disastrous and very costly military campaigns on the continent – one against Spain, the other against France – parliament decided that Charles could not be trusted with such a large sum and instead chose to provide the funds on a yearly basis and only if Parliament approved of the king's handling of the previous year's funds.

This greatly undermined Charles authority for without funds he had no way of governing the country. This made parliament the de facto rulers of England and reduced Charles to being their puppet. As mentioned above, Charles was not one to have his "divine right" to rule be reduced by a body of men he should not have to contend with in the first place. In violation of his constitutional authority, Charles responded by confiscating all the duties that had been collected by the custom houses and imposed compulsory "loans" on private individuals. The loans were actually taxes which, by giving them another name, Charles argued was outside the constitutional purview of parliament. This act was rightly seen as being illegal and many refused to "loan" money that they knew they would never see again. Once again, Charles demonstrated his lack of respect for the law. Over eighty gentlemen were immediately thrown in jail for non-payment and many others were forced into military service. More shockingly, Charles had the army posted throughout the country; often billeted in the homes of those who refused to pay the loan. Tensions between the people and the army increased. The country appeared to be on the verge of rebellion. Martial law was declared and exactions soon followed.

This was a time when the members of parliament saw themselves as the defenders of the constitution and keepers of the rights of Englishmen. They were outraged when they saw Charles willful disregard for the rule of law and his arrogant scorn for the constitution. When Parliament was called in 1628, it was like no other parliament ever seen before. The first order of business in the Commons was to draw up a document which has gone down in history as one of the most pivotal in the history of individual freedom. Known as the Petition of Right, Parliament demanded that 1) no tax or loan be exacted "without the common consent of parliament"; 2) that no man should be detained or imprisoned without due process or legal cause; 3) the billeting of soldiers in private residences should be discontinued; and 4) martial law be ended.

While these rights would become the basic rights of Englishmen and echoed in the founding documents of the United States, presenting such a petition to a 17th century king was not something that was done lightly. It is said that many of the members – even those in favor of the petition – openly wept as they debated its adoption. One observer of the proceedings wrote, "Sir Robert Philips mingled his words with weeping; and Sir Edward Coke, seeing the desolation likely to ensue, was forced to set down when he began to speak through an abundance of tears; the Speaker himself in his speech could not refrain from weeping and shedding tears." From Charles' previous actions, the members knew that they were pledging their lives, fortune, and sacred honor. Charles already had one of the opposition leaders, Sir John Eliot, tried for sedition and thrown into the Tower of London, where he soon died of maltreatment. Charles refused appeals from Eliot's family to take the body home for burial. Instead, Charles had Eliot buried along with the other common prisoners. The men debating the petition could only imagine what he would do to those he saw as committing an act of treason. Yet, that is not why they wept. It was the state in which their once free country now found itself in that drove them to tears.

Like a bill passed by Congress, the petition had no legal authority unless Charles signed it into law. The idea that the king would even consider such a restraint on his authority was preposterous. It appeared that the petition would be more symbolic than an effective attempt to rein in a power hungry monarch. Fortunately, Charles was once again planning another military campaign against France and he was in desperate need of money. Although parliament was opposed to the funding of another of Charles' military fiascos, they realized that the preservation of their rights as Englishmen was more important. They agreed to provide Charles with his much desired money on one condition, that he signed the Petition of

Right. This infuriated Charles and for several days he refused to sign the document. Finally, realizing he had no choice, Charles set the Petition on the Statute Book, which placed it alongside the Magna Carta as a seminal document of English liberty.

Parliament had won a great victory, but it would prove to be just a check on Charles' unconstitutional actions. During this time, his chief advisor was George Villiers, Duke of Buckingham. Buckingham was rightly seen as the architect of Charles' actions and Parliament demanded his resignation. Besides being the king's advisor, he was also his closest companion and Charles baulked at the request. It appeared that a battle of wills was again brewing between Parliament and the king. Buckingham was touring Portsmouth when we was assassinated by a disgruntled and crazed veteran of the previous French campaign. Buckingham has been the commander of that ill-fated campaign and the veteran saw him as the source of all the problems that had plagued him since his return. The fact that the assassination was not politically motivated mattered not at all to Charles. In his grief, he vowed revenge on the people he believed responsible for the death of his friend.

As mentioned above, Charles was incapable of questioning whether his beliefs and action were correct or not. Just as the veteran saw Buckingham as the source of all his trouble, so Charles saw Parliament. With his heart full of vengeance, Charles decided that if Parliament would not confirm to his vision of government, then he would rule without them. In the spring of 1629, he called for their adjournment. News of the adjournment was sent to the House of Commons, where tempers were already flaring. This put the House into a state of near rebellion. and when the Speaker rose to mark the closing of parliament, two members rushed to his side and forced him back into his seat. Shouts were exchanged as members squared off with each other. In the chaos, some took the key from the door and hid it. Upon hearing of the ruckus, Charles marched on Westminster Abbey, where the Houses of Parliament are located. Accompanied by a contingent of soldiers, Charles was determined to once and for all rid himself of the troublesome, rebellious, and treasonous Parliament.

The House of Commons is considered the people's house and to this day no monarch can enter it without a formal invitation from the members. Charles entrance to the House was quickly barred and a proclamation denouncing his actions was read. That done, the House adjourned. It would be eleven years before Parliament would meet again. And when it did, it was with the spirit of rebellion.

Without the opposition of the House of Commons, Charles ignored 500 years of constitutional growth which started with the Magna Carta and ruled with the autocratic authority of even the most absolute of kings. As predicted, Charles' campaign against the French resulted in failure and, having spent his money funding the campaign, he was destitute. Although desperate for money, he refused to call Parliament since they would insist that he rule within the limits of the Constitution. Instead, he found in William Noy a crafty Attorney General who had a knack for redefining and reinterpreting laws in novel, if not unconstitutional, ways. One of those laws was the application of the "Ship Tax."

Traditionally, during times of war, English kings could impose a ship tax to maintain the navy. This ship tax was assessed against coastal towns, which benefitted economically from the seaborne trade that the navy protected. Noy argued that it was within the king's power to assess the 'Ship Tax' not only in a time of peace, but also across the whole nation. The tax was imposed in 1634 and within a year was producing 90% of the king's required annual income. "This was the Holy Grail," as David Starkey writes, "of royal administration, which had eluded English kings ever since the Middle Ages: a large scale permanent income, which came in regularly, year by year, without the bother of consulting troublesome parliaments." It proved to be the answer to all of Charles problems, but it was also extremely unconstitutional.

The tax was bitterly resented and many, including one of the leading members of Parliament, John Hampden refused to pay it. Having full faith in the English legal system, Hampden chose to fight the constitutionality of the tax in court. Hampden did not have to wait long. He soon found himself confronted by the full force of the royal government. He was promptly hauled into court. The resultant trial would be the test case for whether England was a nation of laws or that of royal decree. "With a servility unworthy of the English bench," Robinson would write, "the majority of the judges voted" in Charles favor by ruling that the king had the authority to levy taxes whenever he liked "for the preservation and safety of the commonwealth." With this decision by agenda driven judges, English liberty was all but destroyed. Charles now had the legal authority "to confiscate private property and punish people at will." All legal and property rights were at his mercy. As famous poet John Milton observed at the time, "Grant him this and the Parliament hath no more freedom than if it sat on his Noose, which when he please to draw together with one twitch of his Negative, shall throttle a whole nation." Through legal activism, England went from a nation governed by a constitutionally limited monarch to one no less despotic than the authoritarian King of France.

The judges' decision sent a shockwave throughout the nation. The English had come to see the courts as the protector of the Constitution and stunned by the realization that the judges they trusted to defend their freedom were just as willing to throw away the Constitution as Charles was to violate it. With the courts squarely on his side, Charles' plan to rule the English with the same absolutist power that the French king had over his subjects might have succeeded as it did in France, but the English were not like the French. As Robinson observed, the English were not a "tame race" and, when the time came, they would see that Charles and his "evil" advisors would be properly punished for the treachery they committed against the Constitution and the English people.

It is also during this time that one of the biggest proponents of the state being intimately entwined with the church, William Laud, became the Archbishop of Canterbury.

One of the prime provisions of the Magna Carta was that the English church should be free and independent of royal (political) authority. This provision ended when Henry VIII severed ties with Rome and proclaimed himself "Supreme Head on Earth of the Church of England." This virtually put the religious sphere under the control of the political sphere. Fortunately, just as there are today, there were several Protestant sects which challenged the Church of England's monopoly on the religious beliefs of the nation. England was very tolerant of these "non-conforming" sects and by the reign of Charles, the "Puritans" (so called because of their literal interpretation of the Bible) had become second only to the Church of England in terms of numbers and influence. The Parliament of 1625 highlights the popularity and power of the Puritans. In that Parliament, three quarters of the 500 members elected to the House of Commons identified themselves as Puritans.

Puritanism was seen as a product of the Anglo-Saxon society from which it developed. Unlike the Roman church, or even the Church of England, it was decentralized. Puritans despised the top-down authoritarianism of the state church. They rejected the idea of religious thought being dictated from theological aristocrats in opulent cathedrals. A person's relationship with God was personal and between him and God, no one else. Therefore, there were no popes or bishops to tell the churches what the topic of their sermons would be on any given Sunday. In fact, they had no churches – most services were held in businesses or homes – and each one was independent of the others. Each group appointed its own ministers and set the agenda for Sunday meetings. In other words, there was no organized Puritan church. The one common factor they all had was the unquestionable belief that the Bible, as the true word of God, was to be the focus of all their teachings. This gave their Sunday services more of a Bible study feel than that of an actual church service. This lack of organization and centralization meant that Puritanism was a religious movement of the people. It was bottom up, which matched the Anglo-Saxon political and economic temperaments. It is not a coincidence that the movement would come to dominate the religious and political character of the Anglo-Saxon domains of East Anglia, Essex, and Sussex. Throughout Europe, Protestantism would take various forms. Puritanism, it could be said, was the form produced by the Anglo-Saxons.

Archbishop Laud believed that serving the king and state was just as Christian as serving Christ himself and he disliked what he saw as fake Christianity. More importantly, he feared the challenge they posed to the state church. Seeing Puritanism as a false religion, he abhorred their extremist views of the Bible which included dedicating Sundays as a day for religious study, reflection, and prayer. Traditionally, Sunday afternoons were a time for sport and fun. At the urging of Laud, Charles issued the *Book of Sunday Sports* and a declaration to be read in churches "which positively commanded everyone to take part in them" regardless of their religious belief. This meant that all Englishmen must participate in a sporting activity on Sunday's even if they consider it to be a day reserved for religious activities. As ridiculous as this sounds, it was not a trivial matter. Laud was demonstrating to all, but especially to the Puritans, that the Church of England was the "High Church" and as such had the power of the state behind it. In Charles' England, the political and religious spheres united to destroy freedom of conscience.

Under the influence of Laud, Charles' attack on independent religion wasn't restricted to England. He was also King of Scotland and under Laud's guidance he attempted to establish domain over the Scottish church, which was mostly Presbyterian and independent of political control. Charles ordered it to be restructured under the Church of England model with royal prayer books replacing the Bible and bishops ensuring compliance. The Presbyterians rejected this state takeover of their church and rose up in rebellion. Charles was faced with two options; either abandon his plan to reform the Scottish church or impose it through the use of force. Stubbornly Charles chose force. He decreed that an army be raised to suppress the Scottish rebellion. The problem was that he had no money to raise a proper army without the proper funds. Finding himself without lucre and with Scotland in full rebellion, Charles had no option but to reconvene Parliament.

Although it had been eleven years since the Parliament had last met, many of the members still remembered how Charles had threatened force when it refused to adjourn. Furthermore, they resented being forced to sit on the sidelines as Charles imposed his will upon the people. Nor did the people forget and many of the same members of the previous Parliament were reelected for the new one. This resulted in giving the Parliament a Puritan appearance. This meant that the Parliament was more interested in restraining Charles' despotic rule than they were in suppressing a rebellion to which many were sympathetic. After a month of quarrelling, Charles dismissed the Parliament. Hence, it is remembered by history as the "Short Parliament."

Undeterred Charles set out to create his army by any means possible. He extorted money from the middle and upper classes while pressing those without financial means into military service. The Parliamentarians were under no illusions. They understood that if Charles created an army that could suppress the Scots, then it could easily be used to suppress the English. And there was nothing in Charles' behavior that led them to believe he would hesitate to do so. Realizing the seriousness of the situation, the Parliamentarians, led by John Pym, negotiated a secret understanding with the Scots and in autumn 1640 the Scottish army invaded northern England. Encountering little resistance the Scots captured Newcastle, where it awaited Charles. Charles immediately recognized that his still untrained army was no match for the Scots. He had no option but to accept whatever the Scots demanded. It was at this point that the Scots fulfilled their agreement with the Parliamentarians. Rather than demand political and religious freedom, the Scots demanded a huge sum of money to withdraw from England. In order to comply, Charles was forced to reconvene another Parliament.

Led by Pym, Parliament started to immediately attack the hapless Charles. Almost in complete unity, they focused on the political, constitutional, and religious grievances against the king. Charles was forced to abolish the "Ship Money" and all other objectionable aspects of his reign. He had to rid himself of anyone the Parliament regarded as 'evil' councilors, including Archbishop Laud. Lastly, Charles was forbidden from disbanding Parliament without the consent of its members. It appeared that Parliament would serve as a permanent opposition to royal authoritarianism. But now it was the Puritans' turn to overplay their hand. In a direct attack on the Church of England, they demanded that the king abolish the bishops. The king refused. Pym the called for a vote on a document titled the "Grand Remonstrance." Although addressed to the king, this document was really a manifesto that stripped Charles of all his power, including control of the army. It was passed on the 1st of December, 1641 by the narrow margin of eleven votes (159 to 148). This amount to nothing less than a constitutional revolution that made Parliament the rulers of England and the monarch nothing more than a figurehead.

Surrendering the power Charles had enjoyed while Parliament was adjourned was one thing, giving up all power to rule was quite another. Charles responded by charging Pym, Hampden, and three others with high treason for conspiring with the Scottish army in 1640. When he demanded that Parliament give them up for arrest, they voted the king to be in breach of parliamentary privilege. The queen, who was French, knew how a French king would deal with such rebelliousness. Turning to her husband she exclaimed, "Go you coward! And pull those rogues out by the ears or never see my face again."

On 4 January 1642, Charles entered the House of Commons with the intent of arresting the five men. As his fully armed soldiers surrounded the building, Charles strode to the Speaker's Seat where he proceeded to seat himself. Once in the chair, he immediately demanded that the House produce the five men which he listed by name. The Speaker, falling prostrate the king's feet, declared that he could not answer without permission of the House. Even if he could answer, it would not do Charles any good. Forewarned, the five men escaped out a rear exit as Charles was arriving. Upon hearing the news, Charles murmured, "All my birds have flown".

Charles unconstitutional invasion of Parliament convinced many, including most of those in Parliament, that Charles was indeed a tyrant who would never accept constitutional limits on his authority. The City of London turned against the king and was soon followed by the Anglo-Saxon and Puritan dominated southeast. Charles fled to Nottingham, where he "raised his standard in a war against his Parliament and half his people." The English Civil War had begun.

Although the English Civil War (1642-1649) would tear the nation apart and result in the beheading of Charles I (the only case of regicide in English history) it was a strident step towards England becoming a free and prosperous modern society. During the war, the privileged elites – known as Cavaliers – rallied to the King's standard "by a consciousness that, if his crown should fall, their coronets and titles would soon be sure to follow." In them we see the rise of the political elites who would comprise the political sphere of pre-modern England. The Parliamentarians were an altogether different group. They were the merchants, shopkeepers, brewers, attorneys, clerks, yeoman farmers, and lesser-country gentlemen that made up what the French would call the bourgeois (or middle) class. It would be these middle class businessmen who would create a vibrant, prosperous, and independent economic sphere. Lastly, it would be the Puritans and other non-conforming protestant sects that would preserve the independence of the religious sphere granted by the Magna Carta. This was only made possible by a people, as de Tocqueville observed, whose values are based on Saxon principles.

From the Civil War the three essential spheres would emerge. But it would take another revolution to bring them into the balance that would allow England to break the cycle of predation and leap into the modern age.

Chapter 17
The Reluctant Revolutionary

It was during the chaotic period of the civil war that one of the most controversial figures in English history, Oliver Cromwell, would arise. Cromwell was a Puritan farmer who became a parliamentarian and the creator of the 'New Model' army. As a leader of Parliament and a commander of the army -- second only to Lord Fairfax -- Cromwell was in the unique position of being the only politician with the power to actually do anything. It was under his leadership that pro-Royalist members of Parliament were driven out; leaving what is known as the Puritan controlled "Rump Parliament" to sentence Charles to death. Charles' trial took place in the House of Commons on the 21st of January 1649 with the Members of Parliament acting as a jury. With parliament having been reduced to just the pro-Parliamentary members, Charles' guilty verdict was never in doubt. Characteristically, Charles was as stubborn as ever. He refused to concede that any of his policies were unconstitutional and even rejected the right of parliament to try him. For Charles, "a subject and sovereign are clear different things" and only God can judge a sovereign.

As expected, Charles was found guilty and sentenced to death. Many members soon found out it was easier to say a man should be sentenced to death than it is to actually sign the death warrant. Out of 135 members acting as judges, only 59 had the courage to affix their name to the document that would serve for all of posterity as a permanent record of their gruesome deed.. This did not change the outcome of the trial and on 30th of January Charles was marched out to the black draped scaffold. Even in the face of death, Charles remained stubborn. After disrobing, he said one word, "remember", before placing his head on the cutting board. His head was severed with one blow. As the executioner raised it for all the crowd to see, "there arose," a contemporary account states, "such a groan as I have never heard before and desire that I may never hear again."

The death of Charles I did not bring an end to England's troubles, it only compounded them. Internationally, the new government was a pariah. The other states of Europe refused to recognize it as a legitimate government, ambassadors and representatives were executed on sight. Not having a legally recognized government to protect them, English shipping was considered fair game to any vessel seeking plunder. France and then Holland gave sanctuary to Charles' sons, Charles and James, who were already making plans to avenge their father. England's primary and most troublesome colony, Ireland, was once again aflame with rebellion and Scotland itself was on the verge of civil war. While the lowland Presbyterians were friendly to the new English government, the highland tribes remained loyal to Charles and, after his death, his eldest son; the younger Charles.

The rupture that had developed between the Puritan dominated army and the politicians in Parliament left the government without the ability to effectively deal with all these issues. Bookmakers in London were offering 20 against one that the government would last a year. Moreover, many were appalled by the beheading of Charles and there was a growing sentiment among the people that the younger Charles should return to take his father's place as king; especially if it would bring peace to this troubled and suffering land. The Parliamentarians were on the verge of losing in the peace what they had won in the war.

Correctly believing that there was no else who could save the situation, Cromwell immediately set out with his army to end the rebellion in Ireland. This was a very risky move. With the army gone – and without Cromwell's strong hand – England lay undefended and open to invasion from her various foes. Cromwell knew he had to make quick work of the Irish. In August 1649, he and his army landed in Dublin Bay. What confronted him was utter chaos. Ireland had descended into a bloody religious war with atrocities being committed by both sides. Stern measures would be required if order were to be reestablished. But Cromwell would be more than stern, he was "abominably cruel" and – with "his soul filled with the passion of a blinding hate" – he committed a level of barbarity that is remembered by the Irish to this day.

At the Battle of Boyne, in which Cromwell won a decisive victory over the Irish army, no quarter was given. Irish soldiers, whether they fought or surrendered, were mercilessly slaughtered. Those who ran for their lives were hunted down and killed. As his forces captured the town of Drogheda, its garrison sought sanctuary in the town's church; which was then promptly set afire by pursuing English soldiers. "That night," says Cromwell, "we put to sword about two thousand men…Their friars were knocked on the head promiscuously…I forbade them to spare any that were in arms in the town." Whether he intended it or not, the massacre continued for days and its victims included women and children. The brutality had its affect and town after town, fort after fort surrendered to Cromwell without a fight. Only the castle at Wexford resisted. When it was finally taken, its inhabitants suffered the same fate as those of Drogheda. By spring, except for a few towns in the extreme west, Cromwell was master of all of Ireland.

It is unclear why Cromwell was so ruthless in Ireland. In all his conflicts with the Royalist Cavaliers and the Scots he showed amazing restraint and mercy. It is easy to assume that – since all his other enemies were Protestant – is must have been the Catholicism of the Irish that drove him to commit such atrocities. But as ruler of England he would demonstrate a great degree of religious tolerance. All sects of Protestantism (including Puritan, and Baptist)were free to have open services and even churched. Jews established synagogues and Catholics were left relatively undisturbed. Only the Church of England was prohibited from having services and that was out of fear that it might encourage a Royalist revolt. The other explanation was that he was avenging the atrocities that the Irish committed against the English living in Ireland during the 1641 Irish Rebellion. This may have been part of it, but it is more likely that Cromwell knew that everyday spent in Ireland was a day that England remained vulnerable and the measures he took was the quickest way to end the rebellion. And he did so just in time.

Although the lowland Scots were friendly to the English Republic, their highland countrymen had very different sympathies. Charles, being a Stuart, had Scottish blood in is veins and the Highlanders saw his beheading as a direct attack on their clans. As a result, their loyalty laid with the younger Prince Charles living in exile in Holland. Seeing Cromwell occupied in Ireland, Prince Charles landed in Scotland with the goal of joining forces with the Highland leader, Marquis of Montrose. But before they could meet, Montrose was captured and executed by the Lowland Scots. In an amazing turn of events, the Presbyterians then offered to support the prince's campaign to establish him as King of England if he would agree to allow Presbyterianism to be the religion of England. At this point, as Robinson points out, Prince Charles would have "turned into a Mahomedan with equal zeal" if it gave him the ability to avenge his father. Upon receiving Prince Charles promise, the Kirk sent out a call to arms. Soon, David Leslie, a veteran of the battles of the English Civil War, found himself at the head of a 30,000 strong army comprised of lowland and highland Scots.

Cromwell was very much aware of the threat developing in Scotland. Leaving a garrison force behind to ensure that there will be no more trouble in Ireland, Cromwell set off for London. Allowing just a few weeks to resupply his army, Cromwell was once again on the march. This time north into Scotland. The Scottish forces were located in fortifications just outside the town of Stirling. He soon discovered that, while the Prince was the nominal leader of the army, the Kirk had the real power. Not wanting to fight his fellow Protestants, Cromwell attempted to use reason on the leaders of the Kirk. He appealed to their faith by citing scripture that supported his cause. The Kirk countered with scripture proving him wrong. He knew that as long as the Scots remained in their fortifications he did not have the manpower to force the issue. His only hope was to lure the Scottish army out from behind its fortifications. Again, he would find himself frustrated by the Scots lack of willingness to oblige him.

By the beginning of September, Cromwell was running out of patience and supplies. His already inferior force was further reduced by illness. Recognizing the futility of the situation, he decided to withdraw to England. In a lightening move that took Cromwell by surprise, Leslie skirted around the English forces to take the heights above the town of Dunbar, effectively trapping Cromwell in Scotland. "We cannot get through," Cromwell wrote, "without a miracle." Yet, a miracle he did receive in the form of political interference. The leaders of the Kirk, who were impatient for a Scottish victory, ordered the Scottish army to descend from the hilltops and attack their English foes. This was the opportunity Cromwell had been praying for and in the predawn hours of 3 September 1650, he attacked in full force. As the sun rose, it did so on a scene of a complete rout. The Scottish army was thoroughly defeated. "Never was an escape more wonderful," Robinson would write, "nor a defeat more crushing than Dunbar." Leslie was unable to rally his forces and the next day Cromwell took Edinburgh.

While the victory at Dunbar did eliminate the threat of a Scottish invasion, it did not end the rebellion. A significant Scottish force still remained in Stirling. All that winter and well into the next summer Cromwell, try as he might, could not breakthrough the Scottish fortifications. This gave Prince Charles, with the help of the Presbyterians, time to raise another army. In a daring move, Cromwell struck out to the northeast and into the town of Perth. This left the road to London wide open and Prince Charles leapt at the chance to regain the throne for the Stuarts. The only problem was that Cromwell was ready and shadowed the Prince on a parallel road. The Prince had been assured that the English people would support his return and that his ranks would swell with English volunteers. This support never materialized and he soon found himself outnumbered. With Cromwell on his heels, the Prince's only hope to reach London was to defeat Cromwell. Pausing at the town of Worcester, the Prince prepared his army to meet the English. Once again, Cromwell's soldiers won a decisive victory. Over 10,000 Scots were captured and another 3,000 were killed. Prince Charles fled and for several days lived the life of a fugitive. Only with the help of Catholic and Royalist friend would he reach Brighton and from there Holland.

Worcester, fought in 1651, was the last of a series of battles that started in 1641. As such, it is considered to be the final battle of the English Civil War. Never again would Cromwell lead men into battle, never again would he personally raise an arm against a foe. Instead, he would become a man who became king in all but name.

With the end of the Irish rebellion and the blunting of the Scottish invasion, Parliament and the army was once again at each other's throats. This internal strife threatened to do what the Irish and Scottish could not, end the English Republic before it had a chance to get started. After his victories over the Irish and Scottish, many had come to believe that Cromwell was the only man who could save the Republic. Although this would make Cromwell the "indispensable man" of his time, he was, as Starkey describes him, a "reluctant revolutionary." He was a fervent believer in the limiting and decentralization of government power. His ultimate goal was for England to have a legitimate constitutional republic led by parliament with the nation's leader the "first among equals" or a constitutional monarchy with most of the power securely in the hands of parliament. Unfortunately, Cromwell found himself trapped between an immovable object (Parliament) and an irresistible force (the army).

For Cromwell, the English Civil War went beyond being a fight for who controlled the power of government, it was struggle against the power of government itself. As commander Cromwell was very aware of the Puritan zeal that ran through the army. He understood that this zeal, if left unchecked, threatened to empower government to a level that would be as oppressive as it would be authoritarian. Yet, there was no other entity that could stop the army from taking control of the government. Their rivals in Parliament would only be able to offer words of protest, but little else.

Still, the politicians in Parliament saw themselves as the "watchmen" of the Constitution and of the fundamental rights of Englishmen as granted in such documents as the Magna Carta. They supported an independent religious sphere which, by necessity, would include religious toleration. They wanted to limit the government by having its powers placed in the safe hands of Parliament, whose members they argued were representative of the will of the people. More importantly, they were very jealous of their place in English society. Fueled by mutual distrust and outright hatred, Parliament and the army engaged in a bitter, yet non-violent, fight for control of the government. And Cromwell was the only person who had the power to keep it from turning violent.

Even though it was Cromwell's power that prevented the army from doing away with the Parliament altogether, the Rump Parliament moved to strip Cromwell of all his authority. This was partially done out of fear, but the politicians were motivated mostly out of jealousy. Being politicians, they were envious of Cromwell's power and voted for it to be transferred to Parliament. Unlike the politicians, Cromwell knew that such an action would not stand with the army. The truth is that the Rump Parliament had become a nuisance. It had refused to hold elections and those members who protested that it was becoming nothing more than an oligarchy were driven out of the House. By spring 1653, it had been reduced to just about a dozen or so men and could no longer make any claim to representing the people.

On 20 April 1653, Cromwell went to Westminster. Dressed as a mere citizen, in plain black coat and grey worsted stockings, he sat in his seat as a member of the House. Rising to address the assembly, Cromwell removed his hat as a sign of respect. He then proceeded to try to reason with his fellow members. They refused to listen. Frustrated, Cromwell placed his hat back upon his head and exclaimed, "You are no Parliament. I say you are no Parliament. I will put an end to your sittings." He then proceeded to the Speaker's chair where he told the assembled members that "some of them were Whoremasters. The others of them were Drunkards, and some corrupt and unjust men, and scandalous to the possession of the Gospel, and it was not fit they should sit as a Parliament any longer." Finishing he yelled, "Call them in. Call them in." Upon which soldiers of his personal regiment "The Ironsides" marched in and escorted the astonished members from the hall. Cromwell, being the last to leave, locked the door on his way out. England had lost her king, now it was losing her parliament.

For the next five years Cromwell governed England as a military dictator. This was a position he did not like and he worked feverishly to create a legitimate government. He wrote a constitution to replace the one that had been destroyed. Amazingly, this constitution placed most of the power of government in the hands of the still nonexistent Parliament. Out of fear that any new Parliament elected by the people would lack the religious spirit needed to avoid conflict with the army, Cromwell asked the churches throughout all of England to nominate men for Parliament. From those, 140 "godly and sainted" were chosen to settle the future shape of the government. This assembly, known as the "Barebones Parliament" (after one of its members), became the laughing stock of history. Instead of trying to establish good and orderly government, the assembly, deciding that "the godly have no need of learning," attempted to destroy the universities and then to replace English common law, the basis of English liberty, with Mosaic law. Cromwell saw that his plan had failed. To end the fiasco, he had the body vote to dissolve itself. "Discouraged and disappointed," Robinson writes, "Cromwell stood once more alone; and it was clear that the future constitution must be settled by some other means than appeal to the consciences of saints and cranks."

With the assistance of his advisors, Cromwell drew up a new written constitution. Titled the "Instrument of Government," it set up a position of Protector who would rule the land with the assistance of a permanent Council of State. Power would be shared with a parliament which would sit every three years for a minimum of five months, whereupon it could be dissolved by the Protector. The weakness of the plan was that the sharing of power between the Protector, the Council of State, and Parliament was not made clear. It is interesting to note that even under a military dictatorship, the English strove to establish a limited form of government that would protect an individual's political and economic freedom. Also, within this process, we see a foreshadowing of what the Founding Fathers of the United States would go through in establishing a workable and legitimate government for their new nation.

The first parliament to be formed under this new format was a complete disaster. The Parliament spent its whole session quarreling with Cromwell, now titled the Lord Protector, over its power. It demanded that Parliament have control of the army, something that Cromwell knew the army would never accept. After the mandatory five months, it was dissolved. The second parliament did much better but that was mostly due to over a hundred members of the previous Parliament being prohibited from participating. Those that remained presented a document they called their "Humble Petition and Advice." This document amounted to nothing more than offering the Lord Protector the throne of England.

This was not as crazy or even pro-Cromwell as it sounds. It harkens back to the Anglo-Saxon political traditions that the nation was founded on. Seeing itself as the 17th century version of the Witan, the Parliament saw nothing wrong with it exercising the traditional practice of the Witan to elect the king. Furthermore, tradition and custom limited the power of the English king and authorized, as in the case of John, the use of force if he should exceed his constitutional limitation. There were no such restraints on the power of the newly created and undefined position of Protector. It was a very brilliant move on the part of Parliament for King Oliver would have a lot less authority than Protector Cromwell.

Unfortunately for Parliament, Cromwell was too clever to fall for such a maneuver and the army was strongly against it. He also felt no "clear call" to accept such a title. To do so would be to become what he had despised, royalty. So he rejected it and Parliament dissolved with nothing to show for its efforts. The next Parliament permitted the previously excluded member and fared no better than the first. And, with its failure, went Cromwell's second attempt to establish decentralized representative government.

Incredibly, by most accounts, the English people were still supportive of Cromwell. Many saw his attempts to establish good government as sincere and blamed Parliament for the failures. This did not mean that there was not discontent among some of the people. England had suffered fourteen years of political instability and the inability of Cromwell, the politicians, and the army to work together to bring about the much needed stability led many to ask if it would not be better to return to the monarchy. Prince Charles was just across the channel. Surely he would be willing to accept the crown. By 1655, such attitudes led Cromwell and the army to become fearful of an insurrection. This drove Cromwell to commit his greatest blunder. In an overt use of pure military force, Cromwell divided the nation into eleven provinces with a Major-General in charge of each one. With wide powers of control, and cavalry to enforce that power, the Major-Generals took on the airs of a despot. They watched all foreigners, collected a penalty tax called the "decimation" which was assessed against the manors of known royalists, and even limited the free movement of English citizens.

These were actions that many English were willing to accept if they prevented another civil war. But the army demonstrated that it was "puritanical" as well as Puritan. The Major-Generals extended their duty to impose "the godly life" unto the English people. They outlawed public houses (commonly known as pubs), idlers and minstrels were banished, actors were forbidden to act, the exercising of horses on the Sabbath day was prohibited, newspapers were regulated, and the holding of town markets were not allowed on weekends. "In short, the Major-Generals were turning England into a reformatory," as Robinson notes, "and the Puritans, harmless enough so long as they kept their rules to themselves, were proving them more intolerable tyrants than [Archbishop] Laud had been." Cromwell was wise enough to end the Major-Generalships after a one year trial but the damage had been done. He had lost the trust of the English people and the Puritans were forever marked as enemies of liberty.

On 3 September 1658, Oliver Cromwell died and with him went the English experiment with republicanism. Prince Charles would be invited to take the place of his father and the monarchy was restored. After getting a taste of Puritan tyranny, the English people once again embraced the Church of England. It resumed its place as the "high church"; its supremacy uncontested. All the religious tolerance of Cromwell's republic was erased as members of the nonconforming Protestant sects, Jews, and Catholics were prohibited from holding government positions. Once again, the political and religious spheres would become one and the same.

As chaotic as Cromwell's reign was, it did produce some very important successes. By the time of his death, Cromwell had reestablished England's reputation as a European power. After victorious wars with the Dutch and Spanish, England became the maritime power of the world. In America the colonies flourished. Domestically, Cromwell had reformed the education system. He had built new schools and repaired old ones. Although religious tolerance would be all but nonexistent under Charles II and James II, it was still more than what most other European countries had and would be reasserted less than three decades later. Furthermore, under Cromwell's stewardship, England prospered financially and the concept of a 'Greater Britain', which included Ireland as well as Scotland, was beginning to be realized.

More importantly, it demonstrated that even during a period of military dictatorship, the Saxon principles of limited government, individual freedom, private property rights and economic freedom remained alive and well in the hearts of Englishmen. It was these principles that Cromwell tried— often unsuccessfully – to establish and maintain.

Chapter 18
The Defeat of Absolutism

Upon the death his brother, Charles II, James succeeded him as King of England and Scotland. Known as James II he had converted back to Catholicism several years earlier when he publicly refused to take communion in an Anglican church. Initially this disturbed many Anglicans but James promised that despite his own faith he would support the established church. In a statement to the Privy Counsel James said, "I shall make it my endeavor to preserve this government both in church and state as it is by law established. I know the principles of the Church of England are for monarchy and the members of it have shown themselves good and loyal subjects; therefore I shall always take care to defend and support it. I know too that the laws of England are sufficient to make the king as great a monarch as I can wish; and as I shall never depart from the rights and prerogatives of the crown, so I shall never invade any man's property." In return he asked that the Anglican Church support his role by counseling passive obedience to the monarchy. This was readily given and James II became a Roman Catholic king governing an Anglo-Saxon Protestant dominated England.

"James was a convert to Rome," Churchill writes. "He was a bigot, and there was no sacrifice he would not make for his faith" and that "his accession to the throne seemed to him to be the vindication of the downright conceptions for which he had always stood for." Therefore, shortly after his coronation, James II decided that he was going to fundamentally transform England. One of his first acts, in June of 1685, was to summon Parliament with the objective of repealing the Penal Laws and the Test Acts of 1673 and 1678. The purpose of these laws and acts were, after the Puritan experience, to keep the supremacy of the Anglican Church in England. The Penal Laws and the Test Acts insured that the Anglican Church, being the established state church, had primacy over England's religious life.

Unfortunately for James, only Parliament had the power to change the laws and they were not being cooperative. Being an ideologue, James was not going to let the will of the English people stop him and in an unprecedented move used what were called his "dispensing and suspending powers" to circumvent the Penal Laws and Test Acts. He set up an unofficial Council of Catholics to advise him and granted amnesty to those imprisoned under the penal laws. Additionally, in clear violation of the Test Acts, he began to grant commissions to Catholics in the Army. This led to lawsuits asking whether it was within the power of the King to dispense with the Test Acts and, in response, James dismissed the six judges hearing the case and replaced them with a court that would ensure a verdict in his favor. And this they did! Contrary to all of England's established traditions and laws the judges ruled that:

We think we may very well declare the opinion of the court to be that the King may dispense in this case… Upon these grounds:

1. *That they Kings of England are sovereign princes.*

2. *That the laws of England are the Kings laws.*

3. *That 'tis inseparable prerogative of the Kings of England to dispense with penal laws in particular cases, and upon particular necessary reasons.*

4. *That of those reasons and those necessities the King himself is sole judge.*

5. *That this is not a trust invested in… the King by the people, but the ancient remains of the sovereign power and prerogative of the Kings of England.*

As David Starkey points out, this ruling effectively "transformed Parliament into a mere sleeping partner in the Constitution: it might pass what laws it like; whether and on whom they were enforced was purely up to the King."

As a Catholic who was also the head of the Church of England, he ordered bishops to ban anti-Catholic sermons. When this order went unheeded, and in violation of the independent church clause of the Magna Carta, he issued a "directions to preachers" that banned controversial sermons and "abstruse and speculative notions." James also created an Ecclesiastical Commission to discipline the clergy and regulate the teachings in universities. At the time Oxford and Cambridge were strong supporters of the Anglican Church and required that all the students and fellows take an oath of allegiance and supremacy to the church. In 1686 James suspended that requirement and in April of 1687 he ordered Magdalen College, Oxford to elect his candidate president. Instead the fellows of the College elected their own candidate. In response James's Ecclesiastical Commission declared their actions void and ordered another election. The fellows refused again. In September James went to Oxford and told them, "I am your king. I will be obeyed and I command you to be gone. Go and admit the Bishop of Oxford head, principal, what do you call it of the college, I mean president of the college. Let them that refuse it look to it; they shall feel the wrath of their sovereign's displeasure." When several bishops petitioned the king to express their grievances they were summarily thrown in the Tower of London. This convinced many Anglicans and nonconforming Protestants that James was a Roman Catholic zealot out to destroy their church.

In the meantime James had disbanded the Parliament that had refused to do his bidding and begun preparations for elections of a new parliament he hoped would be more compliant. Realizing that parliamentary elections could not be affected without first changing the local officials he set out to replace them with those more sympathetic to his cause. In October 1687 he ordered Lord Lieutenants of the various counties to put three questions to the justice of the peace, sheriffs and other local officials:

1. Would they support the repeal of the Test Acts of 1673 in 1678 and the Penal Laws?

2. Would they support parliamentary candidates who did?

3. Would they live peaceably with men of all

religions?

Predictably, the replies James received were not very promising and in the months of October and November officials who gave unsatisfactory responses were dismissed. James then proceeded to use his newly expanded dispensing power to appoint Catholics to military, government, church, and university offices. This was followed in January 1688 by sending agents into the constituencies who would help ensure that James got the parliament he desired. Even more threatening were the changes that James was making to the military. Traditionally, England had no standing army and relied on local militia for its defense. This changed in 1685 with the rebellion of Lord Monmouth who was James nephew and the illegitimate son of the former King Charles II. Believing that he was the rightful heir to the throne, Monmouth and his supporters took up arms against the newly established King James. In initial conflicts the local militia either performed miserably or deserted to the other side. In order to remedy this James raised a regular army and made Louise Feversham, a French Protestant, commander. During the rebellion the army had increased to 15,710 men and by the end of 1685 numbered almost 20,000. Although this army was not recognized under English law James kept it in place even after it successfully defeated the rebellious forces of Lord Monmouth. Using his "dispensing and suspending powers" James began to appoint Catholics as officers and filled the army's ranks with Irish Catholic soldiers. He furthermore appointed Catholics to vital military bases around the country and kept a large section of the Army camped at Hounslow Heath, 12 miles from London. Lastly, James employed, as Edward Vallance writes, "wide-ranging confiscation" of firearms in private hands. This attempt to restrict English citizens to weapons that can only be used for hunting was never fully implemented, but it did highlight the intentions of James II.

What made these acts even more threatening was the suspicion that they were the product of James authoritarianism and not the parliamentary process. James did very little to alleviate this fear. The preamble to the Excise (tax) Act of 1685 starts with the declaration that these laws were created under the "sacred, supreme, and absolute power" of the king. For many Englishmen James's actions from 1685 to 1688 were those of a Romanized king who had set out to destroy their Anglo-Saxon traditions of liberty, their religion and their way of life. In their minds it confirmed that he was a monarch determined to return to Rome and the doctrines of divine right and absolutism. This was unacceptable to the English people and it put in play a plan that would not only change the English monarchy but also create the foundation of both American exceptionalism and the birth of the Modern Age.

Three years of James' reign had brought England to one of the most crucial points in world history. Would the country allow James to fundamentally transform England into a feeble version of France with its tyrannical government led by an all-powerful king who was nothing less than "God on earth"? Or would the English defend the traditional liberties they inherited from their Anglo-Saxon ancestors and thus remain a nation of freemen?

Fortunately, by 1688, it became obvious to many of the nobles who comprised England's ruling class that having a Catholic sovereign was leading to the destruction of their way of life. As written above, there were two schools of political thought that emerged from the Civil War. One was the Whigs, who believed in the supremacy of Parliament and the other was the Tories who believed the king to be the final authority. Not surprisingly, the

Whigs were the most fervent in their opposition to the king's actions and urged the removal of James from the throne. Although agreeing in principle to the removal, the conservative Tories counselled a less radical approach. The elder leadership of the party had witnessed the consequences of the forcible removal of a king. It had resulted in the only case of regicide in English history and a nine-year civil war. Wishing to avoid another such incident, the Tories hoped that time and nature would make forcible removal unnecessary. James was nearly the same age that his brother, Charles II, was when he died. Furthermore, James had no son and his only two daughters were both faithful Protestants. James' oldest daughter, Mary, was married to the Prince William of Orange. Prince William was the leader of the very prosperous United Dutch Republic and, although he was not Anglican, he was a devout Calvinist Protestant.

As Winston Churchill would write, "The accession of either Mary, the heir presumptive, or Anne, the next in order, promised an end to the struggle between a Catholic monarch and a Protestant people. Peaceable folk [those desiring a non-violent solution] could therefore be patient until the tyranny was passed."

This all changed when James' wife, Queen Mary Beatrice, announced that she was pregnant in November of 1687. This announcement was received with much skepticism since the last time she had given birth to a son was twelve years earlier. He, like several of her other children, died in infancy and it had been assumed that she could not have any more children. Regardless, the announcement of the queen's pregnancy shifted sentiment from a wait-and-see approach to one in which James II must be removed from the English throne. The question now became who or what would replace James.

Even before James became King several powerful Englishman,

including Winston Churchill's grandfather and the future Duke of Marlborough, John Churchill, started a dialogue with William of Orange. As the Stadtholder, or leader, of the continent's largest and most prosperous Protestant nation, William was seen as the defender of the Protestant faith. Winston Churchill would later write that, "Protestant Europe and England alike looked to him [William] as their champion against the tyrannies and aggression of Louis (King of France)." More importantly, as David Starkey writes, "William was a very different ruler from Louis, the Sun King, the absolute monarch of all he surveyed. For the head of the House of Orange was not a sovereign of the Dutch Republic, but first among equals. Sovereignty instead resided in the Estates (legislative bodies) of the seven provinces." This meant that William was not only Protestant, he was also someone who respected Parliamentary supremacy. Thus, the English Protestants saw him as the only viable alternative to James' Catholic tyranny.

William, who was not only married to James' daughter but was also his nephew, did not wish to see James lose the English crown, but he was determined to prevent England from returning to Catholicism. William had previously established security for the Dutch Republic when he led their armies to victory over Louis XIV, the Catholic King of France. Having England return to the Catholic faith would jeopardize that security by trapping the Dutch Republic between two powerful Catholic countries. He could not allow this to happen and he supported an aggressive propaganda campaign against James II. The goal of this campaign was to prevent England from becoming Catholic and to keep James' attention on internal political matters. He was not concerned with gaining the English throne for himself since his wife Mary would inherit it upon James' death. Thus making William the de facto, if not de jure, King of

England.

This all changed when, on June 10, 1688, James Francis Edward, the Prince of Wales, was born. This meant that there was not only an heir but an heir who was Catholic and whose claim to the throne superseded Mary's. Even if James should die while the Prince of Wales was still a child, his fervently Catholic mother, Queen Mary Beatrice, would reign as regent until the Prince came of age. William of Orange could no longer take a passive approach and he let it be known to his supporters in England that he would be open to accepting the English crown if invited to do so.

It is not surprising that the English were enthusiastic about having the Prince of Orange as their monarch. Not only was he a Protestant leader who had defeated England's archenemy, France, but the Dutch Republic offered a lot about which to be envious. The Dutch Republic was not only the richest Protestant country on the continent it was *the richest country* in all of Europe, perhaps even the world. In the 17th century it had the biggest empire in the world, an empire that stretched from one side of the globe to the other. More important, its form of government appealed to the English character.

In the meantime, in England, James II doubled his efforts to return England to Catholicism. He issued a Declaration of Indulgence which promised religious toleration for all his subjects and proclaimed a new parliament that would meet by November of that year. He then ordered the Anglican clergy to read the declaration to their congregations. To this the Anglican bishops refused on the grounds that it was a challenge to the primacy of the Church of England. This sent James into a rage. "This is a standard of rebellion," he exclaimed and several bishops were sent to the Tower of London without bail. To James' surprise not only did the Anglicans demand the release of the bishops but so did the nonconforming Protestants who, along with Catholics, the declaration was intended to help.

James ordered the bishops tried for seditious libel and had every reason to believe that they would be found guilty. This was mainly because in the 17th century judges usually guided jurors to the outcome desired by the government. But from the start the proceedings did not go as James had hoped. Even though the jury had been stacked in James's favor they could not resist the attitudes of the crowds that hissed at the prosecution witnesses. The final verdict, to James's dismay, was not guilty on all counts for all the bishops. Upon the reading of the verdicts spectators in the courtroom cheered over half an hour and church bells rang throughout all of England.

"The government was quite powerless," recorded historian J. P. Kenyon, "to halt the wave of rejoicing that spread out from London to the whole of England, sweeping most of the dissenters with it. The birth of a Prince had given them the prospect of a Catholic dynasty in perpetuity: the trial of the seven bishops was a gratuitous demonstration of how a Catholic monarch treated Protestants." James had lost all support. The church, the peers, the majority of people, including even the dissenters (nonconforming Protestants), wanted him gone. Only the Catholics supported him but they were too small a minority to make a difference. His last hope was his Catholic led Irish manned army camped just 12 miles outside of London. The question was, would he use it?

The same day that the bishops were acquitted several of the leaders of the movement against James met at the London home of the Earl of Shrewsbury. Their goal was to draft a formal invitation requesting that William invade England in order to remove James from the throne. These men, who would become known as the

"Immortal Seven," wrote to William, "We have great reason to believe, we shall be everyday in a worse condition than we are, and less able to defend ourselves, and therefore we do earnestly wish it might be so happy as to find a remedy before it is too late for us to contribute to our own deliverance." They continued to state that, in their opinion, "19 out of twenty in the nation" were dissatisfied with James and called on William to intervene. Then, risking everything they had including their lives and sacred honor, they each signed the document. By doing so, as Churchill puts it, "Never did the aristocracy or the Established Church face a sterner test or serve the nation better than in 1688."

Since the summer of 1688 William had been secretly preparing for invasion and now, watching all this from across the channel, he knew it was time to act. With invitation in hand William had all the justification he needed but he still had to get approval from the national assembly for his actions. On September 19, 1688 a secret session of the national assembly was convened at The Hague. It was recognized that once James was strong enough he would not hesitate to join forces with France against the Dutch Republic. Invasion by William and the creation of a free Parliament, which would not be under Catholic and French influence, was seen to be the only way to guarantee the Republic's security. Recognizing that it was also a way to advance representative government and guarantee liberties the national assembly unanimously approved William's plan.

The news of a possible invasion by William sent James's government into a panic. James offered to undo all that he had done to undermine the Anglo-Saxon traditions of England. But it was too late and the damage was done. Those around James, including his closest advisers, decided it was time to think about their own futures rather than the future of the Catholic monarchy.

On November 5 William landed in England at Torbay, on the coast of Devon. Upon disembarking, he was reminded that it was anniversary of the Gunpowder Plot when a Catholic attempted to blow up Parliament in 1605. To this the Calvinist Prince replied, "What you think of predestination now?" And with those words began the Glorious Revolution of 1688.

Once in England, William had one task ahead of him and that was to decisively destroy the English army in its first battle. To not do so would threaten to send England into another bloody civil war that would tie down the Dutch army and leave the Dutch Republic virtually defenceless. This was something that William could not afford to do as he would be forced to return to the Dutch Republic, leaving the English to sort everything out for themselves. William had to destroy James' army as decisively and as quickly as possible.

While William was drawing up his battle plans, James started to see the consequences of his policies against the Protestants. It initially started when an officer of the Royal Dragoons, Lord Cornbury, defected to William's side with three regiments of cavalry. Other officers soon followed, often taking large numbers of men with them. This coincided with revolts that broke out all over the country. Yorkshire, Derbyshire, Cheshire, and Plymouth all declared for William. In Portsmouth, the Navy offered its services to the Prince of Orange. All across the country city after city rose in rebellion. As Winston Churchill described it, "By one spontaneous, tremendous convulsion the English nation repudiated James."

With his army disintegrating around him, rebellion across the country, and mobs rioting in London, James withdrew to his Palace in Whitehall. The few advisors he still had at his side beseeched him to enter negotiations with William. William, always the keen observer, began to realize that he may be able to get what he wanted without a fight. He redirected his army towards London with the objective of keeping pressure on James without exposing it to battle. Realizing that William was just days away from London, James sent his wife, Queen Mary Beatrice, and his infant son out of the country. James followed a few nights later when on the night of December 11th he snuck out of Whitehall and rode to the coast. James, recognized by the local fishermen and townspeople, was captured and returned to London. His presence created a problem for William. As long as James continued to be held captive, he would be a uniting and motivating symbol for the pro-James forces. Similarly, executing James was not an option since it would just create a martyr for the struggle. So, William arranged for James' escape, and James left England never to return, thus making the Glorious Revolution a bloodless one.

This left England without an effective or legitimate government and even though William was the master of England, he was not the rightful king. Parliamentary elections were held and the first post-revolution Parliament met on 22 January. The first objective was how to legally remove James II from the throne. The Tories offered a resolution "that King James II having voluntarily forsaken the government, and abandoned and forsaken the kingdom, it is a voluntary demise of him." In return the Whig's proposed "that James II has abdicated government by breaking the original contract" with the people. The Lords preferred the Tory version but recommended using "abdicated" in place of "demise." Eventually, Parliament accepted the statement that "the said late King James II having abdicated the government and the throne be thereby vacant."

In the meantime, Parliament was also working on a governmental system that would prevent a situation like the one with James II from ever happening again. The difficult issue was how to prevent a king from nullifying the powers of Parliament, as James attempted to do, through the use of his "suspending and dispensing powers." A committee under Sir George Treby was established to examine the problem. Within a day, the 39-member committee produced a document listing 23 "grievances" against the actions of James II. These grievances provided for Parliament the justification they needed to legitimize their actions against James II. But the grievances did not do anything to prevent a similar situation from arising in the future.

This led Parliament to create *The Act Declaring the Rights and Liberties of the Subject, and Settling the Secession of the Crown, December 16, 1689*. This document, often referred as the *Declaration of Rights*, included clauses preventing the monarch from curtailing sessions of Parliament, for religious toleration, and for judges to serve on merit rather than as directed by the king. It increased the power of Parliament by requiring parliamentary elections to be held at regular intervals and made it illegal for the crown to levy money or maintain a standing army within the kingdom without the permission of Parliament. Individually, subjects had the right to petition the government (the King) without the fear of being prosecuted and to keep arms for their defense. Subjects were also protected from excessive bail and fines as well as cruel and unusual punishment. Finally, it addressed the issue of the monarchy and hereditary rule. Since English common law is based on precedence, and there was none stating otherwise, it was decided that offering the crown of England to William and Mary jointly would not violate the rules of heredity and kept with the Anglo-Saxon tradition of the Witan selecting the king. William would be made king for life with the crown going to Mary upon his death and then to Princess Anne. In addition, Parliament added that upon the death of all three the closest Protestant heir would be offered the monarchy.

If William accepted the crown under these conditions it would be one of the greatest leaps of representative government in history. It would limit the power of the government, in this case "The Crown", dictate who would inherit the throne and, in writing, guarantee rights to the individual subjects of the kingdom. No other monarch in Europe had such limits on his powers since, as previously noted, his powers were absolute and came from God, not the people. Accepting Parliament's terms, on 13 April 1689 William and Mary were crowned William III and Mary II, King and Queen of England.

This would have great repercussions for the future. As David Starkey observed, "while there is no doubt that the Norman conquest changed England radically, the consequences of the Dutch conquest of 1688 were similarly profound, and not for just this country but, arguably, for the whole world. It turned England from a feeble imitator of the French absolute monarchy into the most powerful and most aggressively modernizing state in Europe. In short, it invented a modern England, a modern monarchy, perhaps even modernity itself."

Chapter 19
The Sun Never Sets

The Glorious Revolution and the Declaration of Rights marked the end of the struggle between Anglo-Saxon individual-centered liberty and Roman state-centered authoritarianism that was forced upon the English by the Norman Conquest six centuries earlier. During his reign, William III would enact three major changes that would further create England's modern government. The same year that he accepted the crown of England, he endowed Parliament the power of the purse by giving it oversight of all public accounts. With the Triennial Act of 1694, William surrendered the ability of a monarch to call and dissolve parliament at will. Instead, parliament would automatically be summoned every three years. Lastly, in 1697, he gave parliament complete control of the army and navy. This would result in the king not being able to move a single regiment or even a single ship without parliament's approval.

On the continent the prevailing belief was that kings were not created by God for the benefit of the people, but that people were created for the benefit of the king. This had always been rejected by the Anglo-Saxons who were to become the English. For them, the Glorious Revolution settled the debate that, if England was to have a king, he would be a servant of the people. Eventually, "The solid realities of the crown's power," as Robinson notes, "were done away with forever, only the husk and appearances were suffered to remain. The ministers were still in theory his Majesty's ministers, but they were no longer answerable to him alone."

This provided England and later Great Britain – after the Act of Unification with Scotland in 1707 – a stable form of government that has lasted to this day. Although there were some who flirted with the revolutionary ideas that resulted in the bloody French Revolution and the revolutionary wars that would wreak havoc throughout continental Europe in the mid-19th century, these ideas never gained much traction in England (nor its offshoot the United States). Over the next three centuries – while France had her Napoleon; Germany had her Hitler; Spain had her Franco; Italy her Mussolini; and Russia her Czars, Lenin, and Stalin – Britain would enjoy continuous liberal democracy based on the Anglo-Saxon system of government. It is telling that Britain would be the only nation to remain at war for the entire struggle against the tyrannical regimes of Napoleon (1803-1815) and Hitler (1939-1945).

During the four decades of political turmoil that started with the Civil War and ended with the Glorious Revolution, over 20,000 Puritans left England for the colonies in the New World. This exodus would have great impact on the character and future of the New England colonies. Yet, it is estimated that only one in 12 Puritans made the treacherous journey. This would leave nearly a quarter of a million Puritans who were mostly concentrated in the traditionally Anglo-Saxon counties of East Anglia, Essex, and Sussex. As previously noted, these Puritans dominated the Parliament (as high as 70%) that resisted the absolutism of Charles I, made up the majority of Cromwell's 'New Model' army, and they were at the forefront of the Glorious Revolution. Even though the restoration of Charles II also restored the primacy of the Church of England, the Puritans – along with the other nonconforming protestant sect such as the Baptists, Quakers, Presbyterians, and Lutherans – created a strong, thriving independent counter to the state church. The growth of their influence would result in the Church of England losing its special status as the official state church in 1714.

The 15th century political philosopher, John Fortescue, observed that the "French king's ability to tax without restraint made him very wealthy, but the French people very poor." Contrarily, the limits on the English king's power to tax made the English king poor, but the English people wealthy. While he was the one to make the connection between taxation and individual wealth, he was not alone in his observation of the prosperity of the English people.

In a report to his government, the Venetian ambassador to England wrote in 1497, "the riches of England are greater than those of any other country in Europe…everyone making a tour of this island will some become aware of this great wealth…there is no small innkeeper, however poor or humble he may be, who does not serve his table with silver dishes and drinking cups; and no one, who has not in his house silver plate to the amount of at least £100 sterling is considered by the English not to be a person of any consequence."

The ambassador's observations were echoed a century later by the Duke of Wirtemburg who was visiting England on one of his many "bathing excursions". As he noted in his diary, the English people "dressed out in exceedingly fine clothes" and "one does not hesitate to wear velvet in the streets". In the countryside, "peasants dwell in small huts, and pile up their produce out of doors in heaps, and so high that you cannot see their houses." About the same time, another German named Paul Hentzner was struck by the prosperity of the average Englishman. "The inhabitants consume less bread and more meat than the French, and put a great deal of sugar in their drinks…their beds are covered with tapestry, even those of farmers…their houses are commonly of two stories." He also noted that houses with glass windows, which on the continent was a luxury that only the wealthy could afford, were very common in 16th century England. More profoundly, Hentzner, with the keen eye of a jurist, noted that along with being wealthy, the English were "impatient of anything like slavery".

When Alexis de Tocqueville visited England in the mid-1800s he was struck by its general affluence. "A Frenchman on seeing England for the first time is struck by the apparent comfort and cannot imagine why people complain." In England, he found "a nation among whom the upper classes are more brilliant, more enlightened and wiser, the middle class richer, the poorer class better of that anywhere else."

These observations by foreign visitors to England demonstrates that not only was England an extremely wealthy nation, but that the wealth was distributed throughout the society. The Duke's comment regarding surplus of produce stacked higher than their houses indicates that the average Englishman was secure in his property, protected by their governmental and legal systems from the predation, by both the state and individuals, which kept the common man on the continent in a perpetual state of squalor and dependency. As Fortescue observed on his trips to France, that although the French "dwell in one of the most fertile realms in the world", the common Frenchman "lives in the most extreme poverty and misery". They "drink water [rather than mead and ale like the English], they eat apples with very brown bread made of rye, they eat no meat other than very seldom a little bacon, or the entrails or head of beast slain for the nobles…they wear no wool, unless a poor coat under their outermost garment which is made of great canvas and is called a frock. Their hose [stockings] are of the same canvass, and do not pass their knees, wherefore they are gartered and their thighs bare. Their wives and children go barefoot." They "can live no other way" since internal predation in the form of taxation denies them the ability to reap the rewards of their labors.

What is significant about these accounts is that they demonstrate that the wealth of the common Englishman precedes the world trade, colonization, mercantilism, Protestantism, industrialization that modern academics, using failed Marxist theories of exploitation, use to explain the origins of such wealth. It is true that these are anecdotal accounts. Fortunately, the history of England is one of, if not the, most documented in the history of man. The Anglo-Saxon Chronicles details the history of the Anglo-Saxons into the 12th century and clearly shows that economic freedom (aka capitalism) was an established part of English society. The Domesday books, started by William III in the 11th century, provide in explicit detail the individual wealth of the English people. The extensive tax rolls of the villages and towns provides the modern researcher with a very thorough picture of the social and economic mobility of English society throughout the ages. It is within these documents that anthropologists such as Dr. Alan MacFarlane of Cambridge have discovered the origins of English liberty and prosperity.

MacFarlane's extensive research, which spans nearly four decades, indicates that by the 15th century economic freedom had eliminated peasantry from England. This does not mean that there were not poor people in England. There definitely were. But being poor in England was a temporary situation that could be escaped. Anthropological evidence reveals that there was great social and economic mobility in England 400 years prior to the Industrial Revolution. There were thriving real estate and labor markets that allowed an individual the opportunity to make his own way through life. This is reflected in the village and town rolls which show that through the generations a family's economic status would rise and fall. The grandson of a servant would be the lord of a manor and vice versa. Furthermore, there was great geographical mobility with family members disappearing from their birthplace only to reappear in another part of the country; or even the New

World. Such economic, social, and geographical mobility is impossible in peasant societies where individuals are restricted by land and familiar obligations. It is estimated that it would not be until late into the 20th century that the common man in most countries would acquire the wealth that the average Englishmen had in the 16th century.

The research conducted by anthropologists like MacFarlane disproves the commonly taught narrative that England become wealthy through the same colonialism/imperialism/mercantilism that had made Spain and France wealthy. The undisputed fact is that the English were wealthy long before England had a single colony and that the wealth – unlike in France and Spain – was widely distributed throughout its society. The fact is, as MacFarlane writes, "England was as 'capitalist' in 1250 as it was in 1550 or 1750. That is to say, there were already a developed market and mobility of labor, land was treated as a commodity and full private ownership was established, there were very considerable geographical and social mobility, a complete distinction between farm and family existed, and rational accounting and the profit motive was widespread." This means that if England's wealth predates world trade, colonization and even Protestantism, then there had to be something else that led the nation to become the world's first nation-state, first industrialized nation, and the dominant world power from the 18th century and well into the 20th century; when it would be superseded by its offspring, the United States.

That something is the Anglo-Saxon system of government that developed in the woods of Germany, resisted the authoritarianism of the Roman Empire, made the Dutch a free and prosperous people, and England even more so.

As covered in the Dutch section of the book, the United Dutch Republic was a continental power and was, therefore, constantly spending its blood and treasure defending itself from the predatory attacks by its neighbors; notably Romanized France and Spain. England, on the other hand, was protected by the sea. This created a natural buffer that allowed the Saxon system of government to flourish nearly unhindered. It was this sea that saved the still vulnerable English from the Spanish Armada in 1588 and would do so again against France's Napoleon in the early 19th century and Hitler's Germany in the 1940s. Even when it was invaded – and sometimes conquered – the system proved itself to be very resilient. Even the subjugation by William after the Norman Conquest in 1066 could not eliminate the Saxon system and within 150 years the English would start reasserting their traditional Anglo-Saxon rights with the Magna Carta. England's natural water barriers gave the island a very distinct history and development very different from that of the continent. This is especially true when the history is seen through the prism and chronology of Marxism. As the Marxist-influenced medieval historian A. E. Kosminsky admitted, Marxism provides no explanation for "this all-conquering growth of capitalism in a country which apparently occupied a very modest place in the economic life of medieval Europe." The fact is that England – and the Saxon principles it is founded on – breaks the Marxist mold that is at the center of the narrative currently being propagated in academia.

More significantly, it allowed the English to establish the elements of a balanced society; independent and separate political, religious, and economic spheres. "The secret of liberty," writes Macfarlane, "was thus firstly a separation of spheres – economy from polity, religion from polity, religion from economy, and society (kinship) from polity, religion, and economy...what [is] needed is both separation and balance...power should be a check to power." It is this check on power that the three spheres produce that allowed England to overcome the yet insurmountable cycle of predation that for 10,000 years has kept the common man in a state of servitude and poverty. For the first time, men – regardless of position – was secure in his rights to life, liberty, and possessions. Each man being the king of his castle. As de Tocqueville would ponder, "Is there any single country in Europe, in which the national wealth is greater...society more settled and more wealthy [than England]?"

In the Act of Union of 1707, England would unite with Scotland to become Great Britain. The seat of government would remain in London and the Anglo-Saxon principles of limited government, individual liberty, private property, and free-market economics would remain at the foundation of the new nation and lead it to found the largest empire in the history of mankind. By the end of the 19th century, the British Empire would span the globe. Three quarters of the world's land mass and its population was under British rule. Her Royal Navy "rule the waves" and eliminated scourges such as the Atlantic slave trade and piracy; scourges which have just recently started to once again plague mankind. Britain's power and prosperity stymied the tyrannical and despotic ambitions of Napoleon and Hitler. As the empire grew, London would replace Amsterdam as the financial center of the world. Her merchant fleet dominated global commerce and her military brought law and order to parts of the world where anarchy and chaos reigned. It is no mere boast when historian David Starkey and anthropologist Dr. Alan MacFarlane claim that England created the modern world and, I might add, the modern concept that every individual is entitled to basic human rights; rights that began with the "rights of freeborn Englishmen."

Part IV

The Modern World

Chapter 20
The New World

The most common narrative of the American Revolution tells us that it was a fight for independence from a tyrannical British monarch. Although, it would ultimately lead to independence, the Revolution did not start out that way. In fact, there were fourteen months of warfare that raged from as far north as Canada and as far south as the Bahamas before the Declaration of Independence was adopted. While some, like Samuel Adams, wanted independence from the beginning, the majority of the delegates at the Continental Congress overwhelmingly rejected the idea of separation from Britain. Yet, during those fourteen months, a war was being fought and people were dying. It is estimated that over 25,000 participated in the battles – including Bunker Hill – with approximately 2,500 losing their lives. If it was not independence they were fighting and dying for, what was it that made North American Englishman bear arms against their fellow English- born countrymen?

The basic truth is that they were fighting – and dying – for their "rights as freeborn Englishmen".

Today, we take our rights for granted to the point that it just seems natural that the colonists should consider themselves to have rights. But this was the 1770s – not the 1970s. The majority of people at the time did not have the benefits or even the concept of individual rights. The average Frenchman did not have any, neither did the Spaniard. And the inhabitants of their colonies definitely did not have any. The reality is that the vast majority of the people in the 18th century would not have been to able conceptualize the idea of having rights, much less fighting for them. In fact, to try to explain the concept of rights to the majority of people at that time would be akin to trying to explain the internet to them. It would be beyond their understanding.

Yet, not only did Englishmen in Britain understand that they had rights, so did their brethren born in her New World colonies. They did so because they were aware that they were inheritors of a system of government that originated in the 'savage forest of Germany', resisted Roman tyranny, was brought to England, was almost lost during the Norman Conquest, was resurrected by the Magna Carta, and guaranteed for all Englishmen in the Declaration of Rights of 1688. Great men like Benjamin Franklin and Thomas Jefferson had to be conscious of this when they proposed having the image of Hengist and Horsa – the two chieftain brothers credited in *The Anglo-Saxon Chronicles* with bringing Saxon rule to England – on the reverse of the Great Seal of the United States. They understood that there was something special about being Englishmen. That is why they didn't demand their human rights or their rights as men. They knew that in the 18th century that no one but Englishman had rights and those rights were based on the Saxon principles for limited government, individual liberty, ownership of private property, and freedom to engage in economic activity without government interference.

Jefferson was especially impressed with the Saxons and the form of governance they created. He studied them with great interest and even taught himself the already extinct Anglo-Saxon language. During his presidency he attempted to get the language taught in grammar schools so that "future Americans would learn of their liberty in the tongue from whence it comes". He even designed the grammar book that the schools should use. He soon found that there was not much support for his proposal and it was quickly abandoned, but not forgotten. When Jefferson founded the University of Virginia and became its first rector, he mandated that the great Anglo-Saxon tale, *Beowulf,* be performed in the original Anglo-Saxon language.

So when the question arose as to what type of government would replace the British monarchy and parliamentary system, it was no surprise that Jefferson would look to the Saxons for the answer. As he told the delegates debating the Declaration of Independence, "Has not every restitution of the ancient Saxon laws had happy effects? Is it not better now that we return at once into that happy system of our ancestors, the wisest and most perfect ever yet devised by the wit of man...?" This statement echoes the sentiment he expressed in the pamphlet that established his reputation as a skillful political writer. In *A Summary View of Rights of British America,* which Jefferson penned at the beginning of hostilities between Britain and her North American colonies, he noted that the "their [the colonists] Saxon ancestors had left their wilds and woods in the north of Europe, had possessed themselves the island of Britain, then less charged with inhabitants, and had established there that system of laws which has so long been the glory and protection of that country." He knew that their system of government was the only one that had a proven track record of producing liberty and prosperity for not only the elites, but also for the commoner. And furthermore, so did the other delegates.

As Kevin Phillips writes in The Cousins' Wars, the Anglo-Saxon struggle against tyranny "was a heritage of liberty New Englanders were proud to share – and would refer to many times in 1774-1775…John Adams, James Otis and others cherished the Saxon analogy because it stood for politics more resembling self-determination, free male suffrage, and consensual social contract – the open-air folk-moots and assemblages in place like Spellow, Norfolk (which meant "hill of speech)." New England firebrand and mentor to Samuel Adams, James Otis, "lauded the ancient Saxon origins of the English constitution: Anglo-Saxon England, in Massachusetts eyes, was a kind of pre-feudal elysium until it was conquered and yoked by the Normans."

Such strong sentiment for the Anglo-Saxon model and New England being the hotbed of "radicalism" in the years leading up to the Revolutionary War is not a product of mere chance. The New England colony was founded by Puritans who were escaping the religious persecutions and political upheaval that started during the reign of Charles I in 1625 and ended with the Glorious Revolution in 1688. Over 20,000 English Puritans would attempt to escape the political and bloody chaos that ravaged England for more than sixty years. Nearly all of these Puritans would come from the southeast of England – notably East Anglia. This part of England was the most Saxonized. Their Saxon traditions persevered through the Norman Conquest and were very much alive in the hearts and minds of those who settled the New England colony. The famed New England town hall meetings were reminiscent of the open meadow assemblies of their Anglo-Saxon ancestors; their charters similar to those that were used in Alfred's time; and their resistance to anything that threatened their liberty was equal to that of the

Saxon resistance to Roman authoritarianism and the Anglo-Saxon opposition to Norman absolutism. Furthermore, it would be their friends and family that remained in England who would lead the struggle against the tyranny of Charles I and fill the ranks of Cromwell's 'New Model' army. It is also clear that the they were very much aware that the Glorious Revolution not only established the current Constitution that governed all Englishmen, including those in North America, but was also a reaffirmation of the "free and antient [sic] principles" of the Saxons. A young country lawyer from Braintree, Massachusetts noted in his diary that upon entering a pub during his first visit to Boston, he saw the portraits of two kings on the walls. The young man was John Adams and he immediately recognized them as the "tyrannical kings Charles II and James II". If their ancestors fought and died for their Anglo-Saxon principles in the 1600s, was it not their sacred duty to do so in the 1700s?

Ironically, it would be the Glorious Revolution and the Declaration of Rights – both of which brought stable government to England – that would cause political chaos in British North America. Many of the colonies were established by people fleeing the political turmoil England was suffering between 1625 and 1689. As mentioned above, the first were the Puritans seeking to escape the religious persecution of Charles I. The next wave was Royalists and Anglicans seeking to escape England's one experiment with republicanism led by Cromwell and his Puritan dominated Parliament. Wanting to get as far from the Puritans as possible, these colonists established settlements in what would become the middle and southern colonies. Mainly starting from Maryland downward, these colonies were separated from the Puritan colonies by the Dutch colony of New Amsterdam until 1664 when it would be ceded to England and become the colonies of New York and New Jersey.

One of the results of these colonies being established during such a tumultuous period of English history is that the English were too preoccupied with their internal strife to pay much attention to the colonies. This meant that the establishment and governance of the colonies was haphazard and, in many cases, on an ad hoc basis. Depending on when they were established, a colony was formed under one of three types;

- The Provincial colonies (New Hampshire, New York, Virginia, North Carolina, South Carolina, and Georgia) were governed by commissions that were created by the king, who would appoint a governor and council. The governor would be the king's executive in the colony and had the authority to establish the assembly. This assembly had two houses. The lower house was comprised of local freemen who were elected by a franchised electorate and it was empowered to create laws. The upper house was the governor's council and all laws coming out of the lower house needed its approval. The governor was the final authority in the colony and had the power to veto, delay, and even disband the assembly.

- Proprietary colonies (Pennsylvania, Delaware, New Jersey, and Maryland) were granted by the king to an individual or groups of individuals, such as William Penn. These individuals were the colony's proprietors and acted in the same capacity as governors did in the Provincial colonies. Assemblies were organized and formed at the discretion of the proprietor(s).

- The Charter colonies (Massachusetts, Rhode Island, and Connecticut) were established by political corporations that received charters from the king. In most cases the establishment of these colonies were financed by private investment. Investors were often common people whose small investments were pooled together, similar to the way mutual funds operate today. The charters included a constitution that organized the administration of the colony including its executive, legislative, and judicial branches.

It is out of this neglect from the mother country that the colonies were forced to establish their own governments to see to their own needs. By 1683, each colony had a provincial assembly that was responsible for administration of the colony. The assemblies, regardless of the type of colony they administered, had the same basic structure. Being based on the English parliament, the assemblies were bicameral with an upper house that took the function of the House of Lords and a lower house that served as the House of Commons. The assembly met once a year and established new laws, passed budgets, set tax policies, negotiated trade agreements with other colonies and countries, and provided for internal law and order of the colony. As long as the actions taken by the assemblies were within established English law, they were allowed to function with very little interference from London. This gave the colonists an autonomy and level of self-rule that would not have been permissible during a more stable period.

The Glorious Revolution and the Declaration of Rights created a stability in English politics that last to this day. Unfortunately, for colonies it contained the seeds of a conflict that would result in the American Revolution. The colonists considered themselves to be just as much freeborn Englishmen as their cousins did in England. In fact, they considered the colonies not as mere appendages to England, but as an extension of England itself. Therefore, they felt themselves entitled to all that had been won during the Glorious Revolution and as benefactors of the Declaration of Rights. This included the supremacy of parliaments, which they considered their colonial assemblies to be. Historically, the assemblies reported directly to the king and not to parliament. Therefore, the colonists came to believe that the authority exercised by the parliament in London was limited to England proper and had no jurisdiction over the colonies, especially since the colonies had no representation in the parliament. As Jefferson would argue in *A Summary of the Rights of British North America*, "Let no act be passed by any one legislature which may infringe on the rights and liberties of another [legislature]." He petitioned King George III to use his veto power "to prevent the passage of laws by any one legislature of the empire, which might bear injuriously on the rights and interest of another." Furthermore, the colonists believed themselves to have all the rights and privileges granted to freeborn Englishmen by the Declaration of Rights.

Regrettably, Englishmen in England did not feel the same way. While the Declaration of Rights did grant parliamentary supremacy, it did so only for the English parliament and not the colonial assemblies. In fact, they argued that it removed the administrational control of the colonies from the king to parliament. This included regulating trade, negotiating treaties, and the imposition of taxes. Furthermore, they maintained that the rights of Englishmen only applied to those living in England and did not extend to the colonials. This was a shock to the colonists, many of whom fled or were descendants of those who fled the arbitrary rule that the Glorious Revolution and the Declaration eliminated from English politics. Yet, they found themselves no better off than if the absolutists had won. As a consequence of 1688-1689, the colonists lost representative government and their rights as Englishmen were conditional on the temperament of parliament.

While this did give the colonists the status of being second class citizens within the empire, it alone did not lead to an armed conflict. It would be the missteps of British politicians that would result in a bloody conflict that would pit North American Englishmen against their European countrymen. As I wrote above, the English had very little experience in administering their colonies. Amazingly, they turned to their archenemies, the French and Spanish, as examples of how to govern colonies. While they could not impose the level of tyranny that the Spanish and French did on their Latin American colonies, they were able to copy the mercantile system that enriched the mother country at the expense of the colonies. London took control over all trade agreements and regulated inter-colonial as well as international commerce. All shipments from the colonies had to first go through Britain before being transferred to a British based ship for its final destination. This resulted in shipments from the Carolinas having to go to Britain before reaching a destination in Virginia. The colonies were also prohibited from producing their own products from the resources the colonist cultivated through their own labor. Instead, the raw material would be sent to Britain where it would be used to make finished products that would then be shipped back to the colonies. This, Jefferson notes, "raised their commodities to the double and treble of what they sold for before" the regulations were in place.

More offensive to the colonists was that all this was being done by a legislative body in which they, the colonists, had no say. They had no vote or even a means to influence those who did vote. This effectively made the four million colonists in America "the slaves, of not one, but 160,000 tyrants [the British voters]" that the parliament represented. Their only recourse was to petition the king to intercede on their behalf. Unfortunately, the king's knowledge of his colonies was no better than that of his parliament. In fact, he relied on parliament's "colonial experts" to advise him on what actions to and not to take. This put the governance of the colony firmly in the hands of parliament and is one of the reasons why petitions to the king went unanswered.

The colonists rightly saw that having no say in the legislative body that governed their actions and a king who ignored their pleas put all their rights and liberties in jeopardy. If the parliament could arbitrarily impose taxes and the king was unwilling to defend them, what would stop them from taking away all their rights as Englishmen? They came to the new world to escape such arbitrary government and now it was being imposed on them by the very people who ended it in England. Ironically, the event and document that created this crisis also offered the colonists the answer. In the Declaration of Rights, parliament clearly expressed that it was an Englishman's right to overthrow any government that went beyond its constitutional limits. The Barons did it to King John in 1215, the Puritan dominated parliament did it in 1649 when they beheaded Charles I, and the English would do it again in 1688 when they replaced James II with William III. Never did parliament ever imagine that it would be used to justify rebellion against their authority. But that is just what the colonists did in 1774.

Interestingly, it would be the attempt by the British army to confiscate the colonists' weapons that would start the American Revolution since it was the same action by James II that ignited the Glorious Revolution. For liberty-minded people there is a connection between their freedom and the ability to bear arms. It is the check of last resort against a government that no longer serves but people.

The Declaration of Rights provided more than a moral and legal justification for the colonists' rebellion against arbitrary rule. It also provided the template for what are the founding documents of the United States. It is clear that Jefferson was thinking of the Declaration of Rights of 1689 when he wrote the Declaration of Independence. A comparison of the two documents (both are included in the indices) shows that the structure of the 1689 document greatly influenced that of 1776. Like the Declaration of Rights of 1689, Jefferson starts the 1776 document with a list of grievances committed by the king against his subjects. This is followed by justification of why there was no other option left except for the drastic and historic actions being taken. Likewise, the Declaration of Rights is reflected in the structure of the Constitution of the United States and the Bill of Rights. In fact, much of the rights enumerated in the first ten amendments were taken directly from the Declaration of Rights. These include:

- The quartering of soldiers without the consent of the owner
- Trial by jury of one's peers
- No fines or forfeitures without due process
- No imposing of excessive bail or fines
- No cruel and unusual punishments

- The right to "petition government for the redress of grievances"

And, most importantly, the right for freeman to bear arms.

From above, it is clear that the Patriots – especially those in the New England colony – saw the colonies' struggle for their traditional rights in the same light as they did the Magna Carta. That the objective of the rebellion was not to create a new nation with a new revolutionary form of government, but as a return to a system of government that Britain appeared to have abandoned.

This does not mean that the colonists were anti-English. In fact, their complaint against the British government was that the British government was denying them their rights as Englishmen. The reality is that they recognized there was something very unique about being English. As one objector to independence put it, "it is better to be a subject of a British monarch, albeit with diminished rights, than to be slaves under the authoritarian Spanish or the absolutist French monarchs." Even after the commencement of hostilities, there was much soul searching done by the delegates of the Continental Congress. Within the fourteen months that passed between the battles of Concord and Lexington and the adoption of the Declaration of Independence, separation from Britain was voted on and rejected twice. For many, independence was an action only to be taken when all other options had failed.

It is important to note that the flag that the Continental Congress debated the issue of independence under was not the "Betsy Ross" flag. It was a flag that is almost unknown to most Americans today, but it represented everything the men like Jefferson stood for. It was also the flag that the forces of George

Washington fought under and the one which a young lieutenant by the name of John Paul Jones raised on the first American naval ship. It was, in fact, the national flag of the United States of America until 1777.

What is significant about this flag is that it had the British Union Jack where today we have the stars. This would be the first of many former British colonies, including Australia and New Zealand, which would honor Britain in their national flags. This is unique to the English-speaking countries and something that you do not see in former French and Spanish colonies. This is because the Founding Fathers understood that being an Englishmen in the 18th century was something unique. As George Washington would write at the end of the war, the foundation of the British Empire:

Was not laid in the gloomy age of ignorance and suspicion but in an epoch when the rights of mankind were better understood and more clearly defined, than at any other former period.

Whether he was a leader like Washington or the lowest private in the army, had the genius of Ben Franklin or the remedial education of a frontier farmer, the Englishmen of North American understood that they were fighting for their rights as "freeborn Englishmen."

It is significant that the patriots who fought for their rights did not refer to them as their human rights or even their rights as men. The fact that they stated that they were fighting for their rights as *free born Englishmen* meant that they understood that the liberties and rights they were fighting to preserve were unique to a certain people. Those people were not Frenchmen, they were not Spaniards, they were not Russians, they were not Chinese: they were Englishmen!

The Founding Fathers were men who were well-versed in English history and its system of government. They understood that the liberties and rights that they enjoyed had evolved over a period that predates the Magna Carta and back to the fall of Rome. They understood, as renowned historical anthropologist and Cambridge professor Alan MacFarlane notes, that:

England as a whole was different from the rest of Europe… a central and basic feature of English social structure has for long been the stress on the rights and privileges of the individual as against the greater group or the state.

This was unique in a world where the norm for the average man was servitude and subservience to the state.

As Jefferson so eloquently points out, there is only one system of government that has a 500 year track record of bringing freedom and prosperity the every society that embraces it. Based on the Saxon principles of limited government, individual liberty, private property rights, and free market economics the United States resisted despotism and, along with other English-speaking countries with the same foundation, became the freest and most prosperous nation of the modern age.

In 1854, the famed 19th century historian, John Motley, wrote that "every schoolchild knows that the so called revolutions of Holland [1568], England [1688], and America [1776] are all links of the same chain." As the illustration shows, this history was taught well into the 1880s.

Now, it is unknown to the vast majority of Americans.

This is because history tells us that no other ideology could compete with or defeat the Saxon model. Competing ideologies can claim to be a better alternative, but they always fall short – often with bloody consequences. Therefore, the Grand Union flag, like anything else that represents the values and principles that made America (and the English-speaking nations in general) exceptional, had to be purged from the political consciousness of the people. Thus, it became another victim of the Left's distortion of history and the forgotten symbol of freedom.

Just as the Dutch and English became the freest and most prosperous peoples in the world during the four centuries prior to the founding of the United States, Americans would come to be a free and prosperous people in the two centuries that followed. Its form of government, based on the Saxon model, would find that essential balance between the political, economic, and religious spheres required to allow individuals to live free and prosper. Just as this balance allowed Britain to be the first nation to leap into the industrial age, America would lead the world into the space age. Within 200 years, Americans would go from planting plows into the earth to planting a flag on the moon.

At the time of independence, the annual income of the average American would be equivalent to that of the average person living today in Mexico or Turkey. When compared to their fellow countrymen, America's poor appear to be very poor indeed. But that is relative. In terms of absolute poverty, even the poorest American is in the top 1% of the world's wealthiest people. The truth is that America is a nation where "even the poor are fat". This is because the political freedom allowed by the Anglo-Saxon model creates economic opportunity that no other system has ever been capable of producing. America's economy would be the largest in the world and it would dominate international trade. The fact that many Americans take the prosperity they enjoy for granted – or even criticize the system because it does not give them enough – is a testament to the unmatched success of the system. The nation itself would become the most powerful ever known to man.

There was a time when people did not take these rights or the wealth they create for granted. They rejected the unfounded belief that rights were something that every human was naturally entitled to. They understood that the rights given to Americans by its form of government and its founding documents made being an "American" something special. This inspired people from around the world – of all color and nationalities – to forever leave their homelands, families, and friends for the chance to become "Americans". Even those, brought here through the shameful practice of slavery chose to stay rather than return to the lands of their ancestors. And it was all because wise men over 200 years ago took Thomas Jefferson's advice and established a nation based on the "greatest system created by the wit of man".

Chapter 21
Freedom and Prosperity

At a recent presentation I noticed a man who was sitting right in the center of the audience. He caught my attention because he kept shaking his head in a manner that did not provide any indication of what he was thinking. I just could not tell whether he agreed with me or not. So I was a little concerned when he approached me afterwards. He was an older black gentleman – in his mid-70s – and the expression on his face was as serious as it could be. But as he got closer, he began to smile and extended his hand for me to shake.

"I just want to thank you", he said with an accented voice, "for all that you just said. I am from Nigeria and I have been here in the United States for over 40 years. I am from the Nigerian royal family and I can say that everything you just said is true. I can remember my grandfather telling me that the best thing to happen to Africa was when the British came. He used to tell us, 'Before the British came we lived in huts, we could not read or write, our children died before reaching the age of 5, and you could not go out – even in daylight – in a group of less than a half dozen people because you would be robbed, kidnapped, or worse. Our women would be brutally raped. This ended when the British came. Under the British, we began living in proper houses. In British built schools we learned to read and write. British doctors and hospitals provided care that allowed our children to grow into adulthood. Most importantly, even in the dead of night a woman could walk in safety. The British was the best thing that ever happened to our people.'

"You see," the gentleman continued to tell me, "I saw colonialism. I grew up in a country ruled by the British. So it makes me angry when I hear people who are ignorant of what the real story of Africa claim that the problems in Africa are due to British colonialism. It is true that there were bad aspects to it, which I admit, but it did more good for Africa than it did bad. I am convinced I am 100% correct when I say that because of the British there are millions of Africans living today who would not be if the British hadn't come to Africa."

This echoes what Faith Mayo, who represents Zimbabwe's second largest political party, said in an interview in 2012. "Most black Zimbabweans would now prefer Ian Smith [the last white prime minister of Rhodesia] to Robert Mugabe – though the human instinct of freedom remains high on the agenda. For what is the purpose of freedom when freedom kills you, when freedom denies you free speech, when freedom kills your relatives, when freedom starves you, when freedom excludes you on tribal grounds?" As she points out, when Mugabe became leader of Zimbabwe (with the support of U.S. President Jimmy Carter and U.K. Prime Ministers Harold Wilson and James Callaghan, both of the leftist Labour Party), "Up to 20,000 people were massacred by the North Koreantrained Fifth Brigade in the early 1980s." More recently, the former Zimbabwean Prime Minister, Morgan Tsvangirai, confessed that Rhodesia was better than Zimbabwe is.

Coming from a Nigerian prince and Zimbabwean politicians, these statements may appear to be from elites nostalgic for bygone days. But there are plenty of common Africans that share the same yearning for an Africa ruled under the Anglo-Saxon model. As one Zimbabwean wrote, "Back in the Ian Smith days Rhodesia was a paradise. There was food for all, cities were being built, there was peace and prosperity. Today Zimbabweans scratch in the dirt for food. Millions have fled to neighbouring countries – mainly South Africa – to beg for a job and/or food." Along similar lines a Zimbabwean living in London wrote "In Rhodesia we had electricity to light our houses and cook our food, schools that educated our children, and, most importantly, a professional police force and legal system that provided black Africans more justice than that of modern Zimbabwe." "Being a second class citizen in Rhodesia," he concluded, "was better than being a first-class citizen in Zimbabwe." What is significant about this observation is that it comes from a man who actually fought with the ZANU (Zimbabwe African National Union) to end white Rhodesian rule.

At the ceremony celebrating Zimbabwean independence in 1980, Mwalimu Julius Nyerere, the then-President of Tanzania, advised the new ZANU government that: "You have inherited the Jewel of Africa, don't destroy it." Rhodesia was indeed the jewel of Africa. Its economy was second only to that of South Africa and its agriculture was unrivaled. Known as "the bread basket of Africa", its wheat farms feed most of sub-Sahara Africa. This does not excuse its racist policies or the fact that it was a 'pariah state' that needed to be reformed. The problem with the anti-colonialists is that they are at best leftist and at worse Marxists. Their hatred of the Anglo-Saxon model prohibits them from separating the racism from the political and economic principles that made Rhodesia the "Jewel of Africa". It was this tendency to see the world through the prism of Marxism that drove American President Carter and the British Prime Ministers to insist that Rhodesia immediately institute democracy on the principle of "one man, one vote". The Rhodesian Prime Minister at the time, Ian Smith, insisted that the Zimbabweans were not ready for democracy. Until this time, the British and Rhodesians took the extraordinary multicultural policy of allowing the native Zimbabweans to retain their traditional tribal system based on chiefs who represented their people in parliament. Therefore, the Shona and Ndebele peoples did not have experience with direct representative democracy. Smith begged Carter and the British to give the Rhodesians time to educate the Zimbabweans on the principles of democracy. As he warned, "If Rhodesia is forced to implement a 'one man, one vote' policy without properly educating the people it is supposed to empower, then Rhodesia would have one man, one vote, one time." That is effectively what happened.

But to Carter and the British leftist, none of this mattered. They had a fellow ideologue waiting to replace the despised white leadership. Besides, the liberation Marxism of Mugabe would end all the suffering that the black Africans had suffered under the whites. Therefore, there would be no need for further elections. Carter had the ulterior motive of attempting to win reelection. As Smith writes in his book, *The Great Betrayal*, U.S. Secretary of State Cyrus Vance let it be known that Carter needed the black vote to defeat Reagan. Nothing, Vance told Smith, would invigorate them more to reelect the President than Carter getting the credit for ending white rule in Rhodesia. Rhodesia, already a pariah state in the international community, was threatened with crippling sanctions that would have catastrophic consequences for both Rhodesians and Zimbabweans alike. This left Smith with two equally vile options: implement a "one man, one vote" policy or watch his people be starved by horrific sanctions. He choose the former and Rhodesia became Zimbabwe.

So it was that leftist ideology and, in Carter's case, political expediency started the events that would destroy the "Jewel of Africa". Liberation Marxism replaced the Anglo-Saxon model of government and within twenty years the nation went from being the second most prosperous country in southern Africa to being the poorest. In fact, since the nation abandoned the Anglo-Saxon model, its economy has deteriorated to the point that Zimbabwe is currently the second poorest in the world. Only North Korea, also a Marxist-based country, has a worse economy. The destruction of Rhodesia had consequences that went beyond its borders. Agriculture was at the heart of the Rhodesian economy. As Marxist economics destroyed the 'Jewel of Africa' it also devastated the "Bread Basket of Africa". As a result, millions of Africans have died of starvation, malnutrition, and disease over the three decades that has passed since the leftist leaders of America and Britain implemented their plan for the destruction Rhodesia.

As another Zimbabwean named Shamva so eloquently put it:

Those who did not live in Rhodesia will have nothing to compare the current Zimbabwe with. Living in Rhodesia was no bed of roses for reasons already known. Yet life was better. It really was. I was happy. I had a good job. I was never hungry and everything worked. There were no shortages that affected me. Times were good and my memories of yesterday are happy ones.

Of course, it was not right that we were often discriminated against, that we had no vote, that we were prohibited from many things available to the whites. This was so very wrong in every respect. However, looking back now and being many decades wiser, I sense that the white government were changing for the better - perhaps or almost certainly because they had no choice. But this change was too late in the game. Now we have what is left. It is sad. If I could chose right now which country I would live in, warts and all, it would be Rhodesia under Smith, even with the issues that white government brought. Does this make Smith a hero? Absolutely no. It just makes him better than the rubbish we have now.

If only that country had another 10 years or so, perhaps we would have been given equal status to the whites and our history would have taken a different path. We will never know.

Yes Shamva, thanks to Carter, Wilson, Callaghan, and other leftists in the West we will never know if the suffering of the Zimbabweans could have been avoided. But, as they say, being a leftist is never having to say you are sorry nor do you ever have to acknowledge the tragic consequences that your vile ideology repeatedly inflicts on the world.

Fortunately, we do have one example of what Rhodesia might have become if it had been allowed the time to reform its outdated racist policies and still keep the Anglo-Saxon model intact. In many respects, South Africa is very similar to Rhodesia. White rule was maintained by the Afrikaner (South Africans of Dutch ancestry) dominated government. Apartheid made it, like Rhodesia, as pariah state. And, more importantly, it became the target of leftists who were still congratulating themselves for the destruction of the "Jewel of Africa". The left placed their hope in their ideological compatriots in the ANC (African National Congress). Like ZANU, ANC embraced the Marxist Liberation ideology and it looked like

South Africa would go the way of Rhodesia when the ANC won the National Assembly in 1994.

When Nelson Mandela started serving his prison term on Robbins Island in 1964, he was a pro-Marxist revolutionary. When he was release 26 six years later he was a wizened statesman who accepted, if not embraced, the Anglo-Saxon model. It is speculation what caused this transformation. Maybe it was the result of the extensive self-education that Mandela pursued while in prison or maybe it was seeing how much suffering the Marxist Liberation ideology did to the Zimbabweans. Regardless of the reason for the change, he came out of prison with the understanding that the problem with South Africa is not the system that it inherited from Britain but that the system was closed to all but a few South Africans. Therefore, when he became president of South Africa in 1994 he resisted pressure from the Marxist who dominated the ANC. Rather than replace the Anglo-Saxon model with liberation ideology, he maintained and then opened the system so that all South Africans could enjoy the liberty and prosperity that the model creates. This would set South Africa on a path very different than that of Zimbabwe.

Within two decades, the South African economy would explode. Like the model did in the United Dutch Republics, England, and the United States, South Africa's middle class would become the largest in Africa. According to a study conducted by the University of Cape Town, within 10 years of Mandela becoming president the black middle class tripled to 4.2 million. Its spending power of $44 billion per year (2004) makes it more economically significant than the white middle class which has remained stagnant. As John Simpson, one of the authors of the University of Cape Town study, stated, "The growth in this country, both economically and in terms of spending power, comes from the black middle class." Additionally, the Anglo-Saxon model empowered the previously oppressed black South Africans. For the first time in their history, black South

Africans felt themselves in control of their futures. Not only were they politically free, the Anglo-Saxon model ensured that they were also economically free. As one new member of the black middle class states, "I just started working hard, you know, basically to have the sort of values that will see you putting your nose to the grindstone, giving your best, that sort of thing." These are the words of an individual empowered by economic freedom and would be recognized by a 16th century Dutchman, a 18th century Englishman, and 19th century American. Furthermore, in contrast to the near starvation existence of their Zimbabwean neighbors, 39% of black South African women and 10% of men are currently categorized as being obese.

Unfortunately for South Africa, over the last ten years its economy has started to stagnate and then falter. Unemployment rose to over 25% and remains there to this day. Even growth of its black middle class stagnated. While some of this was caused by the Global Financial Crisis of 2008, most of it is self-inflicted. Subsequent governments failed to restrain the Marxist tendencies that Mandela so deftly resisted. In an attempt to eliminate "economic inequality" a progressive welfare state was established. There was ever increasing pressure for those who escaped poverty to help those who were incapable or unwilling to do so themselves. As new and ever increasing taxes were imposed to pay for the social programs of the welfare state the economy began to stagnate and then shrink. As policy analyst Liepollo Pheko observed, "It doesn't encourage the middle class. It doesn't encourage people to work. Because the more you work, the more you get taxed.",

While South Africa still has a lot of problems to overcome, the retention of the Anglo-Saxon model put the nation in a position far superior to that of its neighbors, especially Zimbabwe. The nation is still the political, economic, and military power of the region. It showcased its prosperity by hosting both the Rugby and Soccer World Cups. More importantly, by retaining the Anglo-Saxon model, South Africa has avoided the tragic consequences of Marxism that has plagued post-colonial Africa. Only the future will tell if the politicians of South Africa have the wisdom of Mandela or the foolishness of Mugabe.

The polar examples of the success of the Anglo-Saxon model in South Africa and the tragic failure Marxist-based policies in Zimbabwe have not been lost on other African leaders who want a better life for their people. The fall of the Soviet Union ended the spread of political Marxism around the world and Africa was not immune. Within the twenty years that followed the number of democracies in sub-Sahara Africa increased from three to 23. Most of those nations replaced the failed policies of liberation ideology with some form of the Anglo-Saxon model. As a result sub-Sahara Africa today has the fastest growing middle class in the world. According to the African Development Bank, 313 million Africans are now part of Africa's still growing middle class. This is 34% of the entire population of the sub-continent and is 100% increase in less than twenty years. If the trend continues, it is estimated that Africans living below the poverty line will be less than 33% by 2060. This is incredible considering that The Economist ran an article on Africa in 2000 titled *The Hopeless Continent* which painted a very bleak and pessimistic future for sub-Sahara Africa. The incredible economic turnaround over the last decade forced the financial magazine to publish an updated article in 2013 titled *The Hopeful Continent*. The abandonment of liberation ideology has also created stability in a region that has been continually wracked with war. In the mid-1990s – when Marxism was still the ideology of choice – there were twelve major conflicts raging in the region; in 2013 there were only four.

Nearby India is another example of the prosperity that is created when people are provided the economic freedom of the Anglo-Saxon system. When India gained its independence in 1947, it had an Anglo-Saxon based economy. Under Jawaharlal Nehru India adopted a British variant of Marxism called "Fabian Socialism". Under this ideology India appeared eerily similar to Stalin's Russia. The government produced 5-year plans for all sectors of the economy, heavily regulated business even at the micro level, dictated labor policy, intervened in financial markets, created large state bureaucracies, and, of course, high tax rates to support it all. Even though India was considered a non-aligned country during the East-West standoff of the Cold War, it was squarely in the camp of the Soviet Union, which positioned itself as the benefactor and protector of the world's underprivileged, including its nations.

Like the Soviet sponsored Liberation Ideology that doomed Africans to decades of poverty, the Fabian Socialism promoted by Britain's leftist professors as the antidote to colonialism proved itself just as disastrous for the Indians. As what eventually happens in all communist countries, there were shortages of even the most basic commodities. Poverty in India, which the proponents of Fabian Socialism promised to eliminate, increased as the economy stagnated under the taxation and regulation of the system. For four decades (from 1950 to well into the 1980s) the annual growth rate of the economy was a dismal 3.5%; wholly inadequate for a nation with a birthrate of 4.3%. More shocking is that during the same period the already dreary per capita income of the average Indian rose a measly 1.37% per year.

This was during a period when the rest of the world was experiencing the growth produced by the post-World War II boom. Throughout the same period, the annual growth rates of the economy of Pakistan, which was part of India under British rule, was 5%. What infrastructure was left in India by the British soon fell into disrepair as government owed enterprises gained monopolies over public works. As the state established its dominance over the economy and extended itself into the lives of the average Indian, it invited corruption, which flourished without restraint. By 1985, Indians were waking up to the fact that Fabian Socialism was incapable of fulfilling its promises and by the end of 1990 India was facing a severe economic crisis. The government was close to default and its central bank refused new credit. The nation's foreign exchange reserves were reduced to the point that it could not finance even three weeks' worth of imports. Fabian Socialism – and the abstract theories it was based on – had brought India to the brink of financial ruin.

Starting in 1991, India implemented reforms designed to undo the disastrous effect of Fabian Socialism. Known as the Liberalization of India's Economy, these reforms were basically India's embracement of the Anglo-Saxon model. The government privatized state-owned businesses, deregulated industries, eliminated the business licensing bureaucracy, reduced tariffs and interest rates, and ended many of the monopolies that the state had in various sectors of the economy. More importantly, taxes were reduced and the government created fiscal policies aimed at reducing its deficits and debts. While India has not been able to eliminate all the growth retarding policies of Fabian Socialism, by the turn of the 21st century it had progressed towards the Anglo-Saxon model with a substantial reduction in state control of the economy and increase financial freedom.

As a result of these changes, the paltry 3.5% annual growth rate that Fabian Socialism produced, increased to 9.6% in 2006 and then settled to average 7.5% per year. This made the Indian economy the second fastest growing in the world. At this rate, according to the Organization for Economic Co-operation and Development (OECD), the income of the average Indian would double within a decade. In 1996, the middle class numbered a pitiful 25 million out of a total population of 955 million, which equates to the middle class being just 2.6% of the population. The National Council for Applied Economic Research (NCAER) estimates that in 2015, the middle class would make up 20.3% of the population (267 million people) and by 2026 that will grow to 37.2% (547 million people). In fact, according the NCAER research, Indians are becoming so prosperous that the average middle class household "spends 50% of their total income on daily expenses with the remaining going into savings." This prosperity has also benefited Indian society in non-financial ways. The life expectancy of the average Indian has increased, literacy rates are up, and the food scarcity that kept most Indians on the edge of starvation throughout the decades of Fabian Socialism has been eliminated. In fact, the caloric intake of Indians has increase to the point that the Indian Heart Association is now issuing warnings about the dangers of obesity.

Opponents of the Anglo-Saxon model love to characterize it as a system that allows powerful -- mostly white -- nations to exploit poorer nations populated by darker skinned people. That it is the Anglo-Saxon model, a product of white colonialism and rooted in racism and exploitation, which forces the majority of the world to live in squalor and poverty. Yet, it is clear from these examples that nations that embraced the Anglo-Saxon model, both politically and economically, are better off than those that base themselves on the failed theories of Marxism. In India alone, the Anglo-Saxon model has made it possible for hundreds of millions of Indians to escape the poverty that socialism would have imposed on them. By no means can the nations highlighted above be considered developed states. They still have their problems and it is yet to be seen if they are able to overcome them. But they are examples of the prosperity that the Anglo-Saxon model produces regardless of a nation's financial situation or racial make-up.

Research also shows that the experiences of these countries is not unique or an anomaly. According to an IMF ranking of countries by their per capita GDP (2009), eleven of the top 20 were, at some point in time, part of the British Empire. Additionally, according to a United Nations report on life expectancy, five of the top 20 are former British dominions or colonies (dominions are colonies started by English settlers such as Canada, Australia, and New

Zealand), which indicates a high standard of living. In stark contrast, there was not one former French or Spanish colony in the top 20 of either list. In almost every region of the world, except Latin America, a former British colony is one of the regional political and/or economic powers. This includes India, Pakistan, Hong Kong, and Singapore in Asia; Nigeria and South Africa in sub-Saharan Africa; Egypt in North Africa; Australia in Australasia; and of course the United States in North America. Only in Latin America are the former colonies of other imperial powers dominant (Spain's Mexico and Portugal's Brazil). But this is due more to the fact that Britain did not have any significant colonies in the region than it is to the political system that these colonies inherited from their mother countries. From these studies, it is clear that those countries that have retained the British influence (i.e. the Anglo-Saxon model) after their independence fared better than those who rejected it.

Chapter 22
Conclusion

It may be hard for some people to comprehend the impact the Romans and Saxons had on creating the modern world. To many, the struggle between these two very divergent societies is ancient history that no longer has relevance to today's problems. The fact remains that there are very few parts of the world that were not affected by the colonialism of the European powers. It is hard to imagine the how different the world would be if the European empires never existed. But they did exists and they greatly influenced what would become the modern world.

As de Tocqueville observed nearly 200 years ago, "If you want to know the values of a nation, then look at its colonies." This is because the values that a colony receives from the mother country is greatly magnified or exaggerated. As we have seen, the American colonists took English liberty to a degree that their cousins in England could not comprehend. This difference in the understanding of English liberty would result in a bloody conflict that ended with the birth of a new and independent nation based on values of liberty that far exceeded that of the Britain.

The former Spanish and French colonies are no different. Within them we see an echo of Roman authoritarianism with centralized governments that benefit a few elites, a top-down legal system, insecure property rights (sometimes collectivized through state ownership) and economies that deny the average person the freedom to prosper. As mentioned in the previous chapter, it is not by chance that the former colonies of the Romanized European powers are less free and prosperous than those of their Anglo-Saxon counterparts. As one Mexican adage so honestly states, "Mexico is a ranch and the president is the owner." While such sentiment would be rejected by most people living in Saxonized countries, it is far too accurate of nations that inherited the Romanized system of their masters.

The U.S.-Mexican border is where the Roman and Saxon worlds meet. There is no other place on earth where we can observe the striking impact the two systems have had on the formation of the modern world. To the south are the former French and Spanish colonies of Latin America; to the north the former colonies of British North America. One is known for the poverty, history of political instability, and despotism that marked Romanized Europe through the ages. The other is known for its freedom, prosperity, and political stability that the Saxon system produces. It is noteworthy that Latin America has a history of dictators -- from Iturbide and Bolivar in the 1800s to Castro and Chavez in modern times-- while neither the United States or Canada ever had to experience such tyranny. This is the reason, as Daniel Hannan (MEP) states, "Barbados is not Haiti (former French colony) or the Dominican Republic (former Spanish colony) and Singapore and Hong Kong are not like Malaysia or Indonesia." It is ironic that those who oppose the Anglo-Saxon model point to the horrendous history of the Romanized colonies in justifying the model as being unfair, unjust, or even evil.

It is politically correct to blame the wealthy nations for the poverty of the rest of the world, but as we have seen in the last chapter it has more to do with a nation's form of government than it does with colonialism, capitalism, racism, or even exploitation. The people in countries that have never embraced or have abandoned the Saxon model suffer unimaginable poverty, often under oppressive governments. Even good intentioned governments, such as Nehru's in India, that adopt Marxist policies in order to help the poorest of their citizens (often under the guise of ending "economic inequality") eventually discover that all they have accomplished is the destruction of their middle class. Only the Anglo-Saxon model, with its inherent economic freedom, has a 500-year track record of reducing poverty by growing the middle class. And, as Africa and India demonstrated, it is a model that works for all regardless of race, religion, ethnic background, or colonial master.

It is also politically correct to point to the indigenous peoples who have "suffered" under the Anglo-Saxon system as evidence of it being a failure. While atrocities were committed during the age of colonization, they were not limited to the proponents of the model. The non-Anglo-Saxon powers treated their colonies with more brutality than the Anglo-Saxon powers did. As the previous chapter illustrates, British colonialism did far greater good than bad. As Cambridge professor of Historical Anthropology points out, "In Australia, 300 generations of hunter-gatherers never led to anything different until the white colonists arrived." As much as we want to glorify the lifestyle of the indigenous people of the world, the reality is that they barely eked out an existence. They often succumbed to the cycle of subsistence. People died if the land could not provide what was needed to maintain the population. The first to go were the weaker members, which were usually the children and the elderly. The fact is that the life of the indigenous people was more akin to a UNICEF commercial than it is to Disney's *Pocahontas*. Lawlessness was the norm. People were killed or enslaved by other indigenous groups. Cannibalism, piracy, slavery, and mass murder marked much of the pre-colonial world.

It would be the Anglo-Saxon principle of every individual having value -- which is the basis of the modern day concept of human rights -- that would end many of these barbaric practices. The prosperity that the model produced ended starvation and malnutrition around the world. For the first time in history, man was not only able to feed himself but also his neighbors. It is no coincidence that life expectancy, literacy rates, standards of living, and individual prosperity increased -- and infant mortality, diseases, famines, and poverty decreased -- in the 300 plus years that the Anglo-Saxon countries dominated the world. As the Nigerian prince pointed out, "there are a lot more black Africans alive today because of the British than there would be without them. Those who do not see this do so because they are blinded by either hatred or their ideology."

As mentioned above, the Anglo-Saxon countries have dominated the world for over 300 years. It is during this period that most of humanity made the great leap from subsistence farming that barely fed their families, to the industrial age, and lastly into the modern age. This evolution is the product of one people's system of government. And they were people who defended individual liberty from Roman authoritarianism, defeated the absolutism of Romanized Europe, produced documents such as the Magna Carta in 1215, the Acts of Abjuration in 1561, the Declaration of Rights in 1688, the Declaration of Independence in 1776, the Constitution of the United States in 1787, and the Bill of Rights in 1789. As de Tocqueville, a Frenchman, admitted, "In their time, there were no other people on earth who could have produced such documents since they are a product of a people who value the principles that are inherent therein."

Edmund Burke wrote that "Liberty is a contract between the dead, the living, and those yet to be born." We inherited the freedom we enjoy from previous generations -- going back 1,700 years to the Saxon warriors who fought "as if life without liberty is a curse". Sadly, it is today's generation which, out of ignorance, is about to lose liberty for future generations to come. By embracing systems based on the abstract theories of academics and madmen, we are destroying the model that has blessed humanity with the liberty and prosperity we take for granted. Furthermore, by abandoning the model that liberated the common man from poverty and servitude, we risk condemning future generations to that awful state of existence.

It is important to recall the wise and prophetic words of de Tocqueville,

Despotism often presents itself as the repairer of all the ills suffered, the supporter of just rights, the defender of the oppressed, and the founder of order. Peoples are lulled to sleep by the temporary prosperity it engenders, and when they wake up, they are wretched.

We have a choice. We can remain asleep until we wake up wretched or we can take the advice of Mr. Jefferson and "*return at once into that happy system of our ancestors, the wisest and most perfect ever yet devised by the wit of man.*"

Part V

Historical Documents and Bibliography

Document 1

The Magna Carta (The Great Charter)

Preamble: John, by the grace of God, king of England, lord of Ireland, duke of Normandy and Aquitaine, and count of Anjou, to the archbishop, bishops, abbots, earls, barons, justiciaries, foresters, sheriffs, stewards, servants, and to all his bailiffs and liege subjects, greetings. Know that, having regard to God and for the salvation of our soul, and those of all our ancestors and heirs, and unto the honor of God and the advancement of his holy Church and for the rectifying of our realm, we have granted as underwritten by advice of our venerable fathers, Stephen, archbishop of Canterbury, primate of all England and cardinal of the holy Roman Church, Henry, archbishop of Dublin, William of London, Peter of Winchester, Jocelyn of Bath and Glastonbury, Hugh of Lincoln, Walter of Worcester, William of Coventry, Benedict of Rochester, bishops; of Master Pandulf, subdeacon and member of the household of our lord the Pope, of brother Aymeric (master of the Knights of the Temple in England), and of the illustrious men William Marshal, earl of Pembroke, William, earl of Salisbury, William, earl of Warenne, William, earl of Arundel, Alan of Galloway (constable of Scotland), Waren Fitz Gerold, Peter Fitz Herbert, Hubert De Burgh (seneschal of Poitou), Hugh de Neville, Matthew Fitz Herbert, Thomas Basset, Alan Basset, Philip d'Aubigny, Robert of Roppesley, John Marshal, John Fitz Hugh, and others, our liegemen.

1. In the first place we have granted to God, and by this our present charter confirmed for us and our heirs forever that the English Church shall be free, and shall have her rights entire, and her liberties inviolate; and we will that it be thus observed; which is

apparent from this that the freedom of elections, which is reckoned most important and very essential to the English Church, we, of our pure and unconstrained will, did grant, and did by our charter confirm and did obtain the ratification of the same from our lord, Pope Innocent III, before the quarrel arose between us and our barons: and this we will observe, and our will is that it be observed in good faith by our heirs forever. We have also granted to all freemen of our kingdom, for us and our heirs forever, all the underwritten liberties, to be had and held by them and their heirs, of us and our heirs forever.

2. If any of our earls or barons, or others holding of us in chief by military service shall have died, and at the time of his death his heir shall be full of age and owe "relief", he shall have his inheritance by the old relief, to wit, the heir or heirs of an earl, for the whole barony of an earl by £100; the heir or heirs of a baron, £100 for a whole barony; the heir or heirs of a knight, 100s, at most, and whoever owes less let him give less, according to the ancient custom of fees.

3. If, however, the heir of any one of the aforesaid has been under age and in wardship, let him have his inheritance without relief and without fine when he comes of age.

4. The guardian of the land of an heir who is thus under age, shall take from the land of the heir nothing but reasonable produce, reasonable customs, and reasonable services, and that without destruction or waste of men or goods; and if we have committed the wardship of the lands of any such minor to the sheriff, or to any other who is responsible to us for its issues, and he has made destruction or waster of what he holds in wardship, we will take of him amends, and the land shall be committed to two lawful and discreet men of that fee, who shall be responsible for the issues to us or to him to whom we shall assign them; and if we have given or sold the wardship of any such land to anyone and he has therein

made destruction or waste, he shall lose that wardship, and it shall be transferred to two lawful and discreet men of that fief, who shall be responsible to us in like manner as aforesaid.

5. The guardian, moreover, so long as he has the wardship of the land, shall keep up the houses, parks, fishponds, stanks, mills, and other things pertaining to the land, out of the issues of the same land; and he shall restore to the heir, when he has come to full age, all his land, stocked with ploughs and wainage, according as the season of husbandry shall require, and the issues of the land can reasonable bear.

6. Heirs shall be married without disparagement, yet so that before the marriage takes place the nearest in blood to that heir shall have notice.

7. A widow, after the death of her husband, shall forthwith and without difficulty have her marriage portion and inheritance; nor shall she give anything for her dower, or for her marriage portion, or for the inheritance which her husband and she held on the day of the death of that husband; and she may remain in the house of her husband for forty days after his death, within which time her dower shall be assigned to her.

8. No widow shall be compelled to marry, so long as she prefers to live without a husband; provided always that she gives security not to marry without our consent, if she holds of us, or without the consent of the lord of whom she holds, if she holds of another.

9. Neither we nor our bailiffs will seize any land or rent for any debt, as long as the chattels of the debtor are sufficient to repay the debt; nor shall the sureties of the debtor be distrained so long as the principal debtor is able to satisfy the debt; and if the principal debtor shall fail to pay the debt, having nothing wherewith to pay it, then the sureties shall answer for the debt; and let them have the

lands and rents of the debtor, if they desire them, until they are indemnified for the debt which they have paid for him, unless the principal debtor can show proof that he is discharged thereof as against the said sureties.

10. If one who has borrowed from the Jews any sum, great or small, die before that loan be repaid, the debt shall not bear interest while the heir is under age, of whomsoever he may hold; and if the debt fall into our hands, we will not take anything except the principal sum contained in the bond.

11. And if anyone die indebted to the Jews, his wife shall have her dower and pay nothing of that debt; and if any children of the deceased are left under age, necessaries shall be provided for them in keeping with the holding of the deceased; and out of the residue the debt shall be paid, reserving, however, service due to feudal lords; in like manner let it be done touching debts due to others than Jews.

12. No scutage not aid shall be imposed on our kingdom, unless by common counsel of our kingdom, except for ransoming our person, for making our eldest son a knight, and for once marrying our eldest daughter; and for these there shall not be levied more than a reasonable aid. In like manner it shall be done concerning aids from the city of London.

13. And the city of London shall have all it ancient liberties and free customs, as well by land as by water; furthermore, we decree and grant that all other cities, boroughs, towns, and ports shall have all their liberties and free customs.

14. And for obtaining the common counsel of the kingdom anent the assessing of an aid (except in the three cases aforesaid) or of a scutage, we will cause to be summoned the archbishops, bishops, abbots, earls, and greater barons, severally by our letters; and we will moveover cause to be summoned generally, through our

sheriffs and bailiffs, and others who hold of us in chief, for a fixed date, namely, after the expiry of at least forty days, and at a fixed place; and in all letters of such summons we will specify the reason of the summons. And when the summons has thus been made, the business shall proceed on the day appointed, according to the counsel of such as are present, although not all who were summoned have come.

15. We will not for the future grant to anyone license to take an aid from his own free tenants, except to ransom his person, to make his eldest son a knight, and once to marry his eldest daughter; and on each of these occasions there shall be levied only a reasonable aid.

16. No one shall be distrained for performance of greater service for a knight's fee, or for any other free tenement, than is due therefrom.

17. Common pleas shall not follow our court, but shall be held in some fixed place.

18. Inquests of novel disseisin, of mort d'ancestor, and of darrein presentment shall not be held elsewhere than in their own county courts, and that in manner following; We, or, if we should be out of the realm, our chief justiciar, will send two justiciaries through every county four times a year, who shall alone with four knights of the county chosen by the county, hold the said assizes in the county court, on the day and in the place of meeting of that court.

19. And if any of the said assizes cannot be taken on the day of the county court, let there remain of the knights and freeholders, who were present at the county court on that day, as many as may be required for the efficient making of judgments, according as the business be more or less.

20. A freeman shall not be amerced for a slight offense, except in accordance with the degree of the offense; and for a grave offense

he shall be amerced in accordance with the gravity of the offense, yet saving always his "contentment"; and a merchant in the same way, saving his "merchandise"; and a villein shall be amerced in the same way, saving his "wainage" if they have fallen into our mercy: and none of the aforesaid amercements shall be imposed except by the oath of honest men of the neighborhood.

21. Earls and barons shall not be amerced except through their peers, and only in accordance with the degree of the offense.

22. A clerk shall not be amerced in respect of his lay holding except after the manner of the others aforesaid; further, he shall not be amerced in accordance with the extent of his ecclesiastical benefice.

23. No village or individual shall be compelled to make bridges at river banks, except those who from of old were legally bound to do so.

24. No sheriff, constable, coroners, or others of our bailiffs, shall hold pleas of our Crown.

25. All counties, hundred, wapentakes, and trithings (except our demesne manors) shall remain at the old rents, and without any additional payment.

26. If anyone holding of us a lay fief shall die, and our sheriff or bailiff shall exhibit our letters patent of summons for a debt which the deceased owed us, it shall be lawful for our sheriff or bailiff to attach and enroll the chattels of the deceased, found upon the lay fief, to the value of that debt, at the sight of law worthy men, provided always that nothing whatever be thence removed until the debt which is evident shall be fully paid to us; and the residue shall be left to the executors to fulfill the will of the deceased; and if there be nothing due from him to us, all the chattels shall go to the deceased, saving to his wife and children their reasonable shares.

27. If any freeman shall die intestate, his chattels shall be distributed by the hands of his nearest kinsfolk and friends, under supervision of the Church, saving to every one the debts which the deceased owed to him.

28. No constable or other bailiff of ours shall take corn or other provisions from anyone without immediately tendering money therefor, unless he can have postponement thereof by permission of the seller.

29. No constable shall compel any knight to give money in lieu of castle-guard, when he is willing to perform it in his own person, or (if he himself cannot do it from any reasonable cause) then by another responsible man. Further, if we have led or sent him upon military service, he shall be relieved from guard in proportion to the time during which he has been on service because of us.

30. No sheriff or bailiff of ours, or other person, shall take the horses or carts of any freeman for transport duty, against the will of the said freeman.

31. Neither we nor our bailiffs shall take, for our castles or for any other work of ours, wood which is not ours, against the will of the owner of that wood.

32. We will not retain beyond one year and one day, the lands those who have been convicted of felony, and the lands shall thereafter be handed over to the lords of the fiefs.

33. All kydells for the future shall be removed altogether from Thames and Medway, and throughout all England, except upon the seashore.

34. The writ which is called praecipe shall not for the future be issued to anyone, regarding any tenement whereby a freeman may lose his court.

35. Let there be one measure of wine throughout our whole realm; and one measure of ale; and one measure of corn, to wit, "the London quarter"; and one width of cloth (whether dyed, or russet, or "halberget"), to wit, two ells within the selvedges; of weights also let it be as of measures.

36. Nothing in future shall be given or taken for a writ of inquisition of life or limbs, but freely it shall be granted, and never denied.

37. If anyone holds of us by fee-farm, either by socage or by burage, or of any other land by knight's service, we will not (by reason of that fee-farm, socage, or burgage), have the wardship of the heir, or of such land of his as if of the fief of that other; nor shall we have wardship of that fee-farm, socage, or burgage, unless such fee-farm owes knight's service. We will not by reason of any small serjeancy which anyone may hold of us by the service of rendering to us knives, arrows, or the like, have wardship of his heir or of the land which he holds of another lord by knight's service.

38. No bailiff for the future shall, upon his own unsupported complaint, put anyone to his "law", without credible witnesses brought for this purposes.

39. No freemen shall be taken or imprisoned or disseised or exiled or in any way destroyed, nor will we go upon him nor send upon him, except by the lawful judgment of his peers or by the law of the land.

40. To no one will we sell, to no one will we refuse or delay, right or justice.

41. All merchants shall have safe and secure exit from England, and entry to England, with the right to tarry there and to move about as well by land as by water, for buying and selling by the ancient and right customs, quit from all evil tolls, except (in time of war) such merchants as are of the land at war with us. And if such are found in our land at the beginning of the war, they shall be detained, without injury to their bodies or goods, until information be received by us, or by our chief justiciar, how the merchants of our land found in the land at war with us are treated; and if our men are safe there, the others shall be safe in our land.

42. It shall be lawful in future for anyone (excepting always those imprisoned or outlawed in accordance with the law of the kingdom, and natives of any country at war with us, and merchants, who shall be treated as if above provided) to leave our kingdom and to return, safe and secure by land and water, except for a short period in time of war, on grounds of public policy- reserving always the allegiance due to us.

43. If anyone holding of some escheat (such as the honor of Wallingford, Nottingham, Boulogne, Lancaster, or of other escheats which are in our hands and are baronies) shall die, his heir shall give no other relief, and perform no other service to us than he would have done to the baron if that barony had been in the baron's hand; and we shall hold it in the same manner in which the baron held it.

44. Men who dwell without the forest need not henceforth come before our justiciaries of the forest upon a general summons, unless they are in plea, or sureties of one or more, who are attached for the forest.

45. We will appoint as justices, constables, sheriffs, or bailiffs only such as know the law of the realm and mean to observe it well.

46. All barons who have founded abbeys, concerning which they hold charters from the kings of England, or of which they have long continued possession, shall have the wardship of them, when vacant, as they ought to have.

47. All forests that have been made such in our time shall forthwith be disafforsted; and a similar course shall be followed with regard to river banks that have been placed "in defense" by us in our time.

48. All evil customs connected with forests and warrens, foresters and warreners, sheriffs and their officers, river banks and their wardens, shall immediately by inquired into in each county by twelve sworn knights of the same county chosen by the honest men of the same county, and shall, within forty days of the said inquest, be utterly abolished, so as never to be restored, provided always that we previously have intimation thereof, or our justiciar, if we should not be in England.

49. We will immediately restore all hostages and charters delivered to us by Englishmen, as sureties of the peace of faithful service.

50. We will entirely remove from their bailiwicks, the relations of Gerard of Athee (so that in future they shall have no bailiwick in England); namely, Engelard of Cigogne, Peter, Guy, and Andrew of Chanceaux, Guy of Cigogne, Geoffrey of Martigny with his brothers, Philip Mark with his brothers and his nephew Geoffrey, and the whole brood of the same.

51. As soon as peace is restored, we will banish from the kingdom all foreign born knights, crossbowmen, serjeants, and mercenary soldiers who have come with horses and arms to the kingdom's hurt.

52. If anyone has been dispossessed or removed by us, without the legal judgment of his peers, from his lands, castles, franchises, or from his right, we will immediately restore them to him; and if a

dispute arise over this, then let it be decided by the five and twenty barons of whom mention is made below in the clause for securing the peace. Moreover, for all those possessions, from which anyone has, without the lawful judgment of his peers, been disseised or removed, by our father, King Henry, or by our brother, King Richard, and which we retain in our hand (or which as possessed by others, to whom we are bound to warrant them) we shall have respite until the usual term of crusaders; excepting those things about which a plea has been raised, or an inquest made by our order, before our taking of the cross; but as soon as we return from the expedition, we will immediately grant full justice therein.

53. We shall have, moreover, the same respite and in the same manner in rendering justice concerning the disafforestation or retention of those forests which Henry our father and Richard our broter afforested, and concerning the wardship of lands which are of the fief of another (namely, such wardships as we have hitherto had by reason of a fief which anyone held of us by knight's service), and concerning abbeys founded on other fiefs than our own, in which the lord of the fee claims to have right; and when we have returned, or if we desist from our expedition, we will immediately grant full justice to all who complain of such things.

54. No one shall be arrested or imprisoned upon the appeal of a woman, for the death of any other than her husband.

55. All fines made with us unjustly and against the law of the land, and all amercements, imposed unjustly and against the law of the land, shall be entirely remitted, or else it shall be done concerning them according to the decision of the five and twenty barons whom mention is made below in the clause for securing the pease, or according to the judgment of the majority of the same, along with the aforesaid Stephen, archbishop of Canterbury, if he can be present, and such others as he may wish to bring with him for this purpose, and if he cannot be present the business shall nevertheless

proceed without him, provided always that if any one or more of the aforesaid five and twenty barons are in a similar suit, they shall be removed as far as concerns this particular judgment, others being substituted in their places after having been selected by the rest of the same five and twenty for this purpose only, and after having been sworn.

56. If we have disseised or removed Welshmen from lands or liberties, or other things, without the legal judgment of their peers in England or in Wales, they shall be immediately restored to them; and if a dispute arise over this, then let it be decided in the marches by the judgment of their peers; for the tenements in England according to the law of England, for tenements in Wales according to the law of Wales, and for tenements in the marches according to the law of the marches. Welshmen shall do the same to us and ours.

57. Further, for all those possessions from which any Welshman has, without the lawful judgment of his peers, been disseised or removed by King Henry our father, or King Richard our brother, and which we retain in our hand (or which are possessed by others, and which we ought to warrant), we will have respite until the usual term of crusaders; excepting those things about which a plea has been raised or an inquest made by our order before we took the cross; but as soon as we return (or if perchance we desist from our expedition), we will immediately grant full justice in accordance with the laws of the Welsh and in relation to the foresaid regions.

58. We will immediately give up the son of Llywelyn and all the hostages of Wales, and the charters delivered to us as security for the peace.

59. We will do towards Alexander, king of Scots, concerning the return of his sisters and his hostages, and concerning his franchises, and his right, in the same manner as we shall do towards our owher barons of England, unless it ought to be otherwise according to the charters which we hold from William his father, formerly king of

Scots; and this shall be according to the judgment of his peers in our court.

60. Moreover, all these aforesaid customs and liberties, the observances of which we have granted in our kingdom as far as pertains to us towards our men, shall be observed b all of our kingdom, as well clergy as laymen, as far as pertains to them towards their men.

61. Since, moveover, for God and the amendment of our kingdom and for the better allaying of the quarrel that has arisen between us and our barons, we have granted all these concessions, desirous that they should enjoy them in complete and firm endurance forever, we give and grant to them the underwritten security, namely, that the barons choose five and twenty barons of the kingdom, whomsoever they will, who shall be bound with all their might, to observe and hold, and cause to be observed, the peace and liberties we have granted and confirmed to them by this our present Charter, so that if we, or our justiciar, or our bailiffs or any one of our officers, shall in anything be at fault towards anyone, or shall have broken any one of the articles of this peace or of this security, and the offense be notified to four barons of the foresaid five and twenty, the said four barons shall repair to us (or our justiciar, if we are out of the realm) and, laying the transgression before us, petition to have that transgression redressed without delay. And if we shall not have corrected the transgression (or, in the event of our being out of the realm, if our justicial shall not have corrected it) within forty days, reckoning from the time it has been intimated to us (or to our justiciar, if we should be out of the realm), the four barons aforesaid shall refer that matter to the rest of the five and twenty barons, and those five and twenty barons shall, together with the community of the whole realm, distrain and distress us in all possible ways, namely, by seizing our castles, lands, possessions, and in any other way they can, until redress has been obtained as they deem fit, saving harmless our own person, and the persons of our queen and

children; and when redress has been obtained, they shall resume their old relations towards us. And let whoever in the country desires it, swear to obey the orders of the said five and twenty barons for the execution of all the aforesaid matters, and along with them, to molest us to the utmost of his power; and we publicly and freely grant leave to everyone who wishes to swear, and we shall never forbid anyone to swear. All those, moveover, in the land who of themselves and of their own accord are unwilling to swear to the twenty five to help them in constraining and molesting us, we shall by our command compel the same to swear to the effect foresaid. And if any one of the five and twenty barons shall have died or departed from the land, or be incapacitated in any other manner which would prevent the foresaid provisions being carried out, those of the said twenty five barons who are left shall choose another in his place according to their own judgment, and he shall be sworn in the same way as the others. Further, in all matters, the execution of which is entrusted,to these twenty five barons, if perchance these twenty five are present and disagree about anything, or if some of them, after being summoned, are unwilling or unable to be present, that which the majority of those present ordain or command shall be held as fixed and established, exactly as if the whole twenty five had concurred in this; and the said twenty five shall swear that they will faithfully observe all that is aforesaid, and cause it to be observed with all their might. And we shall procure nothing from anyone, directly or indirectly, whereby any part of these concessions and liberties might be revoked or diminished; and if any such things has been procured, let it be void and null, and we shall never use it personally or by another.

62. And all the will, hatreds, and bitterness that have arisen between us and our men, clergy and lay, from the date of the quarrel, we have completely remitted and pardoned to everyone. Moreover, all trespasses occasioned by the said quarrel, from Easter in the sixteenth year of our reign till the restoration of peace, we have fully remitted to all, both clergy and laymen, and completely forgiven, as

far as pertains to us. And on this head, we have caused to be made for them letters testimonial patent of the lord Stephen, archbishop of Canterbury, of the lord Henry, archbishop of Dublin, of the bishops aforesaid, and of Master Pandulf as touching this security and the concessions aforesaid.

63. Wherefore we will and firmly order that the English Church be free, and that the men in our kingdom have and hold all the aforesaid liberties, rights, and concessions, well and peaceably, freely and quietly, fully and wholly, for themselves and their heirs, of us and our heirs, in all respects and in all places forever, as is aforesaid. An oath, moreover, has been taken, as well on our part as on the art of the barons, that all these conditions aforesaid shall be kept in good faith and without evil intent.

Given under our hand - the above named and many others being witnesses - in the meadow which is called Runnymede, between Windsor and Staines, on the fifteenth day of June, in the seventeenth year of our reign.

Document 2

The Act of Abjuration

(United Dutch Provinces 1581)

The States General of the United Provinces of the Low Countries, to all whom it may concern, do by these Presents send greeting:

As it is apparent to all that a prince is constituted by God to be ruler of a people, to defend them from oppression and violence as the shepherd his sheep; and whereas God did not create the people slaves to their prince, to obey his commands, whether right or wrong, but rather the prince for the sake of the subjects (without which he could be no prince), to govern them according to equity, to love and support them as a father his children or a shepherd his flock, and even at the hazard of life to defend and preserve them. And when he does not behave thus, but, on the contrary, oppresses them, seeking opportunities to infringe their ancient customs and privileges, exacting from them slavish compliance, then he is no longer a prince, but a tyrant, and the subjects are to consider him in no other view. And particularly when this is done deliberately, unauthorized by the states, they may not only disallow his authority, but legally proceed to the choice of another prince for their defense. This is the only method left for subjects whose humble petitions and remonstrances could never soften their prince or dissuade him from his tyrannical proceedings; and this is what the law of nature dictates for the defense of liberty, which we ought to transmit to posterity, even at the hazard of our lives. And this we have seen done frequently in several countries upon the like occasion, whereof there are notorious instances, and more justifiable in our land, which has been always governed according to their ancient privileges, which are expressed in the oath taken by the prince at his admission to the government; for most of the Provinces receive their prince upon certain conditions, which he swears to maintain, which, if the prince violates, he is no longer sovereign.

Now thus it was that the king of Spain after the demise of the emperor, his father, Charles the Fifth, of the glorious memory (of whom he received all these provinces), forgetting the services done by the subjects of these countries, both to his father and himself, by whose valor he got so glorious and memorable victories over his enemies that his name and power became famous and dreaded over all the world, forgetting also the advice of his said imperial majesty, made to him before to the contrary, did rather hearken to the counsel of those Spaniards about him, who had conceived a secret hatred to this land and to its liberty, because they could not enjoy posts of honor and high employments here under the states as in Naples, Sicily, Milan and the Indies, and other countries under the king's dominion. Thus allured by the riches of the said provinces, wherewith many of them were well acquainted, the said counselors, we say, or the principal of them, frequently remonstrated to the king that it was more for his Majesty's reputation and grandeur to subdue the Low Countries a second time, and to make himself absolute (by which they mean to tyrannize at pleasure), than to govern according to the restrictions he had accepted, and at his admission sworn to observe. From that time forward the king of Spain, following these evil counselors, sought by all means possible to reduce this country (stripping them of their ancient privileges) to slavery, under the government of Spaniards having first, under the mask of religion, endeavored to settle new bishops in the largest and principal cities, endowing and incorporating them with the richest abbeys, assigning to each bishop nine canons to assist him as counselors, three whereof should superintend the inquisition.

By this incorporation the said bishops (who might be strangers as well as natives) would have had the first place and vote in the assembly of the states, and always the prince's creatures at devotion; and by the addition of the said canons he would have introduced the Spanish inquisition, which has been always as dreadful and detested in these provinces as the worst of slavery, as is well known, in so much that his imperial majesty, having once before proposed it to these states, and upon whose remonstrances did desist, and entirely gave it up, hereby giving proof of the great affection he had for his subjects. But, notwithstanding the many remonstrances made to the king both by the provinces and particular towns, in writing as well as by some principal lords by word of mouth; and, namely, by the Baron of Montigny and Earl of Egmont, who with the approbation of the Duchess of Parma, then governess of the Low Countries, by the advice of the council of state were sent several times to Spain upon this affair. And, although the king had by fair words given them grounds to hope that their request should be complied with, yet by his letters he ordered the contrary, soon after expressly commanding, upon pain of his displeasure, to admit the new bishops immediately, and put them in possession of their bishoprics and incorporated abbeys, to hold the court of the inquisition in the places where it had been before, to obey and follow the decrees and ordinances of the Council of Trent, which in many articles are destructive of the privileges of the country.

This being come to the knowledge of the people gave just occasion to great uneasiness and clamor among them, and lessened that good affection they had always borne toward the king and his predecessors. And, especially, seeing that he did not only seek to tyrannize over their persons and estates, but also over their consciences, for which they believed themselves accountable to God only. Upon this occasion the chief of the nobility in compassion to the poor people, in the year 1566, exhibited a certain remonstrance in form of a petition, humbly praying, in order to appease them and prevent public disturbances, that it would please his majesty (by showing that clemency due from a good prince to his people) to soften the said points, and especially with regard to the rigorous inquisition, and capital punishments for matters of religion. And to inform the king of this affair in a more solemn manner, and to represent to him how necessary it was for the peace and prosperity of the public to remove the aforesaid innovations, and moderate the severity of his declarations published concerning divine worship, the Marquis de Berghen, and the aforesaid Baron of Montigny had been sent, at the request of the said lady regent, council of state, and of the states-general as ambassadors to Spain, where the king, instead of giving them audience, and redress the grievances they had complained of (which for want of a timely remedy did always appear in their evil consequences among the common people), did, by the advice of Spanish council, declare all those who were concerned in preparing the said remonstrance to be rebels, and guilty of high treason, and to be punished with death, and confiscation of their estates; and, what is more (thinking himself well assured of reducing these countries under absolute tyranny by the army of the Duke of Alva), did soon after imprison and put to death the said lords the ambassadors, and confiscated their estates, contrary to the law of nations, which has been always religiously observed even among the most tyrannic and barbarous princes.

And, although the said disturbances, which in the year 1566 happened on the aforementioned occasion, were now appeased by the governess and her ministers, and many friends to liberty were either banished or subdued, in so much that the king had not any show of reason to use arms and violence, and further oppress this country, yet for these causes and reasons, long time before sought by the council of Spain (as appears by intercepted letters from the Spanish ambassador, Alana, then in France, writ to the Duchess of Parma), to annul all the privileges of this country, and govern it tyrannically at pleasure as in the Indies; and in their new conquests he has, at the instigation of the council of Spain, showing the little regard he had for his people, so contrary to the duty which a good prince owes to his subjects), sent the Duke of Alva with a powerful army to oppress this land, who for his inhuman cruelties is looked upon as one of its greatest enemies, accompanied with counselors too like himself. And, although he came in without the least opposition, and was received by the poor subjects with all marks of honor and clemency, which the king had often hypocritically promised in his letters, and that himself intended to come in person to give orders to their general satisfaction, having since the departure of the Duke of Alva equipped a fleet to carry him from Spain, and another in Zealand to come to meet him at the great expense of the country, the better to deceive his subjects, and allure them into the toils, nevertheless the said duke, immediately after his arrival (though a stranger, and no way related to the royal family), declared that he had a captain-general's commission, and soon after that of governor of these provinces, contrary to all its ancient customs and privileges; and, the more to manifest his designs, he immediately garrisoned the principal towns and castles, and caused fortresses and citadels to be built in the great cities to awe them into subjection, and very courteously sent for the chief nobility in the king's name, under pretense of taking their advice, and to employ them in the service of their country. And those who believed his letters were seized and carried out of Brabant, contrary to law, where they were imprisoned and prosecuted as criminals before him who had no right, nor could be a competent judge; and at last he, without hearing their defense at large, sentenced them to death, which was publicly and ignominiously executed.

The others, better acquainted with Spanish hypocrisy, residing in foreign countries, were declared outlawed, and had their estates confiscated, so that the poor subjects could make no use of their fortresses nor be assisted by their princes in defense of their liberty against the violence of the pope; besides a great number of other gentlemen and substantial citizens, some of whom were executed, and others banished that their estates might be confiscated, plaguing the other honest inhabitants, not only by the injuries done to their wives, children and estates by the Spanish soldiers lodged in their houses, as likewise by diverse contributions, which they were forced to pay toward building citadels and new fortifications of towns even to their own ruin, besides the taxes of the hundredth, twentieth, and tenth penny, to pay both the foreign and those raised in the country, to be employed against their fellow-citizens and against those who at the hazard of their lives defended their liberties. In order to impoverish the subjects, and to incapacitate them to hinder his design, and that he might with more ease execute the instructions received in Spain, to treat these countries as new conquests, he began to alter the course of justice after the Spanish mode, directly contrary to our privileges; and, imagining at last he had nothing more to fear, he endeavored by main force to settle a tax called the tenth penny on merchandise and manufacture, to the total ruin of these countries, the prosperity of which depends upon a flourishing trade, notwithstanding frequent remonstrances, not by a single province only, but by all of them united, which he had effected, had it not been for the Prince of Orange with diverse gentlemen and other inhabitants, who had followed this prince in his exile, most of whom were in his pay, and banished by the Duke of Alva with others who between him and the states of all the provinces, on the contrary sought, by all possible promises made to the colonels already at his devotion, to gain the German troops, who were then garrisoned in the principal fortresses and the cities, that by their assistance he might master them, as he had gained many of them already, and held them attached to his interest in order, by their assistance, to force those who would not join with him in making war against the Prince of Orange, and the provinces of Holland and Zealand, more cruel and bloody than any war before. But, as no disguises can long conceal our intentions, this project was discovered before it could be executed; and he, unable to perform his promises, and instead of that peace so much boasted of at his arrival a new war kindled, not yet extinguished.

All these considerations give us more than sufficient reason to renounce the King of Spain, and seek some other powerful and more gracious prince to take us under his protection; and, more especially, as these countries have been for these twenty years abandoned to disturbance and oppression by their king, during which time the inhabitants were not treated as subjects, but enemies, enslaved forcibly by their own governors.

Having also, after the decease of Don Juan, sufficiently declared by the Baron de Selles that he would not allow the pacification of Ghent, the which Don Juan had in his majesty's name sworn to maintain, but daily proposing new terms of agreement less advantageous. Notwithstanding these discouragements we used all possible means, by petitions in writing, and the good offices of the greatest princes in Christendom, to be reconciled to our king, having lastly maintained for a long time our deputies at the Congress of Cologne, hoping that the intercession of his imperial majesty and of the electors would procure an honorable and lasting peace, and some degree of liberty, particularly relating to religion (which chiefly concerns God and our own consciences), at last we found by experience that nothing would be obtained of the king by prayers and treaties, which latter he made use of to divide and weaken the provinces, that he might the easier execute his plan rigorously, by subduing them one by one, which afterwards plainly appeared by certain proclamations and proscriptions published by the king's orders, by virtue of which we and all officers of the United Provinces with all our friends are declared rebels and as such to have forfeited our lives and estates. Thus, by rendering us odious to all, he might interrupt our commerce, likewise reducing us to despair, offering a great sum to any that would assassinate the Prince of Orange.

So, having no hope of reconciliation, and finding no other remedy, we have, agreeable to the law of nature in our own defense, and for maintaining the rights, privileges, and liberties of our countrymen, wives, and children, and latest posterity from being enslaved by the Spaniards, been constrained to renounce allegiance to the King of Spain, and pursue such methods as appear to us most likely to secure our ancient liberties and privileges. Know all men by these presents that being reduced to the last extremity, as above mentioned, we have unanimously and deliberately declared, and do by these presents declare, that the King of Spain has forfeited, ipso jure, all hereditary right to the sovereignty of those countries, and are determined from henceforward not to acknowledge his sovereignty or jurisdiction, nor any act of his relating to the domains of the Low Countries, nor make use of his name as prince, nor suffer others to do it. In consequence whereof we also declare all officers, judges, lords, gentlemen, vassals, and all other the inhabitants of this country of what condition or quality soever, to be henceforth discharged from all oaths and obligations whatsoever made to the King of Spain as sovereign of those countries. And whereas, upon the motives already mentioned, the greater part of the United Provinces have, by common consent of their members, submitted to the government and sovereignty of the illustrious Prince and Duke of Anjou, upon certain conditions stipulated with his highness, and whereas the most serene Archduke Matthias has resigned the government of these countries with our approbation, we command and order all justiciaries, officers, and all whom it may concern, not to make use of the name, titles, great or privy seal of the King of Spain from henceforward; but in lieu of them, as long as his highness the Duke of Anjou is absent upon urgent affairs relating to the welfare of these countries, having so agreed with his highness or otherwise, they shall provisionally use the name and title of the President and Council of the Province.

And, until such a president and counselors shall be nominated, assembled, and act in that capacity, they shall act in our name, except that in Holland and Zealand where they shall use the name of the Prince of Orange, and of the states of the said provinces until the aforesaid council shall legally sit, and then shall conform to the directions of that council agreeable to the contract made with his highness. And, instead of the king's seal aforesaid, they shall make use of our great seal, center-seal, and signet, in affairs relating to the public, according as the said council shall from time to time be authorized. And in affairs concerning the administration of justice, and transactions peculiar to each province, the provincial council and other councils of that country shall use respectively the name, title, and seal of the said province, where the case is to be tried, and no other, on pain of having all letters, documents, and despatches annulled. And, for the better and effectual performance hereof, we have ordered and commanded, and do hereby order and command, that all the seals of the King of Spain which are in these United Provinces shall immediately, upon the publication of these presents, be delivered to the estate of each province respectively, or to such persons as by the said estates shall be authorized and appointed, upon peril of discretionary punishment.

Moreover, we order and command that from henceforth no money coined shall be stamped with the name, title, or arms of the King of Spain in any of these United Provinces, but that all new gold and silver pieces, with their halfs and quarters, shall only bear such impressions as the states shall direct. We order likewise and command the president and other lords of the privy council, and all other chancellors, presidents, accountants-general, and to others in all the chambers of accounts respectively in these said countries, and likewise to all other judges and officers, as we hold them discharged from henceforth of their oath made to the King of Spain, pursuant to the tenor of their commission, that they shall take a new oath to the states of that country on whose jurisdiction they depend, or to commissaries appointed by them, to be true to us against the King of Spain and all his adherents, according to the formula of words prepared by the states-general for that purpose. And we shall give to the said counselors, justiciaries, and officers employed in these provinces, who have contracted in our name with his highness the Duke of Anjou, an act to continue them in their respective offices, instead of new commissions, a clause annulling the former provisionally until the arrival of his highness. Moreover, to all such counselors, accomptants, justiciaries, and officers in these Provinces, who have not contracted with his highness, aforesaid, we shall grant new commissions under our hands and seals, unless any of the said officers are accused and convicted of having acted under their former commissions against the liberties and privileges of this country or of other the like maladministration.

We farther command of the president and members of the privy council, chancellor of the Duchy of Brabant, also the chancellor of the Duchy of Guelders, and county of Zutphen, to the president and members of the council of Holland, to the receivers of great officers of Beoostersheldt and Bewestersheldt in Zealand, to the president and council of Friese, and to the Escoulet of Mechelen, to the president and members of the council of Utrecht, and to all other justiciaries and officers whom it may concern, to the lieutenants all and every of them, to cause this our ordinance to be published and proclaimed throughout their respective jurisdictions, in the usual places appointed for that purpose, that none may plead ignorance. And to cause our said ordinance to be observed inviolably, punishing the offenders impartially and without delay; for so it is found expedient for the public good. And, for better maintaining all and every article hereof, we give to all and every one of you, by express command, full power and authority. In witness whereof we have hereunto set our hands and seals, dated in our assembly at the Hague, the six and twentieth day of July, 1581, indorsed by the orders of the states-general, and signed J. De Asseliers.

Document 3

The Petition of Right
England 1628

The Petition exhibited to his Majesty by the Lords Spiritual and Temporal, and Commons, in this present Parliament assembled, concerning divers Rights and Liberties of the Subjects, with the King's Majesty's royal answer thereunto in full Parliament.

To the King's Most Excellent Majesty,

Humbly show unto our Sovereign Lord the King, the Lords Spiritual and Temporal, and Commons in Parliament assembles, that whereas it is declared and enacted by a statute made in the time of the reign of King Edward I, commonly called Stratutum de Tellagio non Concedendo, that no tallage or aid shall be laid or levied by the king or his heirs in this realm, without the good will and assent of the archbishops, bishops, earls, barons, knights, burgesses, and other the freemen of the commonalty of this realm; and by authority of parliament holden in the five-and-twentieth year of the reign of King Edward III, it is declared and enacted, that from thenceforth no person should be compelled to make any loans to the king against his will, because such loans were against reason and the franchise of the land; and by other laws of this realm it is provided, that none should be charged by any charge or imposition called a benevolence, nor by such like charge; by which statutes before mentioned, and other the good laws and statutes of this realm, your subjects have inherited this freedom, that they should not be compelled to contribute to any tax, tallage, aid, or other like charge not set by common consent, in parliament.

II. Yet nevertheless of late divers commissions directed to sundry commissioners in several counties, with instructions, have issued; by means whereof your people have been in divers places assembled, and required to lend certain sums of money unto your Majesty, and many of them, upon their refusal so to do, have had an oath administered unto them not warrantable by the laws or statutes of this realm, and have been constrained to become bound and make appearance and give utterance before your Privy Council and in other places, and others of them have been therefore imprisoned, confined, and sundry other ways molested and disquieted; and divers other charges have been laid and levied upon your people in several counties by lord lieutenants, deputy lieutenants, commissioners for musters, justices of peace and others, by command or direction from your Majesty, or your Privy Council, against the laws and free custom of the realm.

III. And whereas also by the statute called 'The Great Charter of the Liberties of England,' it is declared and enacted, that no freeman may be taken or imprisoned or be disseized of his freehold or liberties, or his free customs, or be outlawed or exiled, or in any manner destroyed, but by the lawful judgment of his peers, or by the law of the land.

IV. And in the eight-and-twentieth year of the reign of King Edward III, it was declared and enacted by authority of parliament, that no man, of what estate or condition that he be, should be put out of his land or tenements, nor taken, nor imprisoned, nor disinherited nor put to death without being brought to answer by due process of law.

V. Nevertheless, against the tenor of the said statutes, and other the good laws and statutes of your realm to that end provided, divers of your subjects have of late been imprisoned without any cause showed; and when for their deliverance they were brought before your justices by your Majesty's writs of habeas corpus, there to undergo and receive as the court should order, and their keepers commanded to certify the causes of their detainer, no cause was certified, but that they were detained by your Majesty's special command, signified by the lords of your Privy Council, and yet were returned back to several prisons, without being charged with anything to which they might make answer according to the law.

VI. And whereas of late great companies of soldiers and mariners have been dispersed into divers counties of the realm, and the inhabitants against their wills have been compelled to receive them into their houses, and there to suffer them to sojourn against the laws and customs of this realm, and to the great grievance and vexation of the people.

VII. And whereas also by authority of parliament, in the five-and-twentieth year of the reign of King Edward III, it is declared and enacted, that no man shall be forejudged of life or limb against the form of the Great Charter and the law of the land; and by the said Great Charter and other the laws and statutes of this your realm, no man ought to be adjudged to death but by the laws established in this your realm, either by the customs of the same realm, or by acts of parliament: and whereas no offender of what kind soever is exempted from the proceedings to be used, and punishments to be inflicted by the laws and statutes of this your realm; nevertheless of late time divers commissions under your Majesty's great seal have issued forth, by which certain persons have been assigned and appointed commissioners with power and authority to proceed within the land, according to the justice of martial law, against such soldiers or mariners, or other dissolute persons joining with them, as should commit any murder, robbery, felony, mutiny, or other outrage or misdemeanor whatsoever, and by such summary course and order as is agreeable to martial law, and is used in armies in time of war, to proceed to the trial and condemnation of such offenders, and them to cause to be executed and put to death according to the law martial.

VIII. By pretext whereof some of your Majesty's subjects have been by some of the said commissioners put to death, when and where, if by the laws and statutes of the land they had deserved death, by the same laws and statutes also they might, and by no other ought to have been judged and executed.

IX. And also sundry grievous offenders, by color thereof claiming an exemption, have escaped the punishments due to them by the laws and statutes of this your realm, by reason that divers of your officers and ministers of justice have unjustly refused or forborne to proceed against such offenders according to the same laws and statutes, upon pretense that the said offenders were punishable only by martial law, and by authority of such commissions as aforesaid; which commissions, and all other of like nature, are wholly and directly contrary to the said laws and statutes of this your realm.

X. They do therefore humbly pray your most excellent Majesty, that no man hereafter be compelled to make or yield any gift, loan, benevolence, tax, or such like charge, without common consent by act of parliament; and that none be called to make answer, or take such oath, or to give attendance, or be confined, or otherwise molested or disquieted concerning the same or for refusal thereof; and that no freeman, in any such manner as is before mentioned, be imprisoned or detained; and that your Majesty would be pleased to remove the said soldiers and mariners, and that your people may not be so burdened in time to come; and that the aforesaid commissions, for proceeding by martial law, may be revoked and annulled; and that hereafter no commissions of like nature may issue forth to any person or persons whatsoever to be executed as aforesaid, lest by color of them any of your Majesty's subjects be destroyed or put to death contrary to the laws and franchise of the land.

XI. All which they most humbly pray of your most excellent Majesty as their rights and liberties, according to the laws and statutes of this realm; and that your Majesty would also vouchsafe to declare, that the awards, doings, and proceedings, to the prejudice of your people in any of the premises, shall not be drawn hereafter into consequence or example; and that your Majesty would be also graciously pleased, for the further comfort and safety of your people, to declare your royal will and pleasure, that in the things aforesaid all your officers and ministers shall serve you according to the laws and statutes of this realm, as they tender the honor of your Majesty, and the prosperity of this kingdom.

Document 4

The Act Declaring the Rights and Liberties of the Subject, and Settling the Succession of the Crown, December 16,1689

Whereas the Lords Spiritual and Temporal and Commons assembled at Westminster, lawfully, fully, and freely representing all the estates of the people of this realm, did upon the thirteenth day of February in the year of our Lord one thousand six hundred eighty-eight present unto their Majesties, then called and known by the names and style of William and Mary, Prince and Princess of Orange, being present in their proper persons, a certain declaration in writing made by the said Lords and Commons in the words following, viz.:

Whereas the late King James the Second, by the assistance of divers evil counsellors, judges, and ministers employed by him, did endeavour to subvert and extirpate the Protestant religion and the laws and liberties of this kingdom;

1. By assuming and exercising a power of dispensing with and suspending of laws and the execution of laws without consent of Parliament;

2. By committing and prosecuting divers worthy prelates for humbly petitioning to be excused from concurring to the said assumed power;

3. By issuing and causing to be executed a commission under the great seal for erecting a court called The Court of Commissioners for Ecclesiastical Causes;

4. By levying money for and to the use of the Crown by pretence of prerogative for other time and in other manner than the same was granted by Parliament;

5. By raising and keeping a standing army within this kingdom in time of peace without consent of Parliament, and quartering soldiers contrary to law;

6. By causing several good subjects being Protestants to be disarmed at the same time when papists were both armed and employed contrary to law;

7. By violating the freedom of election of members to serve in Parliament;

8. By prosecutions in the Court of King's Bench for matters and causes cognizable only in Parliament, and by divers other arbitrary and illegal courses;

9. And whereas of late years, partial, corrupt, and unqualified persons have been returned and served on juries in trials, and particularly divers jurors in trials for high treason which were not freeholders;

10. And excessive bail has been required of persons committed in criminal cases to elude the benefit of the laws made for the liberty of the subjects;

11. And excessive fines have been imposed; and illegal and cruel punishments inflicted;

12. And several grants and promises made of fines and forfeitures before any conviction or judgment against the persons upon whom the same were to be levied;

All which are utterly and directly contrary to the known laws and statutes and freedom of this realm;

And whereas the said late King James the Second having abdicated the government and the throne being thereby vacant, His Highness the Prince of Orange (whom it has pleased Almighty God to make the glorious instrument of delivering this kingdom from popery and arbitrary power) did (by the advice of the Lords Spiritual and Temporal and divers principal persons of the Commons) cause letters to be written to the Lords Spiritual and Temporal, being Protestants, and other letters to the several counties, cities, universities, boroughs, and cinque ports, for the choosing of such persons to represent them as were of right to be sent to Parliament, to meet and sit at Westminster upon the two and twentieth day of January in this year one thousand six hundred eighty and eight, in order to such an establishment as that their religion, laws, and liberties might not again be in danger of being subverted, upon which letters elections having been accordingly made;

And thereupon the said Lords Spiritual and Temporal, and Commons, pursuant to their respective letters and elections, being now assembled in a full and free representative of this nation, taking into their most serious consideration the best means for attaining the ends aforesaid, do in the first place (as their ancestors in like case have usually done) for the vindicating and asserting their ancient rights and liberties declare

1. That the pretended power of suspending the laws or the execution of laws by regal authority without consent of Parliament is illegal;

2. That the pretended power of dispensing with laws or the execution of laws by regal authority, as it has been assumed and exercised of late, is illegal;

3. That the commission for erecting the late Court of Commissioners for Ecclesiastical Causes, and all other commissions and courts of like nature, are illegal and pernicious;

4. That levying money for or to the use of the Crown by pretence of prerogative, without grant of Parliament, for longer time, or in other manner than the same is or shall be granted, is illegal;

5. That it is the right of the subjects to petition the King, and all commitments and prosecutions for such petitioning are illegal;

6. That the raising or keeping a standing army within the kingdom in time of peace, unless it be with consent of Parliament, is against law;

7. That the subjects which are Protestants may have arms for their defense suitable to their conditions and as allowed by law;

8. That election of members of Parliament ought to be free;

9. That the freedom of speech and debates or proceedings in Parliament ought not to be impeached or questioned in any court or place out of Parliament;

10. That excessive bail ought not to be required, nor excessive fines imposed, nor cruel and unusual punishments inflicted;

11. That jurors ought to be duly impanelled and returned, and jurors which pass upon men in trials for high treason ought to be freeholders;

12. That all grants and promises of fines and forfeitures of particular persons before conviction are illegal and void;

13. And that for redress of all grievances, and for the amending, strengthening and preserving of the laws, Parliaments ought to be held frequently.

And they do claim, demand and insist upon all and singular the premises as their undoubted rights and liberties, and that no declarations, judgments, doings or proceedings to the prejudice of the people in any of the said premises ought in any wise to be drawn hereafter into consequence or example.

To which demand of their rights they are particularly encouraged by the declaration of His Highness the Prince of Orange as being the only means for obtaining a full redress and remedy therein.

Having therefore an entire confidence that His said Highness the Prince of Orange will perfect the deliverance so far advanced by him, and will still preserve them from the violation of their rights which they have here asserted, and from all other attempts upon their religion, rights and liberties:

II. The said Lords Spiritual and Temporal, and Commons, assembled at Westminster, do resolve that William and Mary, Prince and Princess of Orange, be and be declared King and Queen of England, France and Ireland and the dominions thereunto belonging, to hold the crown and royal dignity of the said kingdoms and dominions to them, the said prince and princess, during their lives and the life of the survivor to them, and that the sole and full exercise of the regal power be only in and executed by the said Prince of Orange in the names of the said prince and princess during their joint lives, and after their deceases the said crown and royal dignity of the same kingdoms and dominions to be to the heirs of the body of the said princess, and for default of such issue to the Princess Anne of Denmark and the heirs of her body, and for default of such issue to the heirs of the body of the said Prince of Orange. And the Lords Spiritual and Temporal, and Commons, do pray the said prince and princess to accept the same accordingly.

III. And that the oaths hereafter mentioned be taken by all persons of whom the oaths have allegiance and supremacy might be required by law, instead of them; and that the said oaths of allegiance and supremacy be abrogated.

I, A.B., do sincerely promise and swear that I will be faithful and bear true allegiance to their Majesties King William and Queen Mary. So help me God.

I, A.B., do swear that I do from my heart abhor, detest and abjure as impious and heretical this damnable doctrine and position, that princes excommunicated or deprived by the Pope or any authority of the see of Rome may be deposed or murdered by their subjects or any other whatsoever. And I do declare that no foreign prince, person, prelate, state or potentate hath or ought to have any jurisdiction, power, superiority, pre-eminence or authority, ecclesiastical or spiritual, within this realm. So help me God.

IV. Upon which their said Majesties did accept the crown and royal dignity of the kingdoms of England, France and Ireland, and the dominions thereunto belonging, according to the resolution and desire of the said Lords and Commons contained in the said declaration.

V. And thereupon their Majesties were pleased that the said Lords Spiritual and Temporal, and Commons, being the two Houses of Parliament, should continue to sit, and with their Majesties' royal concurrence make effectual provision for the settlement of the religion, laws and liberties of this kingdom, so that the same for the future might not be in danger again of being subverted, to which the said Lords Spiritual and Temporal, and Commons did agree, and proceed to act accordingly.

VI. Now in pursuance of the premises the said Lords Spiritual and Temporal, and Commons, in Parliament assembled, for the ratifying, confirming and establishing the said declaration and the articles, clauses, matters and things therein contained by the force of law made in due form by authority of Parliament, do pray that it may be declared and enacted that all and singular the rights and liberties asserted and claimed in the said declaration are the true, ancient, and indubitable rights and liberties of the people of this kingdom, and so shall be esteemed, allowed, adjudged, deemed and taken to be, and that all and every the particulars aforesaid shall be firmly and strictly holden and observed as they are expressed in the said declaration, and all officers and ministers whatsoever shall serve their Majesties and their successors according to the same in all time to come.

VII. And the said Lords Spiritual and Temporal, and Commons, seriously considering how it has pleased Almighty God in his marvelous providence and merciful goodness to this nation to provide and preserve their said Majesties' royal persons most happily to reign over us upon the throne of their ancestors, for which they render unto him from the bottom of their hearts their humblest thanks and praises, do truly, firmly, assuredly, and in the sincerity of their hearts think, and do hereby recognize, acknowledge and declare, that King James the Second having abdicated the government, and their Majesties having accepted the crown and royal dignity as aforesaid, their said Majesties did become, were, are, and of right ought to be by the laws of this realm our sovereign liege lord and lady, King and Queen of England, France and Ireland, and the dominions thereunto belonging, in and to whose princely persons the royal state, crown and dignity of the said realms with all honours, styles, titles, regalities, prerogatives, powers, jurisdictions and authorities to the same belonging and appertaining are most fully, rightfully and entirely invested and incorporated, united and annexed.

VIII. And for preventing all questions and divisions in this realm by reason of any pretended titles to the crown, and for preserving a certainty in the succession thereof, in and upon which the unity, peace, tranquility and safety of this nation does under God wholly consist and depend, the said Lords Spiritual and Temporal, and Commons, do beseech their Majesties that it may be enacted, established and declared, that the crown and regal government of the said kingdoms and dominions, with all and singular the premises thereunto belonging and appertaining, shall be and continue to their said Majesties and the survivor of them during their lives and the life of the survivor of them, and that the entire, perfect and full exercise of the regal power and government be only in and executed by His Majesty in the names of both their Majesties during their joint lives; and after their deceases the said crown and premises shall be and remain to the heirs of the body of Her Majesty, and for default of such issue to Her Royal Highness the Princess Anne of Denmark and the heirs of the body of His said Majesty; and thereunto the said Lords Spiritual and Temporal, and Commons, do in the name of all the people aforesaid most humbly and faithfully submit themselves, their heirs and posterities for ever, and do faithfully promise that they will stand to, maintain, and defend their said Majesties, and also the limitation and succession of the crown herein specified and contained, to the utmost of their powers with their lives and estates against all persons whatsoever that shall attempt anything to the contrary.

IX. And whereas it hath been found by experience that it is inconsistent with the safety and welfare of this Protestant kingdom to be governed by a popish prince, or by any king or queen marrying a papist, the said Lords Spiritual and Temporal, and Commons, do further pray that it may be enacted, that all and every person and persons that is, are or shall be reconciled to or shall hold communion with the See or Church of Rome, or shall profess the popish religion, or shall marry a papist, shall be excluded and be for ever incapable to inherit, possess, or enjoy the crown and government of this realm and Ireland and the dominions thereunto belonging or any part of the same, or to have, use, or exercise any regal power, authority or jurisdiction within the same; and in all and every such case or cases the people of these realms shall be and are hereby absolved of their allegiance; and the said crown and government shall from time to time descend to and be enjoyed by such person or persons being Protestants as should have inherited and enjoyed the same in case the said person or persons so reconciled, holding communion or professing or marrying as aforesaid were naturally dead.

X. And that every king and queen of this realm who at any time hereafter shall come to and succeed in the imperial crown of this kingdom shall on the first day of the meeting of the first Parliament next after his or her coming to the crown, sitting in his or her throne in the House of Peers in the presence of the Lords and Commons therein assembled, or at his or her coronation before such person or persons who shall administer the coronation oath to him or her at the time of his or her taking the said oath (which shall first happen), make, subscribe, and audibly repeat the declaration mentioned in the statute made in the thirtieth year of the reign of King Charles the Second entitled, "An Act for the more effectual preserving the king's person and government by disabling papists from sitting in either House of Parliament". But if it shall happen that such king or queen upon his or her succession to the crown of this realm shall be under the age of twelve years, then every such king or queen shall make, subscribe and audibly repeat the same declaration at his or her coronation or the first day of the meeting of the first Parliament as aforesaid which shall first happen after such king or queen shall have attained the said age of twelve years.

XI. All which their Majesties are contented and pleased shall be declared, enacted and established by authority of this present Parliament, and shall stand, remain, and be the law of this realm for ever; and the same are by their said Majesties, by and with the advice and consent of the Lords Spiritual and Temporal, and Commons, in Parliament assembled and by the authority of the same, declared, enacted, and established accordingly.

XII. And be it further declared and enacted by the authority aforesaid, that from and after this present session of Parliament no dispensation by *non obstante* of or to any statute or any part thereof shall be allowed, but that the same shall be held void and of no effect, except a dispensation be allowed of in such statute, and except in such cases as shall be specially provided for by one or more bill or bills to be passed during this present session of Parliament.

XIII. Provided that no charter or grant or pardon granted before the three and twentieth day of October in the year of our Lord one thousand six hundred eighty-nine shall be any ways impeached or invalidated by this act, but that the same shall be and remain of the same force and effect in law and no other than as if this act had never been made.

Document 5

The Declaration of Independence Philadelphia, July 4th, 1776

When in the Course of human events, it becomes necessary for one people to dissolve the political bands which have connected them with another, and to assume among the powers of the earth, the separate and equal station to which the Laws of Nature and of Nature's God entitle them, a decent respect to the opinions of mankind requires that they should declare the causes which impel them to the separation.

We hold these truths to be self-evident, that all men are created equal, that they are endowed by their Creator with certain unalienable Rights, that among these are Life, Liberty and the pursuit of Happiness.--That to secure these rights, Governments are instituted among Men, deriving their just powers from the consent of the governed, --That whenever any Form of Government becomes destructive of these ends, it is the Right of the People to alter or to abolish it, and to institute new Government, laying its foundation on such principles and organizing its powers in such form, as to them shall seem most likely to effect their Safety and Happiness. Prudence, indeed, will dictate that Governments long established should not be changed for light and transient causes; and accordingly all experience hath shewn, that mankind are more disposed to suffer, while evils are sufferable, than to right themselves by abolishing the forms to which they are accustomed. But when a long train of abuses and usurpations, pursuing invariably the same Object evinces a design to reduce them under absolute Despotism, it is their right, it is their duty, to throw off such Government, and to provide new Guards for their future security.--Such has been the patient sufferance of these Colonies;

and such is now the necessity which constrains them to alter their former Systems of Government. The history of the present King of Great Britain is a history of repeated injuries and usurpations, all having in direct object the establishment of an absolute Tyranny over these States. To prove this, let Facts be submitted to a candid world.

He has refused his Assent to Laws, the most wholesome and necessary for the public good.
He has forbidden his Governors to pass Laws of immediate and pressing importance, unless suspended in their operation till his Assent should be obtained; and when so suspended, he has utterly neglected to attend to them.
He has refused to pass other Laws for the accommodation of large districts of people, unless those people would relinquish the right of Representation in the Legislature, a right inestimable to them and formidable to tyrants only.
He has called together legislative bodies at places unusual, uncomfortable, and distant from the depository of their public Records, for the sole purpose of fatiguing them into compliance with his measures.
He has dissolved Representative Houses repeatedly, for opposing with manly firmness his invasions on the rights of the people.
He has refused for a long time, after such dissolutions, to cause others to be elected; whereby the Legislative powers, incapable of Annihilation, have returned to the People at large for their exercise; the State remaining in the mean time exposed to all the dangers of invasion from without, and convulsions within.
He has endeavoured to prevent the population of these States; for that purpose obstructing the Laws for Naturalization of Foreigners; refusing to pass others to encourage their migrations hither, and raising the conditions of new Appropriations of Lands.
He has obstructed the Administration of Justice, by refusing his Assent to Laws for establishing Judiciary powers.

He has made Judges dependent on his Will alone, for the tenure of their offices, and the amount and payment of their salaries.
He has erected a multitude of New Offices, and sent hither swarms of Officers to harrass our people, and eat out their substance.
He has kept among us, in times of peace, Standing Armies without the Consent of our legislatures.
He has affected to render the Military independent of and superior to the Civil power.
He has combined with others to subject us to a jurisdiction foreign to our constitution, and unacknowledged by our laws; giving his Assent to their Acts of pretended Legislation:
For Quartering large bodies of armed troops among us:
For protecting them, by a mock Trial, from punishment for any Murders which they should commit on the Inhabitants of these States:
For cutting off our Trade with all parts of the world:
For imposing Taxes on us without our Consent:
For depriving us in many cases, of the benefits of Trial by Jury:
For transporting us beyond Seas to be tried for pretended offences;
For abolishing the free System of English Laws in a neighbouring Province, establishing therein an Arbitrary government, and enlarging its Boundaries so as to render it at once an example and fit instrument for introducing the same absolute rule into these Colonies:
For taking away our Charters, abolishing our most valuable Laws, and altering fundamentally the Forms of our Governments:
For suspending our own Legislatures, and declaring themselves invested with power to legislate for us in all cases whatsoever.
He has abdicated Government here, by declaring us out of his Protection and waging War against us.
He has plundered our seas, ravaged our Coasts, burnt our towns, and destroyed the lives of our people.
He is at this time transporting large Armies of foreign Mercenaries to compleat the works of death, desolation and tyranny, already begun with circumstances of Cruelty & perfidy scarcely paralleled

in the most barbarous ages, and totally unworthy the Head of a civilized nation.
He has constrained our fellow Citizens taken Captive on the high Seas to bear Arms against their Country, to become the executioners of their friends and Brethren, or to fall themselves by their Hands.
He has excited domestic insurrections amongst us, and has endeavoured to bring on the inhabitants of our frontiers, the merciless Indian Savages, whose known rule of warfare, is an undistinguished destruction of all ages, sexes and conditions.

In every stage of these Oppressions We have Petitioned for Redress in the most humble terms: Our repeated Petitions have been answered only by repeated injury. A Prince whose character is thus marked by every act which may define a Tyrant, is unfit to be the ruler of a free people.

Nor have We been wanting in attentions to our British brethren. We have warned them from time to time of attempts by their legislature to extend an unwarrantable jurisdiction over us. We have reminded them of the circumstances of our emigration and settlement here. We have appealed to their native justice and magnanimity, and we have conjured them by the ties of our common kindred to disavow these usurpations, which, would inevitably interrupt our connections and correspondence. They too have been deaf to the voice of justice and of consanguinity. We must, therefore, acquiesce in the necessity, which denounces our Separation, and hold them, as we hold the rest of mankind, Enemies in War, in Peace Friends.

We, therefore, the Representatives of the united States of America, in General Congress, Assembled, appealing to the Supreme Judge of the world for the rectitude of our intentions, do, in the Name, and by Authority of the good People of these Colonies, solemnly publish and declare, That these United Colonies are, and of Right ought to be Free and Independent States; that they are Absolved from all Allegiance to the British Crown, and that all political connection between them and the State of Great Britain, is and ought to be totally dissolved; and that as Free and Independent States, they have full Power to levy War, conclude Peace, contract Alliances, establish Commerce, and to do all other Acts and Things which Independent States may of right do. And for the support of this Declaration, with a firm reliance on the protection of divine Providence, we mutually pledge to each other our Lives, our Fortunes and our sacred Honor.

Document 6

Constitution of the United States of America
September 17,1787

We the People of the United States, in Order to form a more perfect Union, establish Justice, insure domestic Tranquility, provide for the common defence, promote the general Welfare, and secure the Blessings of Liberty to ourselves and our Posterity, do ordain and establish this Constitution for the United States of America.

Article. I.

Section 1.

All legislative Powers herein granted shall be vested in a Congress of the United States, which shall consist of a Senate and House of Representatives.

Section. 2.

Clause 1: The House of Representatives shall be composed of Members chosen every second Year by the People of the several States, and the Electors in each State shall have the Qualifications requisite for Electors of the most numerous Branch of the State Legislature.

Clause 2: No Person shall be a Representative who shall not have attained to the Age of twenty five Years, and been seven Years a Citizen of the United States, and who shall not, when elected, be an Inhabitant of that State in which he shall be chosen.

Clause 3: Representatives and direct Taxes shall be apportioned among the several States which may be included within this Union, according to their respective Numbers, which shall be determined by adding to the whole Number of free Persons, including those bound to Service for a Term of Years, and excluding Indians not taxed, three fifths of all other Persons. The actual Enumeration shall be made within three Years after the first Meeting of the Congress of the United States, and within every subsequent Term of ten Years, in such Manner as they shall by Law direct. The Number of Representatives shall not exceed one for every thirty Thousand, but each State shall have at Least one Representative; and until such enumeration shall be made, the State of New Hampshire shall be entitled to chuse three, Massachusetts eight, Rhode-Island and Providence Plantations one, Connecticut five, New-York six, New Jersey four, Pennsylvania eight, Delaware one, Maryland six, Virginia ten, North Carolina five, South Carolina five, and Georgia three.

Clause 4: When vacancies happen in the Representation from any State, the Executive Authority thereof shall issue Writs of Election to fill such Vacancies.

Clause 5: The House of Representatives shall chuse their Speaker and other Officers; and shall have the sole Power of Impeachment.

Section. 3.

Clause 1: The Senate of the United States shall be composed of two Senators from each State, chosen by the Legislature thereof, for six Years; and each Senator shall have one Vote.

Clause 2: Immediately after they shall be assembled in Consequence of the first Election, they shall be divided as equally as may be into three Classes. The Seats of the Senators of the first Class shall be vacated at the Expiration of the second Year, of the second Class at the Expiration of the fourth Year, and of the third Class at the

Expiration of the sixth Year, so that one third may be chosen every second Year; and if Vacancies happen by Resignation, or otherwise, during the Recess of the Legislature of any State, the Executive thereof may make temporary Appointments until the next Meeting of the Legislature, which shall then fill such Vacancies.

Clause 3: No Person shall be a Senator who shall not have attained to the Age of thirty Years, and been nine Years a Citizen of the United States, and who shall not, when elected, be an Inhabitant of that State for which he shall be chosen.

Clause 4: The Vice President of the United States shall be President of the Senate, but shall have no Vote, unless they be equally divided.

Clause 5: The Senate shall chuse their other Officers, and also a President pro tempore, in the Absence of the Vice President, or when he shall exercise the Office of President of the United States.

Clause 6: The Senate shall have the sole Power to try all Impeachments. When sitting for that Purpose, they shall be on Oath or Affirmation. When the President of the United States is tried, the Chief Justice shall preside: And no Person shall be convicted without the Concurrence of two thirds of the Members present.

Clause 7: Judgment in Cases of Impeachment shall not extend further than to removal from Office, and disqualification to hold and enjoy any Office of honor, Trust or Profit under the United States: but the Party convicted shall nevertheless be liable and subject to Indictment, Trial, Judgment and Punishment, according to Law.

Section. 4.

Clause 1: The Times, Places and Manner of holding Elections for Senators and Representatives, shall be prescribed in each State by the Legislature thereof; but the Congress may at any time by Law make or alter such Regulations, except as to the Places of chusing Senators.

Clause 2: The Congress shall assemble at least once in every Year, and such Meeting shall be on the first Monday in December, unless they shall by Law appoint a different Day.

Section. 5.

Clause 1: Each House shall be the Judge of the Elections, Returns and Qualifications of its own Members, and a Majority of each shall constitute a Quorum to do Business; but a smaller Number may adjourn from day to day, and may be authorized to compel the Attendance of absent Members, in such Manner, and under such Penalties as each House may provide.

Clause 2: Each House may determine the Rules of its Proceedings, punish its Members for disorderly Behaviour, and, with the Concurrence of two thirds, expel a Member.

Clause 3: Each House shall keep a Journal of its Proceedings, and from time to time publish the same, excepting such Parts as may in their Judgment require Secrecy; and the Yeas and Nays of the Members of either House on any question shall, at the Desire of one fifth of those Present, be entered on the Journal.

Clause 4: Neither House, during the Session of Congress, shall, without the Consent of the other, adjourn for more than three days, nor to any other Place than that in which the two Houses shall be sitting.

Section. 6.

Clause 1: The Senators and Representatives shall receive a Compensation for their Services, to be ascertained by Law, and paid out of the Treasury of the United States. They shall in all Cases, except Treason, Felony and Breach of the Peace, beprivileged from Arrest during their Attendance at the Session of their respective Houses, and in going to and returning from the same; and for any Speech or Debate in either House, they shall not be questioned in any other Place.

Clause 2: No Senator or Representative shall, during the Time for which he was elected, be appointed to any civil Office under the Authority of the United States, which shall have been created, or the Emoluments whereof shall have been increased during such time; and no Person holding any Office under the United States, shall be a Member of either House during his Continuance in Office.

Section. 7.

Clause 1: All Bills for raising Revenue shall originate in the House of Representatives; but the Senate may propose or concur with Amendments as on other Bills.

Clause 2: Every Bill which shall have passed the House of Representatives and the Senate, shall, before it become a Law, be presented to the President of the United States; If he approve he shall sign it, but if not he shall return it, with his Objections to that House in which it shall have originated, who shall enter the Objections at large on their Journal, and proceed to reconsider it. If after such Reconsideration two thirds of that House shall agree to pass the Bill, it shall be sent, together with the Objections, to the other House, by which it shall likewise be reconsidered, and if approved by two thirds of that House, it shall become a Law. But in all such Cases the Votes of both Houses shall be determined by yeas and Nays, and the Names of the Persons voting for and against the Bill shall be entered on the Journal of each House respectively. If any Bill shall not be returned by the President within ten Days (Sundays excepted) after it shall have been presented to him, the Same shall be a Law, in like Manner as if he had signed it, unless the Congress by their Adjournment prevent its Return, in which Case it shall not be a Law.

Clause 3: Every Order, Resolution, or Vote to which the Concurrence of the Senate and House of Representatives may be necessary (except on a question of Adjournment) shall be presented to the President of the United States; and before the Same shall take Effect, shall be approved by him, or being disapproved by him, shall be repassed by two thirds of the Senate and House of Representatives, according to the Rules and Limitations prescribed in the Case of a Bill.

Section. 8.

Clause 1: The Congress shall have Power To lay and collect Taxes, Duties, Imposts and Excises, to pay the Debts and provide for the common Defence and general Welfare of the United States; but all Duties, Imposts and Excises shall be uniform throughout the United States;

Clause 2: To borrow Money on the credit of the United States;

Clause 3: To regulate Commerce with foreign Nations, and among the several States, and with the Indian Tribes;

Clause 4: To establish an uniform Rule of Naturalization, and uniform Laws on the subject of Bankruptcies throughout the United States;

Clause 5: To coin Money, regulate the Value thereof, and of foreign Coin, and fix the Standard of Weights and Measures;

Clause 6: To provide for the Punishment of counterfeiting the Securities and current Coin of the United States;

Clause 7: To establish Post Offices and post Roads;

Clause 8: To promote the Progress of Science and useful Arts, by securing for limited Times to Authors and Inventors the exclusive Right to their respective Writings and Discoveries;

Clause 9: To constitute Tribunals inferior to the supreme Court;

Clause 10: To define and punish Piracies and Felonies committed on the high Seas, and Offences against the Law of Nations;

Clause 11: To declare War, grant Letters of Marque and Reprisal, and make Rules concerning Captures on Land and Water;

Clause 12: To raise and support Armies, but no Appropriation of Money to that Use shall be for a longer Term than two Years;

Clause 13: To provide and maintain a Navy;

Clause 14: To make Rules for the Government and Regulation of the land and naval Forces;

Clause 15: To provide for calling forth the Militia to execute the Laws of the Union, suppress Insurrections and repel Invasions;

Clause 16: To provide for organizing, arming, and disciplining, the Militia, and for governing such Part of them as may be employed in the Service of the United States, reserving to the States respectively, the Appointment of the Officers, and the Authority of training the Militia according to the discipline prescribed by Congress;

Clause 17: To exercise exclusive Legislation in all Cases whatsoever, over such District (not exceeding ten Miles square) as may, by Cession of particular States, and the Acceptance of Congress, become the Seat of the Government of the United States, and to exercise like Authority over all Places purchased by the Consent of the Legislature of the State in which the Same shall be, for the Erection of Forts, Magazines, Arsenals, dock-Yards, and other needful Buildings;--And

Clause 18: To make all Laws which shall be necessary and proper for carrying into Execution the foregoing Powers, and all other Powers vested by this Constitution in the Government of the United States, or in any Department or Officer thereof.

Section. 9.

Clause 1: The Migration or Importation of such Persons as any of the States now existing shall think proper to admit, shall not be prohibited by the Congress prior to the Year one thousand eight hundred and eight, but a Tax or duty may be imposed on such Importation, not exceeding ten dollars for each Person.

Clause 2: The Privilege of the Writ of Habeas Corpus shall not be suspended, unless when in Cases of Rebellion or Invasion the public Safety may require it.

Clause 3: No Bill of Attainder or ex post facto Law shall be passed.

Clause 4: No Capitation, or other direct, Tax shall be laid, unless in Proportion to the Census or Enumeration herein before directed to be taken.

Clause 5: No Tax or Duty shall be laid on Articles exported from any State.

Clause 6: No Preference shall be given by any Regulation of Commerce or Revenue to the Ports of one State over those of another: nor shall Vessels bound to, or from, one State, be obliged to enter, clear, or pay Duties in another.

Clause 7: No Money shall be drawn from the Treasury, but in Consequence of Appropriations made by Law; and a regular Statement and Account of the Receipts and Expenditures of all public Money shall be published from time to time.

Clause 8: No Title of Nobility shall be granted by the United States: And no Person holding any Office of Profit or Trust under them, shall, without the Consent of the Congress, accept of any present, Emolument, Office, or Title, of any kind whatever, from any King, Prince, or foreign State.

Section. 10.

Clause 1: No State shall enter into any Treaty, Alliance, or Confederation; grant Letters of Marque and Reprisal; coin Money; emit Bills of Credit; make any Thing but gold and silver Coin a Tender in Payment of Debts; pass any Bill of Attainder, ex post facto Law, or Law impairing the Obligation of Contracts, or grant any Title of Nobility.

Clause 2: No State shall, without the Consent of the Congress, lay any Imposts or Duties on Imports or Exports, except what may be absolutely necessary for executing it's inspection Laws: and the net Produce of all Duties and Imposts, laid by any State on Imports or Exports, shall be for the Use of the Treasury of the United States; and all such Laws shall be subject to the Revision and Controul of the Congress.

Clause 3: No State shall, without the Consent of Congress, lay any Duty of Tonnage, keep Troops, or Ships of War in time of Peace, enter into any Agreement or Compact with another State, or with a foreign Power, or engage in War, unless actually invaded, or in such imminent Danger as will not admit of delay.

Article. II.

Section. 1.

Clause 1: The executive Power shall be vested in a President of the United States of America. He shall hold his Office during the Term of four Years, and, together with the Vice President, chosen for the same Term, be elected, as follows

Clause 2: Each State shall appoint, in such Manner as the Legislature thereof may direct, a Number of Electors, equal to the whole Number of Senators and Representatives to which the State may be entitled in the Congress: but no Senator or Representative, or Person holding an Office of Trust or Profit under the United States, shall be appointed an Elector.

Clause 3: The Electors shall meet in their respective States, and vote by Ballot for two Persons, of whom one at least shall not be an Inhabitant of the same State with themselves. And they shall make a List of all the Persons voted for, and of the Number of Votes for each; which List they shall sign and certify, and transmit sealed to the Seat of the Government of the United States, directed to the President of the Senate. The President of the Senate shall, in the Presence of the Senate and House of Representatives, open all the Certificates, and the Votes shall then be counted. The Person having the greatest Number of Votes shall be the President, if such Number be a Majority of the whole Number of Electors appointed; and if there be more than one who have such Majority, and have an equal Number of Votes, then the House of Representatives shall immediately chuse by Ballot one of them for President; and if no Person have a Majority, then from the five highest on the List the said House shall in like Manner chuse the President. But in chusing the President, the Votes shall be taken by States, the Representation from each State having one Vote; A quorum for this Purpose shall consist of a Member or Members from two thirds of the States, and a Majority of all the States shall be necessary to a Choice. In every Case, after the Choice of the President, the Person having the greatest Number of Votes of the Electors shall be the Vice President. But if there should remain two or more who have equal Votes, the Senate shall chuse from them by Ballot the Vice President.

Clause 4: The Congress may determine the Time of chusing the Electors, and the Day on which they shall give their Votes; which Day shall be the same throughout the United States.

Clause 5: No Person except a natural born Citizen, or a Citizen of the United States, at the time of the Adoption of this Constitution, shall be eligible to the Office of President; neither shall any Person be eligible to that Office who shall not have attained to the Age of thirty five Years, and been fourteen Years a Resident within the United States.

Clause 6: In Case of the Removal of the President from Office, or of his Death, Resignation, or Inability to discharge the Powers and Duties of the said Office, *(See Note 9)* the Same shall devolve on the Vice President, and the Congress may by Law provide for the Case of Removal, Death, Resignation or Inability, both of the President and Vice President, declaring what Officer shall then act as President, and such Officer shall act accordingly, until the Disability be removed, or a President shall be elected.

Clause 7: The President shall, at stated Times, receive for his Services, a Compensation, which shall neither be encreased nor diminished during the Period for which he shall have been elected, and he shall not receive within that Period any other Emolument from the United States, or any of them.

Clause 8: Before he enter on the Execution of his Office, he shall take the following Oath or Affirmation:--"I do solemnly swear (or affirm) that I will faithfully execute the Office of President of the United States, and will to the best of my Ability, preserve, protect and defend the Constitution of the United States."

Section. 2.

Clause 1: The President shall be Commander in Chief of the Army and Navy of the United States, and of the Militia of the several States, when called into the actual Service of the United States; he may require the Opinion, in writing, of the principal Officer in each of the executive Departments, upon any Subject relating to the Duties of their respective Offices, and he shall have Power to grant Reprieves and Pardons for Offences against the United States, except in Cases of Impeachment.

Clause 2: He shall have Power, by and with the Advice and Consent of the Senate, to make Treaties, provided two thirds of the Senators present concur; and he shall nominate, and by and with the Advice and Consent of the Senate, shall appoint Ambassadors, other public Ministers and Consuls, Judges of the supreme Court, and all other Officers of the United States, whose Appointments are not herein otherwise provided for, and which shall be established by Law: but the Congress may by Law vest the Appointment of such inferior Officers, as they think proper, in the President alone, in the Courts of Law, or in the Heads of Departments.

Clause 3: The President shall have Power to fill up all Vacancies that may happen during the Recess of the Senate, by granting Commissions which shall expire at the End of their next Session.

Section. 3.

He shall from time to time give to the Congress Information of the State of the Union, and recommend to their Consideration such

Measures as he shall judge necessary and expedient; he may, on extraordinary Occasions, convene both Houses, or either of them, and in Case of Disagreement between them, with Respect to the Time of Adjournment, he may adjourn them to such Time as he shall think proper; he shall receive Ambassadors and other public Ministers; he shall take Care that the Laws be faithfully executed, and shall Commission all the Officers of the United States.

Section. 4.

The President, Vice President and all civil Officers of the United States, shall be removed from Office on Impeachment for, and Conviction of, Treason, Bribery, or other high Crimes and Misdemeanors.

Article. III.

Section. 1.

The judicial Power of the United States, shall be vested in one supreme Court, and in such inferior Courts as the Congress may from time to time ordain and establish. The Judges, both of the supreme and inferior Courts, shall hold their Offices during good Behaviour, and shall, at stated Times, receive for their Services, a Compensation, which shall not be diminished during their Continuance in Office.

Section. 2.

Clause 1: The judicial Power shall extend to all Cases, in Law and Equity, arising under this Constitution, the Laws of the United States, and Treaties made, or which shall be made, under their Authority;--to all Cases affecting Ambassadors, other public Ministers and Consuls;--to all Cases of admiralty and maritime Jurisdiction;--to Controversies to which the United States shall be a

Party;--to Controversies between two or more States;--between a State and Citizens of another State;--between Citizens of different States, --between Citizens of the same State claiming Lands under Grants of different States, and between a State, or the Citizens thereof, and foreign States, Citizens or Subjects.

Clause 2: In all Cases affecting Ambassadors, other public Ministers and Consuls, and those in which a State shall be Party, the supreme Court shall have original Jurisdiction. In all the other Cases before mentioned, the supreme Court shall have appellate Jurisdiction, both as to Law and Fact, with such Exceptions, and under such Regulations as the Congress shall make.

Clause 3: The Trial of all Crimes, except in Cases of Impeachment, shall be by Jury; and such Trial shall be held in the State where the said Crimes shall have been committed; but when not committed within any State, the Trial shall be at such Place or Places as the Congress may by Law have directed.

Section. 3.

Clause 1: Treason against the United States, shall consist only in levying War against them, or in adhering to their Enemies, giving them Aid and Comfort. No Person shall be convicted of Treason unless on the Testimony of two Witnesses to the same overt Act, or on Confession in open Court.

Clause 2: The Congress shall have Power to declare the Punishment of Treason, but no Attainder of Treason shall work Corruption of Blood, or Forfeiture except during the Life of the Person attainted.

Article. IV.

Section. 1.

Full Faith and Credit shall be given in each State to the public Acts, Records, and judicial Proceedings of every other State. And the Congress may by general Laws prescribe the Manner in which such Acts, Records and Proceedings shall be proved, and the Effect thereof.

Section. 2.

Clause 1: The Citizens of each State shall be entitled to all Privileges and Immunities of Citizens in the several States.

Clause 2: A Person charged in any State with Treason, Felony, or other Crime, who shall flee from Justice, and be found in another State, shall on Demand of the executive Authority of the State from which he fled, be delivered up, to be removed to the State having Jurisdiction of the Crime.

Clause 3: No Person held to Service or Labour in one State, under the Laws thereof, escaping into another, shall, in Consequence of any Law or Regulation therein, be discharged from such Service or Labour, but shall be delivered up on Claim of the Party to whom such Service or Labour may be due.

Section. 3.

Clause 1: New States may be admitted by the Congress into this Union; but no new State shall be formed or erected within the Jurisdiction of any other State; nor any State be formed by the Junction of two or more States, or Parts of States, without the Consent of the Legislatures of the States concerned as well as of the Congress.

Clause 2: The Congress shall have Power to dispose of and make all needful Rules and Regulations respecting the Territory or other Property belonging to the United States; and nothing in this

Constitution shall be so construed as to Prejudice any Claims of the United States, or of any particular State.

Section. 4.

The United States shall guarantee to every State in this Union a Republican Form of Government, and shall protect each of them against Invasion; and on Application of the Legislature, or of the Executive (when the Legislature cannot be convened) against domestic Violence.

Article. V.

The Congress, whenever two thirds of both Houses shall deem it necessary, shall propose Amendments to this Constitution, or, on the Application of the Legislatures of two thirds of the several States, shall call a Convention for proposing Amendments, which, in either Case, shall be valid to all Intents and Purposes, as Part of this Constitution, when ratified by the Legislatures of three fourths of the several States, or by Conventions in three fourths thereof, as the one or the other Mode of Ratification may be proposed by the Congress; Provided that no Amendment which may be made prior to the Year One thousand eight hundred and eight shall in any Manner affect the first and fourth Clauses in the Ninth Section of the first Article; and that no State, without its Consent, shall be deprived of its equal Suffrage in the Senate.

Article. VI.

Clause 1: All Debts contracted and Engagements entered into, before the Adoption of this Constitution, shall be as valid against the United States under this Constitution, as under the Confederation.

Clause 2: This Constitution, and the Laws of the United States which shall be made in Pursuance thereof; and all Treaties made, or which shall be made, under the Authority of the United States, shall be the supreme Law of the Land; and the Judges in every State shall be bound thereby, any Thing in the Constitution or Laws of any State to the Contrary notwithstanding.

Clause 3: The Senators and Representatives before mentioned, and the Members of the several State Legislatures, and all executive and judicial Officers, both of the United States and of the several States, shall be bound by Oath or Affirmation, to support this Constitution; but no religious Test shall ever be required as a Qualification to any Office or public Trust under the United States.

Article. VII.

The Ratification of the Conventions of nine States, shall be sufficient for the Establishment of this Constitution between the States so ratifying the Same.

done in Convention by the Unanimous Consent of the States present the Seventeenth Day of September in the Year of our Lord one thousand seven hundred and Eighty seven and of the Independence of the United States of America the Twelfth In witness whereof We have hereunto subscribed our Names,

Document 7

United States Bill of Rights
December 15, 1791

Amendment I

Congress shall make no law respecting an establishment of religion, or prohibiting the free exercise thereof; or abridging the freedom of speech, or of the press; or the right of the people peaceably to assemble, and to petition the Government for a redress of grievances.

Amendment II

A well regulated Militia, being necessary to the security of a free State, the right of the people to keep and bear Arms, shall not be infringed.

Amendment III

No Soldier shall, in time of peace be quartered in any house, without the consent of the Owner, nor in time of war, but in a manner to be prescribed by law.

Amendment IV

The right of the people to be secure in their persons, houses, papers, and effects, against unreasonable searches and seizures, shall not be violated, and no Warrants shall issue, but upon probable cause, supported by Oath or affirmation, and particularly describing the place to be searched, and the persons or things to be seized.

Amendment V

No person shall be held to answer for a capital, or otherwise infamous crime, unless on a presentment or indictment of a Grand Jury, except in cases arising in the land or naval forces, or in the

Militia, when in actual service in time of War or public danger; nor shall any person be subject for the same offence to be twice put in jeopardy of life or limb; nor shall be compelled in any criminal case to be a witness against himself, nor be deprived of life, liberty, or property, without due process of law; nor shall private property be taken for public use, without just compensation.

Amendment VI

In all criminal prosecutions, the accused shall enjoy the right to a speedy and public trial, by an impartial jury of the State and district wherein the crime shall have been committed, which district shall have been previously ascertained by law, and to be informed of the nature and cause of the accusation; to be confronted with the witnesses against him; to have compulsory process for obtaining witnesses in his favor, and to have the Assistance of Counsel for his defence.

Amendment VII

In Suits at common law, where the value in controversy shall exceed twenty dollars, the right of trial by jury shall be preserved, and no fact tried by a jury, shall be otherwise re-examined in any Court of the United States, than according to the rules of the common law.

Amendment VIII

Excessive bail shall not be required, nor excessive fines imposed, nor cruel and unusual punishments inflicted.

Amendment IX

The enumeration in the Constitution, of certain rights, shall not be construed to deny or disparage others retained by the people.

Amendment X

The powers not delegated to the United States by the Constitution, nor prohibited by it to the States, are reserved to the States respectively, or to the people.

Bibliography

Ashton, Robert, and Raymond Howard Parry. *The English Civil War and After, 1642-1658*. Berkeley: University of California, 1970. Print.

Black, Conrad. *The Rise to Greatness: The History of Canada*. Toronto, Canada: McClelland & Stewart. 2014. Print.

Campbell, James, Eric John, Patrick Wormald, and P. V. Addyman. *The Anglo-Saxons*. London, England: Penguin, 1991. Print.

Churchill, Winston, and Henry Steele Commager. *Churchill's History of the English-speaking Peoples*. New York, NY: Barnes & Noble, 1995. Print.

Crocker III, H. W. *The Politically Incorrect Guide to the British Empire.* Washington DC. Regnery Publishing, Inc. 2011. Print.

Durant, Will. *The Age of Faith*. New York, NY, Simon & Schuster. 1950.

Ferguson, Naill. Empire: *The Rise and Demise of the British World Order and the Lessons for Global Power*. New York, NY. Basic Books. 2004. Print.

Fortescue, John. *On the Law and Governance of England*. Cambridge, UK. Cambridge University Press. 1997. Print.

Grattan, Thomas Colley. *Holland: The History of the Netherlands*. Dublin Ireland. 1830. Digital.

Hannan, Daniel. *Inventing Freedom: How the English-Speaking Peoples Made the Modern World*. New York, NY. HarperCollins. 2013. Print.

Hannan, Daniel. "The Legacy of the Glorious Revolution." Telephone interview. 20 Oct. 2010.

Hannan, Daniel. *The New Road to Serfdom: a Letter of Warning to America*. New York: Harper, 2010. Print.

James, Lawrence. *The Rise & Fall of the British Empire*. New York, NY. St. Martin's Griffin. 1994. Print.

Lovejoy, David S. *The Glorious Revolution in America*. New York, NY. Harper & Row Publishers. 1972. Print.

Macaulay, Thomas Babington Macaulay, and H. R. Trevor-Roper. *The History of England*. Harmondsworth, Eng.: Penguin, 1979. Print.

Macfarlane, Alan. *The Origins of English Individualism: the Family, Property, and Social Transition*. New York: Cambridge UP, 1979. Print.

MacFarlane, Alan. *The Riddle of the Modern World: Of Liberty, Wealth, and Equity*. New York, NY. St. Martin's Press, LLC. 2000. Print.

Mead, Walter Russell. *God and Gold: Britain, America, and the Making of the Modern World*. New York: Alfred A. Knopf, 2008. Print.

Motley, John. *The Rise of the Dutch Republics Volumes 1-3*. New York, NY. Harper & Brothers Publishers. 1901. Print.

Phillips, Kevin. *The Cousins' Wars: Religion, Politics, & the Triumph of Anglo-America*. New York, NY. Basic Books. 1999. Print.

Robinson, Cyril E. *England: A History of British Progress*. New York, NY. Thomas Y, Crowell Co. 1932. Print.

Starkey, David. "Monarchy." *Monarchy: Series 1-4*. BBC. London. Television.

Starkey, David. *Crown & Country: The Kings and Queens of England, A History*. London: Harper Press, 2010. Print.

Vallance, Edward. *The Glorious Revolution: 1688, Britain's Fight for Liberty*. New York: Pegasus, 2008. Print.

PRAISE FOR LIBERTY INHERITED

John Hancock has traced the origins of American liberty back to their earliest roots, in the political struggles of early modern England. He understands that our two countries are joint inheritors of a great tradition: the tradition of limited government, of parliamentary supremacy, of personal freedom and of the common law. This book is a refreshing antidote to the prevailing historical schools on both sides of the Atlantic. – Daniel Hannan (MEP, Columnist, Author)

John Hancock has written a book that should be required reading for any student of the Founding Fathers, the Declaration of Independence or the Constitution. He describes in a very easy to understand way, how the Founding Fathers arrived at the thought process that resulted in the founding of this great country. So often we focus on what they did, without thinking how they came to do it. – Stefan Bartelski (Political Commentator, Radio Talk Show Host)

In *Liberty Inherited* John Hancock reconnects us with our political heritage and the principles that made this nation great. This book is required reading for anyone concerned that America is losing its exceptionalism.— Congressman Steve Stockman (R-TX)

Made in the USA
San Bernardino, CA
29 August 2017